Gender, Power and Organisations

Also by Susan Halford

Gender, Careers and Organisations (with Mike Savage and Anne Witz)

Gender, Power and Organisations

An Introduction

Susan Halford and Pauline Leonard

First published 2001 by
PALGRAVE
Houndmills, Basingstoke, Hampshire RG21 6XS and
175 Fifth Avenue, New York, N.Y. 10010
Companies and representatives throughout the world

PALGRAVE is the new global academic imprint of
St Martin's Press LLC Scholarly and Reference Division
and Palgrave Publishers Ltd (formerly Macmillan Press Ltd).

ISBN 0–333–61842–4 hardback
ISBN 0–333–61843–2 paperback

This book is printed on paper suitable for recycling and
made from fully managed and sustained forest sources.

A catalogue record for this book is available
from the British Library.

Library of Congress Cataloging-in-Publication Data
Halford, Susan
     Gender, Power, and organisations: an introduction /
     Susan Halford and Pauline Leonard.
          p.cm.
     Includes bibliographical references and index.
     ISBN 0–333–61843–2 (pbk) 0–333–61842–4 (ppc)
          1. Sex role in the work environment.   2. Corporate culture.
I. Leonard, Pauline, 1957-   II. Title.

HD6060.6 .H35 2000
306.3'615—dc21   00–030437

10   9   8   7   6   5   4   3   2   1
10   09   08   07   06   05   04   03   02   01

Printed in China

To Edward, Alice, Emily and Esme

Contents

List of Figures and Tables

Figure

Tables

Acknowledgements

Our very grateful thanks go to Jon Clarke, Department of Sociology and Social Policy, University of Southampton, for his continual support and guidance. We are also most indebted to Frances Arnold and Catherine Gray, for their calm patience and understanding, as our four maternity leaves took their inevitable toll on the original timetable for this book. Pauline would also like to thank William and Frances, who, for her, probably started it all in the first place.

SUSAN HALFORD
PAULINE LEONARD

1

Gender, Power and Organisation: Introducing Power

Gender and organisation in the twenth-first century: a complex and contradictory picture

As we enter the twenty-first century, those of us interested in the world of work are aware that we are faced with a complex and contradictory picture of men, women and organisations. On the one hand, many parts of the picture are optimistic, containing evidence that the divisions between women and men in the workplace are diminishing and real progress is being made towards gender equality. We see that more and more women are entering work organisations, and that many women are the primary breadwinners for the family unit. Further, once in their organisations, many appear to be shattering the glass ceilings and making it to the very top, taking over high-profile positions within organisations of all types. In business, politics, the media and public service, as well as in science, medicine and academia, we are faced with images of women who appear to be transforming the face of organisational life, suggesting that 'the feminist revolution that began 30 years ago has continued to do its work' (Grant 1997:2).

On the other hand, however, some familiar patterns of difference and discrimination persist. Looking at the statistics, we are left pondering the same old sets of figures that catalogue women's secondary status in the workforce. The inequalities that have characterised the working lives of women and men over the last twenty-five years – those to do with pay, occupation and seniority – are still with us. It appears that, for many women, *in spite of* the nearly thirty years of energetic pushing for change, the organisations in which they work are still

1

significantly characterised by gender inequalities. We see that women are still under-represented in the upper echelons of most organisations, and, just as critically, still over-represented in the lower. Men still dominate organisations in almost *every* sense: in terms of jobs, status, rewards and opportunities And women and men remain segregated into different types of work, such that it still makes sense to talk of 'women's work '(where the benefits are lower) and 'men's work' (where they are higher).

For instance, in Britain, although the gender gap in labour market participation has narrowed considerably, the inequalities have not followed suit. Over the last two decades, women have entered the labour market in increasing numbers, while men's participation has declined. In 1975, only 60 per cent of women of working age were economically active. By 1996 this had risen to 71 per cent. In contrast, the economic activity rate of men has declined from 90 per cent in 1975 to 85 per cent in 1996 (EOC 1997a). However, in spite of this trend towards equality in work activity, it can be seen that men still dominate disproportionately in full-time employment, in permanent employ-ment, in management and the professions and, consequently, in pay and personal finance arrangements. In 1996, 92 per cent of male employees worked full-time, compared with 55 per cent of female employees. 84 per cent of all part-time employees are women. Women are also more likely to be in temporary employment: while women make up 48 per cent of all employees, 55 per cent of temporary workers are women. 70 per cent of homeworkers are women, mainly in clerical or secretarial occupations. In contrast, the largest group of men homeworkers is in managerial occupations (EOC 1997a).

In the professions and managerial occupations, while women have increased their share of employment, they still have some way to go (EOC 1977b). Overall, a third of all managers in Britain are women: not a discouraging figure, perhaps. However, they only comprise 13 per cent of middle and senior managers (IoMRE 1996), and the board-room remains an essentially male preserve: in 1996, women made up only 3.3 per cent of directors (IoMRE 1996). The statistics from other research are even less optimistic: these suggest that in many top organ-isations there is still no female representation on the board, and even where women are directors, they tend to be non-executive rather than executive ones (EOC 1997b). There are still very few women in the senior ranks of the British police forces. In 1996, in England, there were six women deputy or assistant chief constables and one chief constable, and no female chief constables in either Scotland or

Wales. In the law, there are still very few female judges, and men dominate the upper levels of the profession, although more women than men are currently admitted each year to the roll of solicitors in England and Wales. In education, men are more likely to be full-time academic staff in universities, and more likely to be employed as head teachers. In medicine, although women comprised 31 per cent of hospital medical staff in Britain, only 21 per cent are on career grades (primarily consultants) (EOC 1997b).

This rather gloomy picture is reflected in the economic rewards that women and men may expect to enjoy. In Britain, women generally earn less than men throughout their working lives (EOC 1996): a fact which is as true for women managers as for women in other jobs. For example, women who work full-time currently earn 80 per cent of men's hourly pay on average. The pay gap widens with age. As a group, women in their fifties are in the worst financial position relative to men of the whole working population, often earning well below half of the weekly earnings of their male counterparts. Women who work part-time have much lower hourly earnings than women who work full-time, because they are more likely to work in lower-paid occupations and at lower grades. Indeed, the difference in hourly earnings between the women who work part-time and men who work full-time has remained virtually unchanged, suggesting that while some of the women working full-time have made some progress towards earnings equality, very few of those who work part-time have done so (EOC 1996). The divisions continue when we look at occupations: women and men tend to work in different industrial sectors. In 1996, women were concentrated in public services (government, health and education) where they made up two-thirds of employees. Men dominated the construction and primary and utility industries. The different occupational choices that women and men make when starting work thus contribute to the sometimes considerable disparities in earnings and income, as well as having a major impact on subsequent career opportunities (EOC 1997a).

These inequalities are even starker for some ethnic minority women. Overall, ethnic minority women have lower economic activity rates than white women and men, and unemployment rates for ethnic minority women and men are high. In 1966, only 6 per cent of white women were unemployed, compared with 19 per cent of black women. When they are employed, black, Indian and Chinese women are more likely to be in full-time employment. Black women who work full-time have higher earnings on average than all other groups including white women: although this may be because many work in London where average earnings are highest, are in younger age groups, and are better qualified (EOC 1996). The pay gap is widest, however, for Pakistani and Bangladeshi women.

In other words, these parts of the picture show that, in spite of dramatic economic changes in global labour markets, as well as dramatic cultural changes in social understandings about men and women, gender still appears to be a major issue within organisational life. While some women have made it to the top, and do earn large salaries (or equivalent salaries to many men), this is still regarded as noteworthy – still something to be written about in the press, and wondered over. Conversely, men are still assumed to be the top dogs in organisations, and anything that complicates this, such as ageism, is again the subject of speculation and contemplation: a cause for concern. The overall picture seems to be that organisations are still deeply inflected with gender traditionalism.

Yet when we look at the picture more closely, it is more complicated than this. Many men and women working in today's organisations deny that gender plays a significant part in their experience or career development. For many people, whether you are a man or a women is *not* seen to be the determining factor for what kind of job you have, where you work, or how much you earn. For some it is their age, their class or their race which is felt to be more important, while for others it is their personality, their training, skills and abilities. Indeed, gender traditionalism jostles alongside evidence that social understanding about women and men are and should be changing. Now, as Coward avers, 'western society is more ambiguous and sexually complex than it was' (1999:6). For many people, gender is an irrelevance, a minor part of their identity, and certainly 'no longer a divider, ascribing men to positions of advantage and women to positions of disadvantage' (Coward 1999:6).

There is also a great deal of evidence, both statistical and anecdotal, to support this more fragmented picture. The shift in work has been away from manufacturing and primary industries – away from the jobs done by men, towards jobs done by women (EOC 1997a). Women now make up half the workforce, and many predict that they will soon overtake men as the major breadwinners (Ghazi 1999). They thus make up a substantial presence in most organisations, and dominate many (for example, the National Health Service in Britain). There has also been a general shift away from full-time jobs, where men still predominate, to part-time jobs, which are mainly taken up by women. 'If, in the main, it has been men who have borne the brunt of unemployment, it has been women who have responded to the need for a flexible workforce' (EOC 1997a:1). Further, the numbers of women and men employed in managerial and professional occupations *has* risen significantly in the last twenty years, suggesting that real progress towards equality is being made. In corporate management and administration, women make up a third of all managers while in professional occupations they now constitute 40 per cent of the category (EOC 1997b). It may, therefore, be just a matter of time before this generation of middle managers and professionals become the chief executives of the future.

Thus, in contradiction to the rather gloomy picture that we gave above, evidence also exists to suggest that gender is declining as a divisive factor within work and organisational life. For many women, as well as men, their work is a major part of their life. Women, as well as men, hold substantial positions of power. Women are now in government, sit on the boards of major corporations, run large companies or own their own businesses, head major charities, have a significant voice through broadcasting, the press, and drama, lead medical teams and make substantial developments in science and academia. In Britain, for example, Margaret Thatcher was the longest-serving Prime Minister in the twentieth century. There are now women in the Cabinet, a woman Director of Public Prosecutions, a woman President of the Board of Trade, a woman director of the Confederation of Business and Industry, women Professors of Science at Oxford University, a woman Head of the Policy Unit at the Institute of Directors, female Chief Executives of major theatres and retail stores....the list goes on (*Guardian* 1997). Women are now seen to be crucially involved not only in organisations but in contemporary decision-making at the most senior levels.

And this is a social revolution that seems set to continue both inside and outside conventional organisational careers and working patterns. For if the future of the workforce is for flexible and multi-skilled workers, then it is women who are most likely to benefit. These new patterns of working, which emphasise self-reliance and independence, may well suit those very women who have been unable to take advantage of the old system of continuous unbroken promotion within a single company until retirement (Grant 1997, Leonard 1998a). Now it is just as common for people at all levels in virtually all occupational sectors to go back and forth between employment with an external organisation and running their own businesses, or to combine working for one or several employers, and/or for themselves. More people work from home, sometimes on a part-time basis, sometimes on a full-time one. Women with caring responsibilities fit well into this style of work; and to assume that this is a secondary style of working, the less preferable option to full-time employment with one organisation is, increasingly, an erroneous assumption. The 'portfolio lifestyle' (Ghazi 1999) is turning out to be a first choice for many people.

Thus, as we enter the next century, it would appear that the gender model of (contented) male full-time employee versus (frustrated) female low-level part-time employee is complicated by people's lived experiences. The pleasures and dissatisfactions from working within organisations are complex and multiple, and may cut across gender. For many men and women, a concrete position within an organisation is essential for both their bank balance and their sense of identity, for others full-time employment for a single organisation costs *them* more than they want to pay. Thus while some cling to the linear career track, dreading redundancy or retirement, others are shifting, by choice, to more flexible working patterns and a different type of relationship with employing organisations. A quick look through contemporary newspapers reveals that they are full of juxtaposed narratives, as much about conventional men and unconventional women as unconventional men and conventional women. For some, gender is key, for others it diminishes into a range of other factors.

Thus while some men find unemployment dispossesses them of their identity: 'I have that normal male thing of valuing myself according to the job I do . . . . when I can't tell someone in one word what I am, then something is missing. I don't represent anything anymore' (Michael Portillo, then a Conservative ex-MP quoted in Radice 1999:10). Others, particularly in unemployment hotspots, have adjusted to a life in which women have stepped in and become the breadwinners: 'Once they got over this male thing about having to be the breadwinner, some of them have actually found it very liberating' (Kevin Flynn, coordinator of Newcastle's Centre against Unemployment, quoted in Radice 1999:10).

Other men actively choose to leave the fast track behind:

> I switched to a three-day week and it's been very liberating and equalising for my wife and I, both working part-time and both seeing those magical moments as they grow up. Now I see fathers in Tesco with their kids, mobile phone in hand, and I think, oh no, are you never free from work? (Colin, male BT middle manager from Milton-Keynes with three young children, quoted in Ghazi 1999:9)

For many people, both men and women, age rather than gender may be a divider. For instance, as men grow older, their relationship with careers, organisations and gender changes and they become caught in a complexity of positions. Youth is king: age counteracts the supposed benefits of gender; as one 45-year-old senior manager of an international banking organisation explains:

> When I turned 40, I knew I could go at any time. Five more years is certainly the maximum. There are lots of young people desperate to get on. Of course the company will lose my experience, but they don't care (Quoted in MccGwire 1999:7)

Some men clearly enjoy their position within their work organisations, and use it as a defining factor in the construction of their identity, while others resent it, and prefer to think of themselves as partner or father first and employee second. Some men are driven by ambition, and want to get to the top of their field, while others prefer simply to find a niche they enjoy. The situation for women is no less complex. Some of the women who are entering those organisations and occupations which have previously been closed to them, dominated by men and the traditions of masculinity, are clearly enjoying their experiences, and using the power they have gained. For example, in a recent survey of the UK's fifty most powerful working women, there is a sense of pleasure in the way they talk about their relationship with their work and organisations, a sense of real achievement and success. Comments such as 'I love working here' 'I work for fun' are common (*Guardian* 1997). The UK president of one of the US's largest telecom companies talks about the tremendous buzz she gets from her job, primarily from managing people and 'watching [them] grow'. She explains: 'I will change the culture of the company just by being here' (Chapman-Pincher in Burden 1997).

For some of these women, their gender is key to who they are in their organisations, what they do and how they do it, while for others it is a non-issue:

> I have tried very hard to make sure women have as many opportunities as men. The environment I work in is tough and unsociable and it is a real obligation to ensure it's a working environment in which women can flourish. When I was first made an editor in the BBC I was the only woman, which I found profoundly depressing. When a member of my staff tells me they are pregnant I will congratulate them. When they tell a man they will still see it as key. (Jenny Abramsky, Director of Continuous News at the BBC, quoted in *Guardian* 1997b:5)

I thought this (being patronised and ignored as a graduate student) was because I was a lowly novice, but subsequently realised it was because I was a woman. There is a Svengali syndrome rife in academia between self-assured male lecturers and impressionable young female students who unwittingly learn a kind of helplessness. (Susan Greenfield, Gresham College Professor of Physics, quoted in *Guardian* 1997b:5)

I have experienced discrimination as a woman, but I do not want to dredge it up. It's very important not to be bitter about these things. (Kay Davies, Professor of Genetics, quoted in *Guardian* 1997a:5)

In work, gender is not an issue, people know that I can add to what they do irrespective of sex. (Dawn Airey, Director of programmes at Channel 5, quoted in *Guardian* 1997a:5)

[W]hen you get to the heavy end of the voluntary sector, the men begin to dominate. But I do not spend too much time thinking about it. If people need convincing of my abilities they will be convinced by the way I am doing the job, not by standing on soap boxes. (Ann Abraham, Chief Executive, National Association of Citizen's Advice Bureaux, quoted in *Guardian* 1997a:5)

While parenting is an issue which affects both men and women, for many women this is often perceived to be the biggest difference between them and their male colleagues. Many working mothers feel that the pull that having children makes on women does not seem to be as strong for men. As the director of the UK's Confederation of Business and Industry explains:

I do feel guilty leaving them. Extremely guilty, especially when they are ill. When I get home in the evenings, they are usually too tired to read to me... Women have different life preferences than men. Men with families hang around at the end of the day, doing very little. Women, by and large, go home. (Barker in Thomas 1997:6)

This is a tension that women at all levels of organisations may feel, not just highly paid managers. It is also one that holds true for many men. Relationships with work and organisation can be complex: a mixture of responsibility, guilt and perhaps enjoyment, of ambition and a desire to get on, coupled with an equally strong desire to 'downshift'. As a 33-year-old woman with a house husband partner sums up:

I enjoy my job, but I really resent being away from my two year old, earning all the money. He loves being with our daughter but feels his own career is going nowhere. Neither of us is really happy with the situation. (Ghazi 1999)

What are we to make of this complex and contradictory picture? On one hand, there is plenty of evidence to suggest that the all too well-known patterns of gender difference and disadvantage continue to characterise women's and men's position in, and experience of, work organisations. On the other hand, we have evidence of some truly remarkable changes. It seems as though there are some instances where women, or men, see unity between themselves as a social group, but others where the profound differences between women, or between men, are striking. And, it seems, that while gender may be highly significant to some individuals' experiences of organisation it may be not at all significant to others. At the very least, the evidence above suggests that the significance of gender may ebb and flow across individual and organisational time and space.

But how can all these impressions be valid? How can organisations be both static – repeating entrenched patterns of gender inequalities – *and* dynamic – upturning traditional gender relations? How can they be both oppressive and enabling for women, and indeed for men? How can the relationship between gender and organisation be at once universal and fragmented? Clear and contradictory?

The initial aim of this book is simply to *find out more*, to reveal the depth and breadth of this complex and contradictory picture. By unpicking and re-presenting the research on gender and organisation we aim to elaborate on the range of ways gender is enacted, sustained and generated across the structures and practices of organisational life. Throughout this exploration, our further aim is to investigate how we might *understand* the complex and contradictory evidence presented above. In this chapter, we will argue that existing accounts of the relationship between gender and organisation can offer only partial explanations. In the following section, we look at three key perspectives; but we show that while each of these can illuminate parts of the picture described above, other parts are – at best – left unaccounted for and – at worst – denied. We suggest that the key to achieving a fuller understanding lies in paying greater attention to the question of *power*.

In the third section of this chapter, 'Gender, Power and Organisation', we review three alternative theories of power to show the integral relationship they have with gender and organisation. We show that these should not be seen as *competing* perspectives, but rather that all three forms of power may be seen to operate in contemporary organisations. Indeed, it is this *multiple* constitution of power that explains the complex and contradictory picture described here, in this section. In this book, we aim to build upon this understanding in order to

construct a more satisfactory account of the relations between gender
and organisation.

Perspectives on gender and organisation

Existing research offers several ways of thinking about the relation-
ship(s) between gender and organisation. In what follows, we outline
the three main alternative perspectives: liberal, structural and
poststructuralist. To a certain extent, delineating three clear perspectives is, of course, to establish three 'ideal types'. That is to say, each
perspective is described so that the concepts used, and the arguments
made, fall perfectly within a clear 'host' framework and are totally
consistent. This is intended to offer a simple introduction to the
different ways of understanding the relationships between gender and
organisation. However, when we come to look at actual examples of
research on gender and organisation, in Chapters 2 to 6, we will see
that not all writers do, in fact, draw clearly on one perspective or
another. The ideal types do not always capture the complexity of the
arguments being made, and it is not always easy to 'pigeonhole' writers
into one of the three alternative perspectives. Having said this, as
Chapters 2 to 6 will show, many writers *can* be clearly placed within
one perspective or another, and almost all show clear tendencies
towards one of these three ways of seeing relationships between gender
and organisation. The following presentation of the three perspectives
should not, therefore, be dismissed simply as a heuristic device but
should be seen as a genuine introduction to much of the research which
is described and analysed in the rest of the book.

Liberal perspectives

The first, and most popularised, way of seeing the relationship between
gender and organisation draws on liberal traditions of theorising both
'gender' and 'organisation'. Liberal perspectives on gender rest on a
conviction about the underlying sameness of women and men. The
political project for liberal feminism has been to reveal this sameness
by exposing the distortions of sex role stereotyping, prejudice and
discrimination – in organisations as elsewhere – and, therefore, to
claim equal rights for women and men. (See for example, Wollstonecraft 1985, Mill H.T. 1970, Mill J.S. 1970, Friedan 1965.) Liberal

feminists argue that women and men possess the same capacities, and in particular the same human capacity for rationality (to think and act with reason and without being swayed by emotion). The fact that such a capacity for rationality is often *seen* principally as a male trait, contrasted with feminine emotionality and lack of reason, says nothing about what men and women are really like 'underneath it all'. Rather, this assumption, reflects a long history of stereotyping which has, in effect, privileged men and discriminated against women, according them fewer resources, less status, less authority and less control over their lives. If (some) women have come to portray these stereotypes, or even to identify themselves with prejudiced notions of femininity, this should not be taken as proof of their 'reality' but rather of the power of sex role conditioning or socialisation. Through the differential treatment of boys and girls, from a very early age, sex roles (what boys and girls do) and even identities (how boys and girls see themselves) come to mirror stereotypes and thus to perpetuate them. These stereotypes and the roles they sustain are understood to be oppressive to women, since they act to prevent women from achieving their full potential. Thus, gender differences and inequalities are seen to reside in prejudice and self-sustaining tradition.

Liberal perspectives offer an account of gender differences across society, revealing examples of discrimination in such diverse arenas as the media, education, politics and social policy, and of course in paid work and organisational life. This pervasiveness is understood as a series of *patterns* of discrimination, caused by a range of ingrained individual and social prejudices, and not as the outcome of orchestrated interests deliberately intended to achieve these patterns. While indeed, men may be able to achieve their human potential more readily than women and, in this sense, to benefit from gender difference and inequality, liberal feminists do not claim that men *as a social group* are acting in consort to sustain their privilege. Some men may do so, but any such actions are understood as a matter of individual prejudice rather than a symptom of any more general or systematic relations of oppression.

The place of organisation within this liberal conception of gender is, then, as one of the arenas in which outmoded beliefs, customs and prejudices continue to operate. Many examples come readily to mind: the company director who, much as he claims he would like to, won't promote a woman to the board because he believes that women simply can't take the pressure above a certain level and are prone to emotional outbursts, crying or hysteria; or the section manager who thinks mothers who work are neglectful, even unnatural individuals, not to be trusted in the workplace; or the personnel officer who asks female candidates about their plans for marriage and children, assuming this will drain their commitment to work, but never asks men similar questions. The fact that attitudes such as these continue to thrive in modern workplaces says little about the real attributes of working women. But because these beliefs are held by some men (and even some women), and they are able to make key decisions, for example about appointments or promotions, women are held back at work and are unable to fulfil their full potential. Clearly this is detrimental for those women. It is also, liberal writers argue, bad for the organisation.

This is because a liberal perspective sees organisation as fundamentally gender-neutral, and prejudice as an inappropriate hangover from earlier times, which serves only to impede the smooth and efficient running of organisational life. Max Weber (1968) initially developed this perspective through his particular concept of bureaucracy (this is discussed fully in Chapter 2), and it has subsequently been used by many researchers and writers within the field of organisational science and management studies in particular. In the bureaucratic concept of organisation, it is an *individual*'s qualities that are valued, and these are assessed and rewarded according to purely objective criteria. Since liberal accounts of gender see no sex-based pattern to individual qualities, emphasising instead the essential sameness of women and men, there is no reason why bureaucratic organisational life should continue to reproduce patterns of discrimination and difference. To the contrary, bureaucracies should see women and men as they really are, as individuals with a range of skills and competencies.

At first sight, then, it may seem as though there is a mismatch between a liberal perspective on gender and a liberal perspective on organisation. While the former emphasises the multitude of ways women and men are still treated differently, including inside bureaucratic organisations, the latter emphasises the gender neutrality of bureaucracy. However, the difference between these accounts lies in the focus of their analysis, rather than in any more fundamental incompatibilities. While liberal writers on gender tend to focus on the actual, everyday experiences of women (and men), rather than the abstract or ideal state of equality which they see as their goal, liberal writers on organisation focus more generally on the gender neutral ideal practice of bureaucracy, rather than the more 'messy' actual practices of organisation. Critically though, those liberal feminists who have concentrated on prescribing reform agree that the Weberian vision of bureaucratic neutrality is an achievable end goal, and can indeed be used to install appropriate rules and procedures which will remove old-fashioned prejudices from work organisations. Similarly, a liberal perspective on organisation accepts that the ideal type bureaucracy may, as yet, be some way off describing everyday life in work organisations, as traditional sexist prejudices do continue to persist. However, these prejudices are seen as illegitimate interlopers in the bureaucratic organisation. They have no place and serve only to impede the proper functioning of the bureaucracy.

At the core of the liberal perspective on gender and organisation is the faith that women and men are the same, should therefore be enabled to become equal, and that – as far as work organisation is concerned – bureaucracy, properly developed, can deliver this gender equality. Thus, liberal perspectives emphasise the potential for achieving a fair and just society. Change can be achieved by ridding society of its stereotypes and prescriptive sex roles and preventing individuals from acting on their prejudices (for example, by refusing to employ a woman for a certain job). The social and political aim, therefore, is to remove the barriers to sexual equality and to allow women and men to realise their shared potential as equal citizens and as equal human beings. For organisations, the way forward is to rid bureaucracies of the prejudices and traditions left over from earlier times by refining rules and procedures to make sure that only rational, bureaucratic (and therefore, by definition, gender-neutral) criteria are taken into account.

Structural perspectives

Structural perspectives share a common belief that social relations between individuals, in organisations as elsewhere, are part of a broader system of relations between unequal social groups, based on gender and/or class and/or race. They stand in direct criticism of the liberal perspective, described above, which they see as recognising only superficial manifestations of deeper social structures of inequality. These structures can be understood as underlying laws governing how social and economic life functions, at least at present. The key to these structures is that they have been constructed in the interests of dominant groups and serve to perpetuate these groups' dominance. The success, in large part, of such structures of dominance lies in their ability to appear as simply common sense or 'just the way things are'.

Structuralists argue that the liberal failure to see these deeper social structures serves only to leave them unchallenged, and therefore to reinforce the system of discrimination and inequality. Gender differences are understood as a fundamental social division, rather than the actions of a few prejudiced individuals, in which women are systematically oppressed directly to serve the interests of other more powerful social groups, particularly men but also whites and the ruling classes (see, for example, Barrett 1980, Walby 1990). Bureaucratic work organisations are seen as a vehicle for this oppression and not held to be even potentially neutral in their form or practice. From this common base, we can distinguish three distinctive structural perspectives on the relations between gender and organisation.

Radical perspectives
Radical feminists claim that men as a social group dominate women, as a social group and use the term 'patriarchy' to describe this system of domination and subordination. Women's oppression by men is understood to be the most fundamental form of human oppression visible across all societies throughout history. Unlike liberal feminism, which suggests that 'underneath it all' women and men are really the same, radical feminism emphasises the *differences* between women and men.

The specific source and manifestation of these differences varies between different radical feminist writers. However, there is most commonly reference to women as mothers and carers. Women's capacity to bear children and sustain new life (through breastfeeding) is thought to be responsible for a range of distinctively feminine characteristics. Rich (1976), for example, argues that women's capacity to bear children is their greatest strength, bestowing on them particular ways of seeing the world and relating to others. Other radical feminists have claimed that women's reproductive capacity generates a distinct spirituality. Characterised by empathy, caring and a sense of connection with others, this spirituality is not only understood as different from men, but superior to male ways of being. (For example, see Daly 1984.) By contrast, men are characterised as uninvolved in the natural rhythms of life, as emotionally restricted, and as aggressors. This is often linked to beliefs about male sexuality, which is understood to be aggressive, domineering and always an expression of man's power over woman. Through sexual violence, and the ever-present threat of sexual violence, men are able to control women through physical domination and fear. (For the clearest articulation of this argument see Brownmiller 1975). Some radical feminists suggest that it is the nature of male sexuality and the distortion and suppression of female sexuality which lies at the heart of patriarchy.

Across these analyses it is not always clear where the root of gender difference lies. In some cases it seems as though the connection between femininity and reproduction is understood to constitute a *biological* foundation for difference, while in other it seems to be more the case that entrenched social processes have generated all-encompassing categories 'man' and 'woman' which provide a solid and persistent foundation for difference. In either case, radical feminists claim universal and coherent categories of difference and oppression. In sum then, radical feminism suggests that women's difference is devalued by patriarchal society, inhibiting women's recognition of their true capacities, and forcing them to accommodate to an alien and oppressive culture which privileges masculinity.

Organisational life can be cast as a fine example of this. The bureaucratic emphasis on rationality, reason and lack of emotion is seen quite clearly to privilege male characteristics over female characteristics. Since men are understood by radical feminists to be rational while women are not (or less so) it is not surprising that men are naturally more at home within bureaucratic organisations than women are. More than this, radical feminists see that the full range of masculine attributes – from aggression to single-mindedness or detachment – come to be positively associated with organisational life (for aggression read competitive, for single-minded read focussed, for detachment read logical). Meanwhile, supposedly feminine attributes – such as emotionality, empathy or the ability to see many sides of the same issue – are interpreted negatively (read illogical, 'soft' and disorganised). In other words, the sex ascription of any particular characteristic (whether it is associated with masculinity or femininity) seems to be more important in determining the value placed on it, rather than any independent or neutral evaluation of what might be best for work organisations. The fact that bureaucracy presents itself as neutral makes the domination even more effective by persuading women that they too can and should emulate the masculine ideal, even though to do so is to deny their true nature.

Not surprisingly then, radical feminism rejects the idea that liberation entails women realising their capacity for reason, fact, objectivity and so on. Rather, the future lies in two possible directions. First, in recognising that women and men are simply different and that the focus for social change should be in re-valuing femininity and all the characteristics associated with it, so that it is no longer simply the negative flip-side to masculinity. For example, it has been argued that feminine qualities would actually benefit organisations and that this should be recognised by managers and taken on board in organisational practice, for example in making appointments and promotions. More cynically, it has been argued that bureaucracy is so alien to feminine ways of being that the only way to realise the organisational potential which femininity offers is to establish separate women-only organisations run according to feminine principles. The second scenario for the future, less commonly suggested, is that we should understand women's view of the world as a privileged view and one which might be adopted as the way forward for all people. This suggests a more radical recasting of all organisational forms, beyond either the mix-and- match combination of masculine and feminine or the separatism suggested above, towards an androgynous alternative for everyone.

Marxist feminism
A second structuralist perspective on gender, derived from Marxism, also sees that women as a social group are oppressed. However, in this case, the primary cause of women's oppression is understood to be capitalism (Barrett 1980). This then is a less universal account than radical feminism, since it confines itself to the analysis of capitalist societies. Women's position in society, and the relations between women and men, are understood to be by-products of the interests of the capitalist mode of production.

Modes of organisation are understood to be constructed in the interests of capitalist profit and gender divisions, as well as those of race, are seen as ways of controlling the working class and keeping wages as low as possible. Differences such as those between women and men (or classes or races) are understood as a social and/or economic fabrication that serves the interests of capitalism and not thought to have any foundation in real differences (such as those posited by radical feminism).

In particular it is argued that women's position in the labour market and their experience inside work organisations is explained by their constitution as a reserve army of labour for capitalism. Because capitalism is seen to progress through periodic cycles of economic slump and boom it requires a large, flexible and easily controllable group of workers who can be pulled into the workplace during times of expansion, and expelled back into the home during times of recession. Marxist feminists argue that it is easier to treat women in this way than men because they have historically been less well organised in the workplace and can be supported by their husbands in the family when not engaged in paid work. Therefore, it is in the interests of capitalist organisations to keep women in poor positions at work, in unskilled work with few rights, so that they are readily dispensable should the need arise. In the household, women also offer special value to capitalism, by discharging many of the tasks required to keep the male workforce in good condition (cleaning, cooking, childcare) and for no direct wages. Thus, it is in the interests of capitalist organisations to perpetuate women's role as housewives by denying them fulfilling jobs or careers. Of course, the male partner has to be paid enough to support his wife and family (and this constitutes the 'family wage') but even so, this constitutes a fraction of the cost of paying for all the services which a housewife provides on the open market.

While the maintenance of these gender relations may seem to benefit men, as a social group, who retain the better-paid and more secure jobs and get domestic service at home, the Marxist feminist perspective understands the primary cause of these relations to be the capitalist mode of production. In fact, Marxist perspectives deny that men really benefit in any way from these arrangements. Under capitalism, *both* men and women are alienated from their true human nature and human potential. Both men and women are oppressed by capitalism and it is only by overturning capitalism that both men and women will be released from the tyrannies of gender and class oppression. The fact that not all women and very few men recognise this is understood within Marxist feminism as a function of ideology and false consciousness, whereby oppressed individuals are led – wrongly – to believe that the dominant values in society are in their own best interests. Through these mechanisms, capitalism is able to encourage us to internalise its values thus dividing women from men in a way that may appear to be a matter of gender conflict but is, at root, a question of class oppression.

Within this analysis, organisations are understood as instruments of class domination. This is clearest in historical analysis of the early factories, where bringing workers together under one roof was as much about control (enabling direct supervision and punishment) as it was about the introduction of new technologies such as steam power (Thompson and McHugh 1990). Marxist analyses of contemporary bureaucracy also emphasise the way organisation facilitates class control. For instance, bureaucracy is precisely about the *division of labour*: breaking tasks down into finer and finer stages, each performed by a different worker. This represents a de-skilling process, whereby individual workers no longer possess the knowledge to complete a full task on their own, and this reduces their bargaining power. Dividing different components of the labour process by sex serves to further fragment the workforce, making it even less likely that groups will combine to reclaim holistic knowledge of production. Another example is offered in analysis of the career hierarchy offered by large bureaucracies. By separating workers hierarchically, often by very fine distinctions, solidarity is undermined (again, this is reinforced by gender divisions) and, furthermore, workers are encouraged to buy into organisational expectations since conformity means a chance of promotion with more money, status and so on.

Black feminist structuralism
Black feminist writers have established convincing critiques of both radical and Marxist theories of gender. In each case, it is argued that the category 'race' and the relations of racism have been subsumed to privileged categories of gender and class. The experience of being black is treated as, at best, secondary and, at worst, irrelevant to an understanding of gender. Black feminist writers argue that 'gender' and 'class' have been conceptualised in essentially white terms and that the experience of black women and men cannot be described or understood through these white concepts. Thus, any analysis of gender and organisation which fails to take into account racism and black/white difference will also fail to account for black women's (and men's) particular relationship to and experience of organisational life.

Many black feminist writers proposed that racism is a structural feature of society in which whites as a social group have systematically dominated and subordinated blacks, as a social group (see for example Carby 1982, Hill-Collins 1990, Mirza 1998: 1). Some black feminists interpet this history of white racism within established structural theories. Angela Davis, for example, builds her argument using Marxist analysis explaining racism as part of the dynamics of class oppression (Davis 1981). Most, however, understand racism as an independent set of structural relations, not derived from any other 'non-race' social and/or economic dynamics.

Fundamental to this structure of racism is the history of black enslavement by whites. This is a history of the most extreme and brutal oppression in which white men, and women, denied black men and women their freedom and their human rights. Slaves and their descendants became located in a culture where norms, values and judgements assumed and privileged whiteness. Black history, culture and consciousness was rendered subordinate under the homogenising force of white supremacism. In the main this history of slavery concerns Afro-Caribbean women and men, particularly those living in the USA. Nonetheless, black feminists argue that all people of colour have been, and continue to be, subjected to related processes of white domination and subordination. Colonialism, from Asia to Australia and the USA and Africa again, established the white domination of native peoples, depriving them of freedom and resources and superimposing a privileged white culture.

In sum, then, black feminists within the structural tradition argue that racism constitutes quite different set of experiences for black women and men compared with their white counterparts. Some take the argument further and explain that experience of being black establishes a distinctive consciousness. Hill-Collins (1990) for instance writes of the 'Afro-centric' consciousness among black Americans.

The place of bureaucracy within this analysis is essentially as a white form of organisation, established by whites (principally, although not only, men) in their own image. In some cases it is argued that blacks and whites do possess quite different characteristics and that this makes it difficult for them to adjust to white organisational life. 'Bureaucratic man' is sometimes represented as uptight, unimaginative and conservative, and contrasted with the freethinking, risk-taking unconventionality of blacks (Davis and Watson 1982). In other cases, it is argued that perceptions of black difference have no substance, but are maintained by white racism. Here we can see loud echoes of the radical–liberal division within feminist theory.

Poststructuralist perspectives

Poststructuralism has its roots in the broader movement of structuralism – in particular in the work of Saussure. Saussure's focus was on language, and his aim was to demonstrate that language is a system, structured through rules and laws, into which we are born. Language is thus a social rather than an individual phenomenon: we cannot make up the rules, only how we are going to apply a pre-existing system to what we want to say. By using the common rules and codes of the language system, members are able to communicate with each other meaningfully (Hall 1997). However, it is this idea of a deep and underlying structure upon which meaning rests in a fixed and secure way which poststructuralists reject. Poststructuralists argue that meaning is always in process, always being constructed and never fixed and finite.

'What we call meaning is a momentary stop in a continuing flow of interpretations of interpretations' (Storey 1993:85). There is nothing that can be finally understood: meaning is always deferred. Although an 'author' may have a particular intent in what she or he says, writes or does, there is no guarantee that this is what the 'reader' receives or adopts.

This idea has important implications for how we understand the notion of the individual self. In liberal theorisations, the self is seen as a free, rational, intellectual agent, who has a fixed and highly individual inner core or essence. In contrast, poststructuralists replace this idea with the notion of the 'subject': the human as a product of the specific cultural and historical locale in which they live – in other words, a social rather than an individual project.

The poststructuralist approach has been widely adopted, not only by linguists and literary theorists, but also by social scientists. In particular, feminists have drawn on these ideas to argue against the fixed and finite analyses offered by both liberal and structuralist accounts (see, for example, Barrett and Phillips 1992, Hollway 1984, Weedon 1987). They stress the transient and precarious nature of social relations, claiming that both 'gender' and 'organisation' are indeterminate, ever-changing, subject to continuous reconstitution by particular individuals, in specific times and places. As a result, a key focus for poststructuralists is the locale and the individual. Research aims to explore how such locales or individuals may differ from each other and how they make interpretations of 'gender' and 'organisation'.

With this focus on specificity, the question of *difference* is central to poststructuralist analysis. This suggests an alternative approach to understanding the relationship between gender and organisations. Poststructuralism does not offer a general theory, adequate (more or less) for understanding and explaining all instances and experiences of gender, across all organisations. Instead, what is offered is a method of understanding the way in which time and space will constitute gender and organisation, and the relationship between the two in distinctive forms. Thus, in their conception of gender, poststructuralists stress the historical and geographical differences that exist between women and between men, across different cultures and time periods, and even within a single culture or moment in time. In fact, one of the principal contributions of feminist poststructuralism to the understanding of gender has been its critical focus on the assumption of stable meanings about gender, such as are implied by the terms 'woman' and 'man'. These terms are usually used as though we all know what they mean (even though, as we discussed in the introduction to this chapter, our common-sense understandings of the boundaries between women and men are becoming blurred). Poststructuralist writers argue that this kind of unthinking use of gendered categories can in fact reinforce essentialist beliefs that the differences between women and men are given and fixed. Rather than reproducing these taken-for-granted meanings about women and men, poststructuralists attempt to deconstruct these categories, pulling apart the ways different meanings of femininity and masculinity have been cemented together. Through this project, the categories 'man' and 'woman' are understood as highly specific creations, with no fixity or inherent stability or reality, but rather as fractured and fluid.

This understanding presents a challenge to the idea of women and men possessing coherent gendered identities. As there are such a wide range of possible alternative constructions of masculinity and femininity, it is seen to be impossible to predict how women and men may behave or identify themselves. There are multiple choices to be made in the construction of gender identity, although many of these may in fact be powerful external constraints. It is through 'discourses': 'the historically, socially and institutionally specific structure of statements, terms, categories and beliefs' (Scott 1988:35), which frame and determine both social knowledge and understanding, that the nature of personal identity (Foucault 1977) is produced. At any one moment in time and space, a range of competing discourses exist, some of which are supported by the more powerful elements in society. Power is thus concentrated in and through discourses. Thus different ideas about gender – understandings of the categories 'woman' and 'man', what is femininity and what is masculinity – will be contained in these competing discourses. The more powerful of these, such as those of patriarchy, are more able to claim the status of 'truth' or reality.

Organisation is one such set of discourses, which may contribute to the construction of the gendered self in particular ways. Particular discourses of organisation (whether liberal or structural) present ideas of what it is to be human or masculine or feminine, to which we, as individuals, are subjected. In some organisations, discourses may be specifically gendered: the appropriate use of space, individual appearances and presentation of the self (for instance) may all be defined in terms of difference for women and men. However, what is deemed to be 'masculine' or 'feminine' is no more constant here than in other social discourses. Following the poststructuralist emphasis on difference, we can see those organisational controls over individual women and men may be cross-cut by age or race. Further, gender is constructed differently in different types of organisation (compare for example, the army with a merchant bank or a record company) and within different parts of organisations (compare public business spaces with private offices or social spaces).

The centrality of the notion of difference in poststructuralism, and its quest to move away from the perceived homogenising tendencies of other feminist theoretical approaches, has meant that poststructuralism has been used convincingly by black feminist theorists (see, for example, Calas 1992, Mohanty 1991), both inside and outside organisational theory. Black feminist poststructuralists have deconstructed contemporary theories and discourses of gender and organisation in order to demonstrate how assumptions of whiteness are embedded within them. Organisation thus not only contributes to gendered identities, but racialised ones, defining what it means to be black or white within organisational life. These writers have demonstrated how dominant constructions of blackness are rooted in colonial histories, such that black people are usually placed into the position of the 'other'. In this way, black people face a (limited) set of identities constructed through a restricted set of organisational discourses. The construction of self may be further constrained by the ways different organisations, and different organisational members, may map these identities onto them.

While this account of organisation may seem to share some of the features of the structuralist perspectives outlined above, it is important to point out that there are critical differences. First, while structuralist perspectives point to the domination of one group over another, poststructuralists see that *all* individuals within organisations – whether bosses or workers, men or women, whites or blacks – are subjected to organisational discourses and controls over their identities and behaviours. Second, unlike structuralist approaches, poststructuralism denies the existence of central, coordinating interests that have designed the system to their own advantage. While it is understood that, on occasion, particular discourses *may* come to serve dominant interests, it is denied that these can ever be seen as a deliberate creation of those interests. In other words, poststructuralists refute the argument that patriarchy, white supremacism or class domination has generated particular gender or organisational arrangements, although it is possible that such arrangements may effectively benefit particular interests over others. Third, and finally, poststructuralists understand that any set of discourses or practices is inherently unstable and open to reinterpretation. While structuralists – in different ways – see some possibilities for social and/or economic change, this takes the form of fundamental transformation, for example, class revolution or feminist separatism. Poststructuralists on the other hand see the possibility for resistance, reinterpretation and change as ever present and there for the taking by individuals.

Evaluation

From our discussion, it can be seen that each of these perspectives offers insights into particular issues and aspects of the relations between gender and organisation. For instance, the liberal perspective enables us to see the broad range of ways in which individuals and organisational life are gendered, without requiring us to understand instances of discrimination as generic, as the essential consequence of men and organisation. Thus we may understand the successes of the women whom we discussed at the beginning of this chapter as examples of organisations where traditional, stereotypical understandings of women and men are being eroded and overcome. Indeed, the fact that a large proportion of these appointments are in public sector organisations where equal opportunities pushes have been most evident goes to show that it is only by deliberate changes in organisational culture and practice that gender discrimination may be tackled. Just as importantly therefore, the liberal perspective offers clear prescriptions towards the practical politics of organisational change. Working within a Weberian model of organisation, liberal accounts can highlight the purely bureaucratic reasons why gender discrimination should be ended. This makes calls for change hard to dismiss as unrealistic, inappropriate or purely political, and may offer the best (if pragmatic) hope for improvement in women's position in modern work organisations. Furthermore, the Weberian model of bureaucracy offers a ready-made framework for new gender-neutral polices, emphasising as it does the need for training, job-specific skills, clear guidance on seniority and decision-making and so on.

However, the liberal perspective can be criticised for failing to recognise the broader picture of disadvantage – the pervasive links which may exist between phenomena. For example, we saw from the statistics we discussed on pages 2–4 that gender discrimination at work is consistent and widespread (EOC, 1997a and b), and that in many cases things have changed little over time. The facts are hard. For example, in many occupations, such as teaching, the pay gap between women and men has remained unchanged for twenty years (EOC 1996). In 1995, a third of the women in the UK were reported as low-paid (EOR 1995). The career opportunities in many organisations are still substantially poorer for women than men (EOC 1997c). Sexual harassment is still endemic: 1993 saw a 58 per cent increase in sexual harassment complaints made to the Equal Opportunities Commission. The vague notion of tradition, differential childhood socialisation, and the processes of stereotyping, are all rather soft explanations for what can be interpreted as very entrenched patterns of inequality and constantly recurring discrimination.

By contrast, the structuralist perspectives seem to offer neat and complete accounts that explain how and why different aspects of gender discrimination can be seen as part of a deeper underlying system of inequality. Whether this system is described primarily as patriarchy or capitalism, a theoretically rigorous explanation is given to account for the deep and repeated patterns, which we see not just in twentieth-century Britain or Europe but across history and across the globe. However, these perspectives may also be charged with the criticism that they fail to see the full picture. Difference is understood only along highly prescribed axes – those of gender, class or race, all large categorical groups which are understood to share commonalties. Individual experiences, which may differ from the grand scheme, are dismissed, or explained as 'false consciousness', rather than accounted for as part of the theoretical approach. Relations between the categories are only viewed as conflicting, thus emphasising the fixed and immutable nature of difference. The achievement of change thus becomes almost impossible to admit to; any appearance of change is explained as merely tokenistic window-dressing: part of the larger conspiracy to keep minority groups in the subject position. Whether this explanation is sufficient to explain the kinds of changes we discussed in the first section is debatable.

One of the strengths of poststructuralist accounts is that they do enable us to accommodate the diversity that we see, the awkward instances that don't seem to quite 'fit in'. The examples we gave at the beginning of the chapter 1 of women and men performing against type may be seen as representations of the many differences in experiences which both women and men have, and which do not conform to dominant understandings of gender. The range of competing experiences of both gender and organisation, and the fluid constitution of the relationship between the two, become acceptable from a poststructuralist understanding. However, by virtue of this position, there is also a failure to give any weight to the repeated, mundane patterns of discrimination and disadvantage that certain people share: women, ethnic minorities, the old and the young, gays and lesbians, people with disabilities. The *similarities* in experience that these people may have are not acknowledged, nor are the perpetual advantages that accrue to many (mainly white) men.

Clearly, each of these perspectives contributes some understanding to the complex and contradictory picture that we described at the out set. However, as we have demonstrated, at the heart of each perspective lies the exclusion of the others. Combining their insights, taking bits from each and trying to map them together to form a coherent explanation, is therefore problematic, if not impossible. Liberals deny that 'gender' has any real existence, as do Marxists, as do poststructuralists, but all for different reasons. Poststructuralists deny the human subject and particularly notions of human rationality, which are core to both liberalism and Marxism. Meanwhile, while Marxists see gender discrimination as a systematic expression of dominant economic interests, liberals deny this and propose that bureaucracy can offer a gender-neutral future. The liberal faith in bureaucracy is derided by structuralists of all sorts, who see it only as a bourgeois–patriarchal–white tool and understand the future to lie in the rather utopian construction of new, 'ideal' forms of organisation which would liberate oppressed groups and offer an egalitarian future. Poststructuralists have no such 'holy grail' and offer no clear political agenda, which leaves them prey to accusations from all sides of being apolitical or, worse, unable to challenge manifest examples of discrimination and inequality.

What, then, are we to make of the complex and contradictory picture which we discussed in the introduction to this chapter? There is no single perspective that enables us to see that all of this evidence is valid, or even significant. And we cannot combine the perspectives, because they appear to be fundamentally irreconcilable. We are left, it seems, with having to make some hard decisions about which pieces of evidence we will take as the most important indicators of relations between gender and organisation, and dismissing the rest – or, at least, consigning the remainder to an uncomfortable place at the back of our minds, to deal with later. Or are we?

Gender, power and organisation

In this book we suggest that the key to achieving a more integrated understanding of the relations between gender and organisation lies in focusing attention on the question of 'power'. Power is the common lynchpin in all three perspectives on gender and organisation described above. In each case, gender difference, disadvantage and discrimination in work organisations is commonly seen as the outcome of the operation of power, in which men – individually, collectively or through discourses which privilege the masculine – wield power over women. This gendered power is seen to flourish in work organisations, which fail to challenge it, whether because they operate according to traditional beliefs, because they reflect broader social structures or because discourses of organisation are constructed in conjunction with discourses of gender difference and hierarchy. Indeed, it is in the very nature of organisations that they (attempt to) systematise power relations between members, bestowing official rights of power to certain individuals over others, validating certain cultural and/or normative beliefs or discourses and not others. In sum, all three perspectives see gender as essentially a question of power. Organisations too are understood as mechanisms or fields of power. And the link between gender and organisation – for all three perspectives – is that gendered power relations have become entwined with organisational power relations. Organisational power strengthens gendered power. Meanwhile, gendered power comes to characterise (at least some forms of) organisational power. For example, good management comes to be identified with masculine characteristics. Another example might be the way informal controls over staff can be exercised through sexual innuendo or harassment. In this way, organisational power may actually come to *constitute* as well as simply reinforce gendered power relations.

As we have seen in the previous section, the concepts of gender and (to a lesser extent) organisation have been reasonably well worked through in the literature on these subjects. The perspectives we have discussed do not, however, help us to take on board the range of complex and contradictory evidence about gender and organisation offered in the first section. To the contrary, fundamental incompatibilities in the conceptualisations of organisation, and especially gender, mean that we appear to have reached something of an impasse. Despite its centrality, the concept of 'power' has rarely – if ever – been made explicit in accounts of gender and organisation. In practice, this means that the term is used as if we all know and agree what it means, when in fact it is actually used with a great diversity of meanings. In the following sections we outline in greater detail the specific place which power occupies in liberal, structural and poststructuralist accounts of gender and organisation. We will show that each perspective draws on rather different understandings of power, with their roots in broader social theory debates about the definition, nature and operation of power. Nonetheless, at the end of this chapter we suggest that all three forms of power may operate simultaneously in work organisations, producing the complex and contradictory picture described at the beginning of this chapter.

Liberal perspectives on gender, power and organisation

Liberal perspectives on gender and organisation rest on two distinct but interconnected understandings of power. The first focuses on the level of interactions between individuals. The second is concerned with the question of power in relation to the broader organisational level.

Individualised understandings of power within liberal perspectives on gender and organisation focus on the way that one individual may be able to exert his (or her) prejudices over another individual to her (or his) disadvantage. For example, an interviewer may deny a woman promotion on the grounds of her supposed emotionality or impoverished commitment to the workplace. This dovetails neatly with broader liberal interpretations which recognise the operation of power in instances where one individual is able to realise their will against the wishes of one or more other individuals (Dahl 1957, 1961, Weber 1986, Clegg 1989). This statement contains several key points. First, power is understood to be a matter of *individual* action where one person knows what they want and is able to act in a way which achieves this. Second, power is used *intentionally*, towards clearly defined ends. Third, power is understood to exist only in *observable actions*: we need to be able to see specific instances of the exercise of power to say that it exists. Fourth, power is only present where there is *conflict*, where one individual can override the clearly expressed wishes of another or others; if conflict is not observable then consensus is assumed to prevail.

The concept used to capture these features is that of *episodic agency*. Power resides in specific and observable episodes where sovereign agents overcome the wishes and resistance of others in order to achieve their will. Within this individualised conception, power is understood as dispersed, with individual actors prevailing over different issues. There is no single power elite or underlying system of power relations which privilege particular social group or interests. Overall, power is understood to be negative and prohibitive, wielded by individuals who have it, over those who do not, in a way which prevents them from doing what they would clearly wish. This understanding is character-istic of the liberal perspective on gender, power and organisations. As we saw in the previous section, in this account, patterns of disadvan-tage are understood to be the reflection of multiple individual exercises of discrimination, or power, rather than a coordinated conspiracy.

One of the most frequently cited examples of liberal research on power is the programme pursued by the American Sociologist Robert Dahl during the 1960s. Centring on community politics on the east coast of the USA, Dahl carried out extensive empirical research on local decision-making, examining which actors or interests 'won' in each case where a decision had to be made. His explicit agenda was to disprove the idea that power was in the hands of a ruling elite. Dahl discovered that in fact many different actors were involved in local decision-making, that different actors prevailed in different instances of decision making and that there were rarely any objections to the decisions which were made. From this, he concluded that the American political system was highly inclusive, with strong democratic represen-tation, and that it was not accurate to speak of a power elite (Dahl 1961, 1986). (For useful discussions of Dahl's research see Lukes 1974 and Clegg 1989.)

Liberal research on gender, power and organisation shares this rejection of the existence of a ruling power elite. However, there tends to be less faith that the absence of an elite must mean that gender patterns in organisations are chaotic, with widespread participation of all actors and a range of diverse outcomes. Certainly, liberal perspect-ives see no fixed or absolute domination of power by men, but nor do they recognise an absolutely open system of power relations. In prac-tice, persistent patterns of gender discrimination are identified in lib-eral work on gender and organisation. The extension of Dahl's work by Bachrach and Baratz (1963), still working within the liberal tradi-tion, is useful here. Provoked by Dahl's focus on decision-making as the manifestation of power, Bachrach and Baratz claimed that *non-*decision-making should also be understood as an instance of power. In their study of policy-making, attention was thus directed to the way decisions may be made to keep certain issues off the agenda altogether, forestalling certain actors from fully articulating their interests by confining debates to safe, traditional issues. This fits more fully with liberal accounts of gender, power and organisation, explaining how refusals to even consider questions of discrimination or equal opportunities might prevent women from fully expressing their experiences or openly opposing established practices and procedures.

Nonetheless, in keeping with the liberal tradition, Bachrach and Baratz are clear that power can only be said to exist where there is some expression of conflict, however incomplete or private. As they conclude, if 'there is no conflict, overt or covert, the assumption must be that there is a consensus on the prevailing allocation of values in which case non-decision making is impossible' (quoted in Lukes 1974:19). Thus, if women do not express any resistance or opposition to organisational practices, we can only assume that they willingly consent to those practices and, therefore, that power has not been exercised. Within this approach therefore, we cannot say that individuals' true interests are restricted through the operation of power, unless they themselves explicitly recognise this. If they do not, we must assume that they are making a free choice to act in the way they do.

Let us turn now to broader conceptualisations of power within the liberal tradition. Following from Hobbes, through Weber (in places) to Parsons, here the focus is on power as productive: bringing order to an otherwise uncivilised society. While Hobbes was concerned with the role of the state, and how power vested here could grant social order, Parsons took an even wider focus, examining how power could act to stabilise and maintain whole social systems. In both cases, 'power' becomes a property understood at a social level, not an individual level, and longer-term configurations of power, rather than individual episodes, are the subject of inquiry. However, and this is a crucial point, both Hobbes and Parsons understand this social power as beneficial to all citizens, or at least to all *civilised* ones. Unlike structural perspectives, to which we turn in a moment, the notion of social or systematic power within a liberal tradition bears no sense of oppression or inequality. Rather, this conceptualisation is more closely allied to a pluralist vision of society, in which everyone contributes and where some interests win on some occasions, others at other times (compare with Dahl above). This is understood to be in the long-term interests of society as a whole: 'Power, rather than being a conflictual mechanism which is opposed to social order, is both enabled by and constrained within that social order' (Clegg 1989:132).

This of course bears remarkable similarity to the conceptualisation of bureaucracy within liberal theories of organisation. In this account, bureaucracy is seen to rid society of earlier modes of organisation which were based simply on the possession of power by some groups, which were able to use this for their own ends. Instead, bureaucracy offers a system free from the dictates of power, run instead along lines of legitimate authority. In this sense, a properly functioning bureaucracy would be free from gendered power, operating instead through non-gendered authority. Power – in the traditional sense that men have it simply because they are men – has no rationale in the modern bureaucracy. Authority, by contrast, is bestowed through criteria of qualifications, training, skills, experience (and so on) and as such should not become contaminated with gender (or race, or any other irrational social divisions).

Structural perspectives on gender, power and organisation

The place of power in structural perspectives on gender and organisation lies in the way dominant social groups (men, whites, the ruling class) are able to control social and economic relations. This they do in order to secure their own privilege, at the expense of the oppression of other, less powerful social groups. Structural perspectives on power emphasise two main points, clearly distinguishing themselves from the liberal perspective outlined above. First, it is claimed that there are coherent and systematic power relations that underlie all social relations and interactions. Power is understood to be (largely) in the hands of a dominant social group or several dominant groups. Second, structural perspectives on power claim that power relations can be said to exist even where there is no observable instance of conflict.

The first point is simple enough. Power is not understood to be the property of individuals but of social groups who are able to use their power to ensure their interests across the full range of social arenas. In this formulation, the focus is no longer on individual interactions but on the way society has come to work as a coherent system of power relations. The exercise of power is not contingent on the outcome of particular instances of conflict but is embedded within broad, relatively stable and consistent dynamics in which one set of interests (more or less) constantly prevails over another set of interests. The point is not, then, to study individual decisions but to understand the integrity of the system as a whole. As far as gender is concerned, therefore, individual examples of sex discrimination within work organisations are not seen simply as isolated instances of one individual's power over another. Rather, that individual is understood to be the bearer of broader, socialised relations of power which enable him (in the case of gender) to act in ways which are consistently and repetitively mirrored across other interactions between women and men at work.

The second point also moves us beyond the liberal identification of power, which, as we just saw, claims that unless we can see one agency prevailing over the opposition of another agency, power cannot be said to exist. By contrast, structural perspectives on power claim that even where individuals or groups *believe* that they are *freely* choosing to behave in certain ways, or to hold particular values, they may still be understood to be subject to the power of more dominant interests. Indeed, as Lukes has argued 'is it not the supreme exercise of power to get another or others to have the desires you want them to have?' (Lukes 1974:23). Thus power is no longer recognisable only in those circumstances where conflict is manifest. Instead, beliefs in freedom from oppression and in freedom of choice are reinterpreted as the ultimate effect of power. So, if women fail to resist organisational practices this does not mean to say that all is fair, and power relations are absent, as the liberal perspective might have us believe. Rather, it means that men have exercised the ultimate power by persuading women to see things their way.

Key concepts here are 'ideology' and 'false consciousness'. Dominant social groups promote value-systems, comprised of beliefs and ways of understanding the world, which legitimate their dominance and offer a framework through which subordinated groups can accept their place. The power relations between dominant and subordinate groups are thus obscured and the grounds for resistance to domination weakened or obliterated. A false consciousness is generated within the oppressed, who come to understand their position as fair and equal, failing to recognise their oppression as such, and failing to perceive their true interests. Thus, within structural perspectives, episodic power does not have to be exercised in order for dominant groups to 'hold power'.

According to such a view, individual men do not have to take concerted actions to maintain gender inequality in organisations. This can be explained in several ways. First, the operation of ideology and establishment of false consciousness means that gendered power relations are taken for granted, accepted even as reasonable and just. Second, organisational forms are already a reflection of power, inherently privileging masculinity and male dominance (as well as class and race dominance), and not even potentially neutral. Third, even in those instances where women (or other subordinated groups) *do* glimpse their real interests, direct conflict may not take place because subordinated groups know that the powerful could exert episodic agency if they wanted to, and this is enough to undermine opposition. This latter exercise of power has been labelled dispositional power by Wrong (1979), drawing attention to the way power resides in aware-ness of the *capacity* to act as well as in actually taking action – think, for example, of the woman who decides not to pursue a case of sexual harassment because she knows it might provoke worse action still on the part of her harasser.

Poststructuralist perspectives on gender, power and organisation

Poststructuralist perspectives on gender and organisation rest on quite different understandings of power again. There are three core prin-ciples here. First, power is understood as to circulate between *all* social actors, rather than being restricted in the hands of a dominant few. Second, power is understood to operate through the construction of 'truth' through language and discourse. Third, the way power operates through discourses of truth shapes how each of us perceives ourselves, others, and the world around us. Let us take each of these points in turn.

First, poststructuralists are critical of top-down, functionalist views of power where power is understood as a possession, which is held by some who use it to prohibit the actions and freedom of the powerless. This amounts to a critique of *sovereign* conceptions of power which assume that power is intentional action by 'A' (one actor or agency) which ensures that 'B' (another actor or agency) bends to A's will. While Foucault acknowledged that there are instances where sovereign power is exercised (for example where senior officials can use their position to achieve their wishes), he located this within a more general understanding of power as decentralised. In making this claim, Fou-cault was arguing that power does not belong to individuals or to one group or class over others. Instead, the *practice* of power is decentral-ised and we are all part of its application as well as its subject. To quote Foucault at length:

> Power is not that which makes the difference between those who exclusively possess and retain it, and those who do not have it and submit to it. Power must be analysed as something which circulates, or rather as something which only functions in the form of a chain. It is never localised here or there, never in anybody's hands, never appropriated as a commodity of piece of wealth. Power is employed and exercised through a net-like organisation. And not only do individuals circulate between its threads; they are always simultaneously in the position of undergoing and exercising power. They are not only its inert or consenting target; they are always also the elements of its articulation. In other words, individuals are the vehicles of power, not the points of its application. (Foucault 1986:233–4)

Thus, power is understood as diffuse, as a network in which we are all enmeshed as both subjects and bearers of power relations. Women in work organisations are not simply powerless, oppressed by men who are all-powerful. Rather, both women's and men's relation to power in organisations is complex and shifting. Both women and men may bear power and both may be subject to power. A woman head-teacher, for example, has power over her staff, yet may also be constrained by a male teacher-member on the board of governors. Here, power and gender interact in multiple and complex ways – the head-teacher gains power from her position at work, but this may be challenged by gender and/or other positions, both formal and informal. This understanding of power effectively undermines any notion of women (or men) having objective interests with any degree of coherence or fixity. We are never simply oppressed or dominant.

The poststructuralist focus on language means that power and language are understood as integrally connected. The exercise of power resides in attempts to fix (or change) the meaning(s) of what is true through language. Language thus defines and limits the possibilities of how we understand the world and ourselves. In other words, people, as subjects, are constituted through the possibilities offered to them through language. Power resides in limiting those possibilities which themselves (re)produce power. For example, it is through language that 'categories' are constructed, such as gender, class, race or organisation, and meanings are attached. These exist for people to identify themselves by, yet the ambivalence present in language, the fact that it has to be constantly reproduced by individuals, means that meanings may be contested and identities redefined, never remaining fixed or set. Indeed, Foucault understood resistance to be coexistent with power: 'as soon as there is power there is the possibility of resistance. We can never be ensnared by power, we can always modify its grip' (Foucault in Kritzman 1988:122–3). In this sense, then, the individual is both *produced* by power, and a producer of power, rather than something completely distinct from it. (Compare this with sovereign conceptions of power, where power is something an individual might possess or not possess.)

An interesting example of this process in action can be seen in the changes and negotiations that have occurred in the job of air hostess on many airlines. Airlines have traditionally exercised a great deal of power over the performance of their (at first almost exclusively) female staff – specifying aspects of physical appearance such as height, weight and age, as well as aspects of personal grooming such as hairstyle, make-up and so on. In particular, hostesses were also trained in their personal demeanour: they had to be smiling and pleasant at all times, even in the face of rudeness and abuse from airline passengers. However, employees have challenged and resisted this exercise of power over their personal identity in different ways. For instance, men have challenged the practice of only employing women as cabinstaff. Women and men of all races, sizes and ages have challenged the regulation of personal appearance. Further, the pressure to act out the job through a certain performance has been resisted through personal modifications and interpretations – such as a refusal to smile, or a refusal to 'mean it' (Hochschild 1983). A signature on a work contract no longer means a whole work identity has been bought: people bring their own interpretations and their own politics to their jobs, and these frame how they carry out their tasks.

From this perspective, while power resides in attempts by a variety of agents to fix the meaning of truth, there is no underlying or 'real' truth beneath the meanings established. To be a man or a woman, a hostess or a steward, a nurse or an engineer has no essentialist meaning, merely that people are categorised through language and as such are subjected by meanings thence constructed. Nor are identifiable interest groups engaged in systematic efforts to fix meaning. To the contrary, both the establishment of discourses of 'truth', and any relationship that individuals or groups have with these discourses, are partial and fluid. Attention is thus shifted away from the question of real interests, to how 'real' interests are constructed, through language, discourse and text.

This intertwining of power and subjectivity is captured in Foucault's concept of 'disciplinary power', by which he described how the nature of domination in modern western societies is distinguished from earlier times. Whereas, before industrialisation, control was achieved through a variety of (often extremely violent and public) physical punishments, these were replaced by punishments directed towards the soul, the mind or the will (Burrell 1988). As Foucault (1977) describes, complex and subtle forms of correction and training appeared, which meant that rather than needing any visible forms of coercion, control was achieved through hidden techniques of discipline. These mechanisms of correction were developed principally in the more punitive institutions, such as prisons. For instance, Foucault notes how Bentham's design of the panopticon, a circular prison with a central well, from which prisoners could at all times be observerd, was widely adopted throughout Europe. While extending this analysis to modern work organisations may at first sight may seem rather extreme, these processes of control and scrutiny can be seen to operate at some level within and through all organisations. Whatever the organisation, discipline revolves around subjecting the lives of employees to minute details. Thus many organisations locate their employees in a cellular system, from whence they may be observed, construct timetables of activity and manuals of how to behave, and have clear systems of control and command in operation. For example, (women) nurses in hospitals traditionally had to conform to very exacting prescriptions about their behaviour. (While some of them have been relaxed more recently, their legacy remains). These covered not only how they conducted themselves on the ward, but also how they looked and dressed, where they lived while training – even what time they had to be in at night and who they socialised with. 'Matron' (the senior nurse, always a woman) exerted these principles often with a mere look or comment, and many lived in fear, although no physical retribution was ever given.

Overview

In this book we explore the possibility that all three forms of power described above operate simultaneously within contemporary work organisations, acting to constitute gendered experiences and to gender organisations in a range of diverse and even, sometimes, contradictory ways. We start, in Chapter 2, with a look at organisational structures, the way organisations are designed and formal rules are practised. Chapter 3 looks at organisational cultures – that is, the informal processes and practices, as well as the attitudes and belief systems that coexist within the organisation. In Chapter 4, we focus more specifically on management and leadership: the senior tiers in

organisations. In Chapter 5, we turn to the issue of sexuality in organisations, while in Chapter 6 we explore strategies that have been
pursued to challenge the gendering of organisational life. These are
the issues that have dominated research and writing on gender and
organisation to date and, as such, our book intends to offer an over-
view of research in the area. In each case, we trace the complex web of
relations that can be seen to exist between gender, power and organisation.

Through our exploration, we will show how that complex and contradictory picture of relations between gender and organisation that we
outlined at the start of this chapter has to be taken seriously, and in its
entirety. Indeed, it is representative of the multiple aspects that have to
be taken into account, in order to understand the relationships
between gender and organisation as we enter the twenty-first century.
In Chapter 7 we conclude by showing how power, in all its diverse
conceptualisations, is central to this understanding.

2

Organisational Structures

Introduction

We saw in Chapter 1 that the relationship between gender and organisation has been described in a range of rather different and often
competing ways. We have argued that endorsing any one of these
empirical or theoretical accounts as accurate over and above the others
is to lose sight of the insights offered by the other accounts and to
oversimplify both the empirical phenomena and their analysis. However, allowing this diverse range of empirical evidence and theoretical
argument to remain intact leaves us with a complex and confusing
picture of relations between gender and organisation. At a general
level, we have already suggested that focusing attention on the issue
of power – particularly the range of ways in which power is constituted
inside work organisations – will be helpful in allowing us to see how it
is that diverse and even contradictory relationships between gender and
organisation can coexist. In this chapter, we aim to focus more closely
on the nature of power in relation to one particular aspect of organisation: organisational structures. Precisely what is meant by this term may
vary from one writer to another, but includes reference to the formal
design of an organisation, perhaps conceptualised as a chart showing
job titles, with specific responsibilities arranged into hierarchies of
accountability and command. Reference will also be made to the formal,
documented rules and procedures that are understood to govern organisational practice within these hierarchies. In fact, organisations are
perhaps most popularly understood as structures, as an empty framework of hierarchies and procedures into which employees are simply

slotted. These organisational structures are understood to distribute specific degrees of power to named organisational positions – chief executive, manager, supervisor, and so on – regulating the overall configuration of power within an organisation and the particular degree of power which named individuals have over others, over resources, over decision-making and so on.

The aim of this chapter is to examine what, if anything, these organisational structures, and the power that inheres within them, have to do with gender. What is the place of organisational structures in the gendering of organisational life? To begin with, we know of course that women and men are placed very differently across organisational hierarchies. Women are still concentrated at the lowest levels and face specific constraints on their careers should they try to move up the organisational hierarchy. For black women the situation is even more pronounced. (See Chapters 1 and 4 for further details.) On the other hand, we also know that recent years have seen some significant changes in the position of women across organisational hierarchies. While the numbers of women at the top of organisational hierarchies may be low still, they are rising – often quite dramatically – across most sectors of the economy.(See Chapters 1 and 4 for further details.)

But what causes these gendered patterns? Are organisational structures themselves – the hierarchies and procedures described above – implicated, and if so how? In this chapter we review four different arguments about the place of organisational structures in the gendering of organisational life. In each case, we show that the argument hinges on a distinct understanding of power in relation to organisational structures. Throughout we will show that it is the particular interpretation of power in each argument that defines the relationship which is identified between organisational structures and gender in organisational life. How power is understood determines the way organisational structures are conceptualised and the connection – if any – which these structures are thought to have with gendered patterns of difference and discrimination.

Organisational structure and modern bureaucratic power

The understanding of organisations as structures owes a great deal to the work of Max Weber. Weber specified key features of the modern organisation precisely in terms of specific identifiable organisational structures. He used the term 'bureaucracy' to describe this particular type of organisation. It is widely accepted that the bureaucratic form of organisation emerged in the West during the period of transition from feudalism to modernity and capitalism which took place from the sixteenth century onwards (Ferguson 1984, Morgan 1986, Clegg 1990, Thompson and McHugh 1990). As new economic, social and political relations associated with capitalist modernity became established, bureaucracy assumed an ever more dominant position. By the twentieth century, bureaucracy had commonly ceased to refer to just one type of organisation but had become synonymous with organisation. In the West, when we think of organisation, we think of bureaucracy. Furthermore, as aspects of human social and economic life become ever more organised, for example by the intervention of state institutions such as the law, schools and social services as well as business organisations, some have been moved to speak of the 'bureaucratisation' of modern society (Ferguson 1984).

Weber distinguished a number of key features which he argued contributed to the 'ideal-type' bureaucracy' (Weber 1964). In using the technique of an ideal type, Weber meant to convey that his model would not necessarily be exactly mirrored in empirical reality. Instead, Weber claimed that modern organisations would display tendencies towards the features of the ideal type and, perhaps even more importantly, that the features of the ideal type would come to be agreed upon as sound organisational principles and goals. The key features of Weber's ideal type are as follows:

- *Functional specialisation*: tasks within the organisation are finely broken down into individual jobs. Each job is highly specific and can be carried out by a specialist who is expert in that precise task.
- *Clear hierarchy*: jobs are coordinated into a coherent whole by an orderly structure of command and control. Each person knows precisely their own degree of authority, knows their place in the structure of authority and knows how the hierarchy works.
- *Precise contracts of employment*: these specify, in writing, each individual's duties, and their responsibilities as well as their rights;
- *Standardisation of rules and procedures*: all organisational activity is governed by written rules and procedures, which all staff have clear knowledge of and adhere to. These rules are utterly impersonal, and always carried out in the same way regardless of individual personalities or social relationships. This renders behaviour within bureaucracies uniform and predictable.

- *Credentials*: each member of staff is appointed to a specific job on the basis of their technical skill and competence to perform their task. Skill and competence are measured increasingly through formal qualifications. Individuals may rise up the hierarchy on the basis of their qualifications and other measurable, technical skills. Bureaucracies are meritocratic.
- *Rewards*: these are strictly determined by place in the hierarchy. Pay and conditions are attached to individual posts in the hierarchy and not to individual people. Power belongs to the position in the hierarchy, to the office, and to individuals only in so much as they hold that position.
  (*Sources*: Weber 1947, Morgan 1986, Clegg 1990, Morgan 1990.)

The emphasis on organisational structures within Weber's account of bureaucracy is clear. The finely graded hierarchy linking specific tasks, the standardisation of rules and procedures and, as part of this, the objective allocation of people to tasks and tasks to rewards, all establish the primacy of formal organisational structures over any individuals or personal relationships within those organisations. The abstract structure determines organisational life, independently of any particular individuals who may inhabit that structure. Indeed, Weber believed that individual personalities, personal characteristics and social relationships would cease to be important; they would be overruled and controlled by the bureaucratic structures described above.

F.W. Taylor (1947) was also concerned with the way organisational structures serve to control behaviour and practice in work organisations. Taylor was especially concerned with establishing modern management techniques, which he saw as essential to the success of rapidly expanding organisations in the early twentieth century. As the division of labour increased, organisational hierarchies extended and formalised rules and procedures came to dominate, and the role of managers, who would oversee activity in the increasingly complex organisations, became ever more important. Taylor developed five basic management principles, which he combined into his theory of 'scientific management' (Morgan 1988, Thompson and McHugh 1990). The first principle was to make sure that managers, not workers, were responsible for all planning and control of work. The second was to develop a science for each element of work, breaking each task down to discover its component parts and establish a precise formula for carrying out the task to optimum efficiency. The third principle was to use scientific techniques to appoint the best person for the job. The fourth was to make sure that workers are trained properly in the precise techniques necessary to carry out their job efficiently. Taylor's final principle was to make sure that managers police the production process, once it has been established according to these principles, and that workers are rewarded fairly.

Unlike Taylor, Weber's feelings about what he believed to be the inevitable transition towards bureaucracy were mixed. On the one hand he mourned the loss of less predictable, less mechanistic and more magical forms of social life. Related concerns were echoed by Marx, who saw bureaucracy taking on a life of its own, rendering human beings no more than functional cogs in the bureaucratic machine (Clegg 1990:30). On the other hand, Weber believed that the organising structures of bureaucracy represented a positive progression from earlier forms of organisation.

The positive benefits offered by bureaucracy explained its ascendancy during the transition to capitalism and modernity. This link can be made in two slightly different ways. First, bureaucracy was a way of coping with the increasing scale of production and markets as capitalism advanced. This led to larger and larger factories and businesses, the proliferation of goods, the diversification of production within firms and the rapid expansion of markets within Europe, the US and the countries they colonised. These developments made quite inadequate the 'simple' organisation of earlier times, where few distinctions were made between workers, and single entrepreneurs or families ruled their (relatively) small enterprises through coercion. In its place, bureaucracy offered a way of allowing worker specialisation to deal with technical specificities at the same time as maintaining devolved control through strict hierarchic structures and rules. Bureaucracy facilitated the development of capitalism, enabling firms to deal with the ever increasing complexity of the capitalist world. As horizons expanded and events outside the organisation became less predictable and controllable, bureaucracy promised that inside the organisation all contingencies could be brought under rigid, predictable control. In a changing world, bureaucracy was seen as the technical form of organisation which would allow organisations to work to maximum efficiency and effectiveness. 'Effectiveness' and 'efficiency' were assumed to be universal principles to which all modern organisations would aspire, and bureaucracy was assumed to be the best way of achieving these goals. In this way, bureaucracy came to be seen as a 'necessary feature of modernity' (Clegg 1990: 35). Modernity demanded calculability of results and bureaucracy offered an instrument or tool of unrivalled technical superiority with which to achieve this (ibid.).

A second link between bureaucracy and modernity arises from this over-arching belief in the possibility of finding one best way to create finite order and certainty. This rationalising process is understood as a key feature of modernity of which the emergence of bureaucracy is symptomatic. The transition to modernity involved a shift away from faith in divine, magical and coercive forms of control and authority towards a belief in scientific knowledge and the establishment of 'laws' through which the world could be understood and hence controlled. This belief applied to all spheres of life: to views of nature, to attitudes towards witchcraft and magic, to the long-term decline in religious belief, and to economic organisation. In short, with modernity came the belief in rationality. Bureaucracy was seen to embody the principles of rationality: that science could establish 'one best way'; that complex social and economic processes could be rendered intelligible, manipulable and controllable; and that these forms of knowledge and control were in the best interests of all, so that the only interests served by bureaucracy would be organisational efficiency and success. Thus, as Clegg summarises, Weber's ideal type of bureaucracy 'springs from a modernist vision of a modernist world' (1990:4). Indeed, Weber's vision of bureaucracy and, to a lesser extent Taylor's scientific management, has left a tremendous legacy within organisational theory. The imperative to find the precise 'one best way' of arranging organisational structures to achieve greatest efficiency, and the view of organisations as instruments which can be manipulated to achieve desired ends, have pervaded much organisational and management literature.

The degree of faith in organisational structures suggested by Weber, and others, hinges on a particular definition of power. During the course of his life's work, Weber defined a number of different sorts of 'power', within which perhaps the most significant category was 'authority' (Weber 1986). Within this, Weber distinguished three ideal types of authority. The progressive nature of bureaucracy lay principally in the way it replaced 'charismatic' and 'traditional' authority with 'rational-legal' authority. In this schema, charismatic authority refers to the power held by individuals with such special personal qualities that these define their right to rule (Morgan 1986). Charisma means, literally, gift of grace (Morgan 1986:159). Examples of charismatic authority might include Ghandi or Nelson Mandela (especially prior to democratic elections in South Africa). By contrast, 'traditional' authority refers to the power held by those who symbolise or embody traditional values, such as monarchs or the aristocratic classes. Such people have authority merely by virtue of birth into those social categories which have traditionally held power. Finally, rational-legal authority is achieved only through the correct application of formal rules and procedures (Morgan 1986). Those in authority must 'win their rights to power through procedural means' (ibid:160). Thus, rational-legal authority contrasts strongly with the other two types of authority, principally because of the emphasis on transparent and neutral procedures which enable everyone to at least attempt to win authority. This is not only more equitable and democratic; it also (presumably) ensures that authority is exerted by those best able to do so, as determined by technical means, and not simply by those with charisma or traditional status. So, like Taylor, Weber believed that the establishment of bureaucratic structures could ensure the most efficient form of modern organisation. This efficiency was ensured by the democratic configuration of power which defined bureaucracy.

What then does this imply for thinking about the relationship between gender and organisational structures? If bureaucratic structures determine organisational practice, and are themselves neutral, then gender inequality should not exist in the modern organisation. Indeed, it could be argued that bureaucracy was particularly beneficial to women, as Pringle explains:

> For Weber, bureaucracy is progressive in that breaks down the old patriarchal structures and removes the arbitrary power held by fathers and masters in traditional society (Pringle 1989:85).

Rational-legal authority, unlike traditional authority (and, arguably, charismatic authority) is understood to be gender-neutral. If bureaucratic organisations are ruled by organisational structures which permit only rational-legal authority, then bureaucracies should allow all individuals to be judged by their personal skills and qualities and not according to prejudiced stereotypes attributed to them simply by virtue of their sex. Bureaucracy should thus allow us to see that women and men have the same abilities, and enable all individuals to realise their full potential unencumbered by inaccurate gender stereotypes.

However, despite the rapid advance of bureaucratic forms of organisation in the twentieth century, we know, of course, that a vast range of gender differences and inequalities continue to persist across modern organisations. How can this be explained? It could be argued that the differences we see are the outcome of fundamental differences between women and men: that women and men have different orientations, because of their sex, which mean that women are more committed toward home and family, while men are more concerned with employment and careers. In this argument, these distinctively gendered orientations are seen as a matter of predisposition and choice: women and men choose to concentrate on the activities they are best at and which fulfil them most. In this way, intrinsic qualities of women and men are used to explain the gendering of organisational hierarchies. The cause of gender differences in work organisations is therefore seen to lie *outside* organisations. Any gender differences manifest inside organisations are therefore nothing to do with organisational structures *per se*, but to do with the different qualities and interests which women and men bring with them to work. Once at work, women and men are subjected to rational-legal authority which delivers fair judgements on the basis of organisational criteria and the gendered individuals with which the organisation is presented. So, if women show less interest in attending training courses or in promotion, this is their choice. They will be treated differently by the bureaucracy as a consequence, but this does not constitute discrimination, simply a rational judgement about the qualities and usefulness of that person to the organisation. Women's position within organisational hierarchies is therefore the outcome of their choices about how much time and effort they wish to put into the workplace.

However, others have argued that internal organisational factors may be just as important – if not more important – in explaining sex differences in the organisational hierarchy. Within organisational sociology, Acker and Van Houten (1974) were among the first to claim that gender differences were mobilised *by* organisational structures, rather than simply imported from elsewhere into an essentially neutral organisational arena. In this formulation, gendered power – rather than gender-neutral rational-legal authority – is understood to inhere within organisational structures. Rather than seeing organisational structures as carrying the power necessary to achieve organisational goals in everyone's best interests, Acker and Van Houten opened the door to seeing organisational structures as the mobilisation of male power.

Precisely how do gendered power relations implicate organisational structures in this way? The following sections concentrate on three different arguments. First, we consider Kanter's argument that organisational structures are gendered only in so much as men happened to populate the hierarchies at an earlier time than women. This may mean that organisational structures have come to sustain male privilege and power, but this is seen an unintended outcome and does not indicate that organisational structures are inherently gendered in any way. To the contrary, Kanter's account denies any deliberate or systematic mobilisation of male power through organisational structures and is underlain by an optimistic belief in the rational-legal *potential* of organisational power relations. Second, we consider arguments which suggest that organisational structures serve quite explicitly to keep women and men in their distinctive positions, taking the particular forms they do in order to maintain male power. Here, then, we are moving from a liberal to a social-structural interpretation of organisational structures. Third, and finally, we consider arguments which suggest that bureaucratic organisational structures can never be stripped of this gendered power, and that women must establish alternative forms of organisation for themselves.

Male dominance and the corruption of bureaucratic power

We know that women and men tend to occupy different positions within organisational hierarchies. One explanation for the persistence of this is that once segregation has been established it becomes very difficult to break the pattern. This argument is made by Kanter, a US business consultant and academic, in her book *Men and Women of the Corporation* (1977a), which was one of the first detailed empirical studies of gender and organisation and remains widely cited today.

Kanter begins with an observation about numbers: at the time of writing, 96 per cent of all mid and senior managers in the US were men, and in Indsco (the pseudonym she gave to the organisation she studied) women comprised only 2 per cent of officials and managers but 87 per cent of the clerical and office workers. The explanation for this, she argues, lies with historical factors which are no longer relevant in today's world. Namely, she continues, it is the fact that men were the first to colonise the bureaucracies which expanded in the US from the late nineteenth century onwards. Women were relative latecomers, only entering bureaucratic employment as opportunities in domestic service contracted during the first two decades of the twentieth century. The increase in women's presence was dramatic: in 1870 the US census takers recorded just seven female stenographers (typists); by 1920 the census recorded 500000 women doing the same job. As women entered business organisations they moved into routine clerical work because, Kanter argues, management had already been established as a masculine role – that is, something which men, and not women, carried out. This, she claims, was simply a function of the need for the newly emergent and rapidly expanding occupation of 'managment' to create a

> 'spirit of managerialism' that gave ideological coherence to the control of a relatively small and exclusive group of men over a large group of workers and also that differentiated to viewpoint of the managers from that of the owner-entrepreneurs. (Kanter 1977a:20)

The fact that managers happened to all be men meant that this 'spirit of managerialism' came to work through a masculinised culture and reliance on gender uniformity at the managerial level. (See Chapter 3 below for discussion of the concept of 'homosociability' which Kanter uses to elaborate on this.) Because men had dominated the early bureaucracies, they came to behave in ways which served to perpetuate male dominance. However, it is vital to emphasise that it was the requirements of the management function which established this behaviour and culture, and not any masculine imperative to dominate women. Here, power is vested in managers, who happen to be men. Now, this in turn may have gendered consequences, but in Kanter's account power is derived fundamentally from management positions and is conceptualised as management power and not male power.

Just as the managerial role makes men behave in ways which reinforce male dominance of management positions, Kanter argues that women's segregation into routine clerical positions, with few possibilities for promotion, causes them to behave in ways which ensure that they stay there. At Indsco great status was conferred on those who moved up the ladder. But for those who did not, the message was clear: 'You do not mean much to your company unless you get the chance to move on' (1977:131). In this context, Kanter argues that if you give people opportunities then their ambitions and their capabilities soar. If opportunity is denied, they perish. Using this argument Kanter claims that women stuck in dead-end jobs start to appear disinterested in their work, unmotivated and more inclined to familial and domestic concerns. All these are claims which have been made by those who believe that women and men have fundamentally different orientations because of their distinctive genetic make-up. But Kanter's point is to refute these claims. It is not that women display these tendencies because they are women, but rather because they are stuck in dead-end jobs. Women's relative powerlessness in bureaucratic organisations is thus understood as a consequence of their structural location and not their sex.

Similarly, the few women in management posts may display different behaviour to their male counterparts not because they are women, but because they are seen as 'tokens' in the masculinised managerial world. Kanter argues that 'tokens become encapsulated in limited roles that give them the security of a "place" but constrain their areas of permissible or rewardable action' (1977:231). Women managers do derive authority from their structural location, but their scarcity undermines this. Because it is so unusual to find women in management positions, Kanter argues, the few who do attain management status are only accepted on stereotypical terms. They 'can never really be seen as they are' (1993:230), Rather, if they want to fit in they have little choice but to accommodate themselves to the stereotypical roles on offer: mother, pet, iron maiden and seductress. (See Chapter 4 for a fuller discussion of these roles.) Of course, the fact that they are women is what establishes them as tokens, and the roles offered are defined in terms of femininity but, Kanter argues, women managers' adoption of these roles has nothing to do with intrinsic feminine personalities or values. Rather, the phenomenon is explained by their exceptional location within the organisational hierarchy.

The key point being made, then, is that jobs shape people, their behaviour and their identities. The organisational hierarchy exerts tremendous power, generating different identities at different levels. Managers come to take on certain identities as a consequence of being offered opportunity, autonomy and fulfilment. Routine clerical workers come to take on quite different identities as a consequence of being denied opportunity, autonomy and fulfilment. This enables Kanter to refute entrenched sexist assumptions held about women and men. It is not, she says, that women and men are intrinsically different at all. In fact, given the chance, we would see that, underneath it all, women and men are essentially the same. But at present, differential locations in the organisational hierarchy means that women and men behave differently. In this sense, Kanter argues, 'the corporation is the quintessential contemporary people producer' (1993:1). Like Weber, Kanter believes that people are shaped by the character of modern bureaucracies, but Kanter has discovered a flaw in the smooth transition to fully functioning bureaucracy. Kanter agrees that in principle organisational structures are essentially gender-neutral, impacting on both women and men in the same way. The fact that women and men tend to occupy different places in hierarchy explains the apparent differences in their behaviour and attitude towards work, not the fact that they are different sexes. In sum, structural location becomes self-reinforcing. Once women and men occupy different positions, they stay there.

Kanter's understanding of organisational structures, and their relation to gender, hinges on a particular understanding of power. While she clearly sees patterns of disadvantage present within work organisations, and connects this to the way organisational hierarchies function, she refutes any suggestion that this is the outcome of social structural power wielded by men in order to dominate women. Rather, she sees power as an enabling and productive capacity in organisations. She describes power as 'the ability to get things done' (1977:166) and as 'autonomy and freedom of action' (*ibid*:196). Power in this sense may only incidentally involve power over another person or persons and is seen as positive both for the individual thus enabled and for the organisation as a whole. In practice, Kanter acknowledges, this power has accrued to those in senior hierarchical positions, both by virtue of authority granted to them by the hierarchy and because 'power begets power' (ibid:168): those who have it can attract more, while those who do not are continually denied. We can think of this in terms of positive and negative spirals of power and powerlessness. For example, people have come to prefer men as managers, since men have always had more power than women and therefore are understood to be the more powerful sex. Similarly, women are seen as mean or bossy managers because we are less used to seeing women wield this sort of hierarchical power: it clashes with our preconceptions. Furthermore, women's general powerlessness compared with men causes them to behave in less creative and enabling ways, and this characteristic (borne of powerlessness and not sex) comes to be associated with all women. However, Kanter is certain, once women do get into positions of hierarchical power, these negative stereotypes will cease to function, since 'power wipes out sex' (ibid:200). Once again then, Kanter sees that gender has accidentally become caught up in these cycles of organisational power and powerlessness. However it may appear at present, there is nothing intrinsically gendered about organisational structures or the power which is mobilised through them. This position allows Kanter great optimism about the future of bureaucracy. The deployment of power in organisations should become positive, productive and enabling, accrued and exercised equally by men and women for the collective benefit of the organisation and its members.

Kanter suggests a number of measures to challenge this destructive loop which historical accident has bestowed on modern organisations. One of the most pressing concerns is to equalise the numbers of women and men across the hierarchy. Only by doing so will the masculine character of management be disrupted and replaced by a neutral 'spirit of managerialism'. A more specific problem to be addressed concerns the status of secretarial work. This work, she admits, remains defined in non-bureaucratic and gendered terms even in modern bureaucracies. The problem is, Kanter argues, that secretarial work has never been fully bureaucratised but is a 'bureaucratic anomaly... a repository of the personal inside the bureaucratic' (1977:101). Through the bureaucratisation of secretarial work, this anomaly can be eradicated.

Kanter's emphasis, therefore, is on getting bureaucratic structures to function properly, ensuring that rational-legal authority is fully established. Principally this involves extending opportunities to more people in the workforce and valuing all workers more fully. These changes, she suggests, would be good for organisations:

> In general, organisations with enhanced opportunity would be, I propose, more alive and interesting places. There would be fewer people indifferent to work or considered 'dead wood'. There would be more enthusiasm for innovation and less dysfunctional conservative resistance. And there would be structural supports for more equal treatment of women, minorities and disadvantaged classes. (1993:275)

Thus, making changes to established organisational design is seen as good for everyone including – almost as a by-product – women. This is an approach which has been taken by many liberal feminists in their campaigns for change. Appealing to the widespread popular assumption that bureaucratic organisations should be regulated by rational-legal authority, liberal feminists have been able to make a forceful case for change in those instances where discriminatory structures can be shown to exist. Where it can be shown that sex discrimination persists inside supposedly rational organisations, it is highly effective to argue that, in its own terms, the bureaucracy should make structural changes to (re)establish neutrality. This generally means rewriting procedures, or introducing new rules and regulations to make sure that the structures do indeed deliver their promise of a meritocratic outcome. (See Chapter 6 for an extended discussion of organisational change.) Here, then, sex discrimination at work is thought to persist because we have yet to design the right structures to tackle it. In this sense then, the Weberian vision of bureaucracy as progressive is a worthy and ultimately achievable one. It is simply that we have not got there yet. Organisational structures are still defined in terms of rational-legal authority – at least potentially – and any other configurations of power inside work organisations are understood as anomalous and bad for both staff and the organisation.

In the following section, we will move on to consider a rather different understanding of the relationship between gender and organisational structures which hinges on a totally different conceptualisation of power.

Organisational structures and male power

A rather different argument about the relationship between gender and organisational structures suggests that, far from a contingent outcome of history, gendered organisational structures are actively sustained by men in their own interests. In this argument, it is not simply gender-neutral organisational imperatives which maintain the historic imbalance between women and men across the hierarchy but the mobilisation of male power. Organisational structures do not come to reproduce male power unwittingly, but are in fact designed for this purpose or, at least, actively maintained with this in mind.

Ressner (1987), in her study of Swedish government bureaucracies, argues that bureaucratic hierarchies should also be seen as patriarchal structures and thus that men dominate not only as managers but also as men. Working within a structuralist feminist perspective which recognises the dual systems of patriarchy and class oppression, Ressner claims that bureaucratic organisations privilege dominant interests within both class and gender systems. In relation to the former, Ressner is building on a long history of Marxist interpretations of bureaucracy and scientific management. These emphasise the way bureaucracies allow the separation of control (by management) from execution (by workers), enabling managers to appropriate workers' knowledge and dominate workers more effectively (Braverman 1974, Thompson and McHugh 1990). In relation to the gender oppression, Ressner suggests, patriarchy resides in organisational structures (as well as organisational cultures, see Chapter 3), which serve to constrain women's opportunities at the same time as they enhance men's careers. Thus, male power is understood to reside *within* bureaucratic rules and procedures. Similar points have been made by a range of commentators (see below), who highlight three key aspects of organisational design which contribute to organisational gender inequalities, as follows.

Methods of recruitment and selection
First, attention is drawn to methods of recruitment and selection. Since the 1970s most Western countries have implemented legislation which makes it illegal to specify a preference for either a male or a female in recruitment and selection of staff. (See Chapter 6 for further details of this legislation in Britain.) However, even where they appear to be entirely gender-neutral, procedures in this area of organisational practice have been shown to impact differentially on women and men. In some organisations, 'informal' recruitment still takes place. This means that word of mouth is used to make people aware of a vacancy and/or that appointments are made without the establishment of formal job specifications, selection criteria or interview. While it can still be claimed that the 'best person for the job' is being sought, regardless of sex, this type of recruitment can restrict who even knows about the job to a select band and may allow full rein to any prejudices or stereotypes which managers might hold (Collinson *et al.* 1990; see also Chapter 4). However, some would argue that informal recruitment is not a properly bureaucratic mode of practice – since it is not governed by overt rules and procedures – and that it is precisely in its informality that discrimination is allowed to flourish. By contrast, it is suggested, formalising recruitment and selection – establishing proper bureaucratic structures – will ensure that individuals are treated in their merits alone (Webb 1991). Not surprisingly, such claims for bureaucratic formalisation have been widely used by equal opportunities campaigners for many years.

Nonetheless, there is now a substantial body of evidence to unsettle this faith in formalisation. Even where jobs are openly advertised, decisions made about *where* to advertise might mean that women – and other groups – are less likely to see the advertisement. Connected to this, the advertisement might imply preference for one sex or the other, for example by using a photograph which shows only men performing the task. Even were these prejudices eradicated, the job requirements might persist in favouring men over women. Many examples have been uncovered of hidden assumptions in adverts and selection criteria which have precisely this effect. For instance, qualifications may be asked for which, in fact, are totally unnecessary to perform the job. If these are qualifications which men are more likely to hold (for example, higher-level qualifications in design and techno-logy) the process of recruitment will discriminate against women. Other similar requirements, which are unnecessary to do the job and encourage men rather than women, include the following:

- *Length of experience* (or 'time serving'), which women are less likely to achieve because of the greater probability of discontinuous career histories linked to childcare.
- *Restrictions on age* – for example under 30 or under 40 – which may also result in fewer women applying, since time taken out of the labour market may put them in comparable positions with men at a slightly later age.
- *Mobility and travel* – may be more difficult for those women who have children and women with partners who are less likely than the traditional female housewife to be able to make long distance moves easily.
- *Physical requirements* – for example, being able to lift heavy weights (where mechanical devices could do the job just as well), a require-ment which would also discourage some men from applying.

Similar points can also be made about the selection of staff for promo-tion. All these requirements may inhibit women from applying for jobs or promotions and, even if women do apply, may prejudice selectors decisions about who to appoint.

Even where women and men are recruited to the same posts, recruit-ment practices may contribute to gendered careers. Studies of British high-street banking organisations make this point particularly well. Up until the 1970s, banks recruited women and men to separate clerical posts. The grades, payment and promotion opportunities were quite distinct. In particular, the ceiling for women's grades stopped before management level. Following the attentions of the Equal Opportun-ities Commission (Crompton and Jones 1984, Scouller 1992) banks revised recruitment so that women and men were both recruited to identical clerical posts. However, the common practice of recruiting women with lower-level qualifications gained at 16 years old, and men with higher level qualifications gained at 18 years old, established a tiering system whereby women were denied access to study for Institute of Bankers qualifications and automatically discounted for promotion to senior positions because of their lack of qualifications. Thus, even where the same clerical posts were held by both sexes the structuring of recruitment in these organisations meant that the jobs held very different opportunities for the two sexes. As Crompton and Jones concluded, in their influential study *White Collar Proletariat* (1984), the office proletariat is not a homogenous mass but is structured by sex. Indeed, Morgan (1986) argues that the maintenance of boundaries between workers can be interpreted as one aspect of the exercise of power inside organisations. Certainly, boundaries between women and men have been maintained by formal procedures of recruitment and selection, which supports the argument that male power resides in bureaucratic structures.

Job grading and career ladders
The second aspect of organisational design which has been shown to limit women and enhance men's career opportunities is the way jobs are graded and hierarchical ladders between jobs are constructed. It has been established that the skills associated with jobs typically done by women are less highly rated than those associated with jobs typically done by men. This is partly because the abilities required to carry out feminised work, for example care work, are seen as less difficult to acquire and as involving less complexity and responsibility; and partly because it is assumed that women acquire these skills 'naturally', and that since formal training is not required they need not be highly valued. The introduction of job evaluation schemes, whereby scientific techniques are used to assess job content and to rate jobs according to criteria of knowledge required, skill, complexity, effort entailed and working conditions, has been seen as one way to overcome these sex prejudices. Acker (1990) found that such schemes were used world-wide as a technique assumed to rationalise organisational hierarchies and set fair wages. Apart from issues of equity, Acker points out that, in any case, hierarchies will function more smoothly if the staff within them believe them to be objective and reasonable. So far so good. But, Acker argues, job evaluation rests on criteria which, although they are supposed to be objective, reflect entrenched managerial values which are, in turn, associated with the masculinity of management. Thus, it remains the case that some aspects of particular jobs are ignored or devalued, while others are championed. Complexity and responsibility are defined in terms of managerial and professional tasks, Acker argues, thus:

> The childcare worker who is responsible for other human beings or the secretary who serves six different, temperamental bosses can only be minimally counted if the congruence between position level, responsibility and complexity is to be preserved. (1990:149)

She concludes:

> Job evaluation systems were intended to reflect the values of managers and produce a believable ranking of jobs based on those values. Such rankings would not deviate substantially from rankings already in place that contain gender typing and gender segregation of jobs and the clustering of women workers in the lowest and worst paid jobs. (p. 150)

Here Acker echoes Weber's formulation of rational-legal authority, which he understood to rest on broad approval of the hierarchy which, in turn, rested on the recognition that people in certain posts had a right to exert power, a 'right to rule'. Of course, unlike Weber, Acker reinterprets this authority as gendered. The 'right to rule' is established by gendered organisational values and gender stereotyping, not by purely abstract criteria. Alternative criteria for job evaluation could be established and might pose more a more fundamental challenge to existing 'organisational logic' (Acker 1990) and established hierarchies (Cockburn 1991). Such fundamental challenges are rare but important, and we discuss them in Chapter 7 below.

Linked to this issue of rules and procedures which position particular jobs in the organisational hierarchy or structure, an important point has been made about the way different jobs are – or are not – linked together. Clerical work offers a good example. At the level of the labour market as a whole, this category of work is done by both women and men, although not in equal proportions. However, particular organisational structures may mean that men doing clerical work have more opportunities to advance up the career ladder than women. Some clerical jobs are located at the bottom of long career hierarchies, making it possible for individuals to advance from routine clerical work at the bottom of the hierarchy right up to senior management at the top – although, as we have already seen, recruitment procedures might in fact structure this hierarchy by sex. Other clerical posts are segregated into much shorter hierarchies, some of which are comprised of just two or three rungs. In a US study of hierarchies in 100 organisations, Barron *et al.* (1986) found that women were significantly less likely than men to be in jobs that were linked into long ladders of opportunity. Women were segregated into posts (including manufacturing as well as clerical posts) which were tightly bound into short hierarchies, whereas men were in ladders that were longer. The study identified 283 promotion ladders and found that as many as 71 per cent were exclusively male while only 6 per cent were exclusively female. Clearly, men dominated the lower-level posts which had opportunities while women were segregated into organisational dead-ends. This is frequently because the skills involved in feminised jobs are undervalued and hence not seen as having anything to contribute at a higher level of the organisation. Halford *et al* (1997) found good examples of this in their study of banking, nursing and local government organisations. Nursing, for instance, is seen to be incompatible with management. Despite strong evidence that nurses are increasingly developing managerial skills at ward level, the managerial career ladder for nurses has been significantly truncated in recent years (see also Davies 1995). Similarly certain kinds of routine clerical work in local authorities are tightly segregated into organisational 'dead-zones' despite the multiple skills developed by staff in these posts. Meanwhile in banking, the managerial work most frequently done by women – 'operations management' which entails everyday coordination of branch staff and activities – is not generally seen as suitable experience for promotion to more senior levels. Cockburn (1991) makes the same observation in her study of retailing, reporting women's complaints that 'their chances were "ceilinged out" a grade or so higher, while men had the whole organisational tree to play in' (p. 63). Here again, we see how the creation of boundaries between male and female workers acts as a structural form of male power in modern organisations.

Organising hours of work
The third and final aspect of organisational design which has been shown to shape gendered opportunities is the way organisations structure working hours. Most organisations continue to offer workers contracts which commit them to 35 or more hours per week and expect that these hours are carried out between 9 a.m. and 5 p.m. or thereabouts. The full-time worker with a continuous, life-long career has been established as the norm in modern organisations. By contrast, part-time working, job-sharing and discontinuous careers are understood as exceptional, as 'other' to the established norm. Although there has been a dramatic increase in part-time work since the 1950s and especially during the late 1980s and 1990s, part-time work is often structured by different terms and conditions (for example, lower *pro rata* pay, or ineligibility for pension schemes). Furthermore, part-time work is not structured into mainstream organisational hierarchies, but is considered suitable only for certain lower level functions. For example, in a recent study part-time work was found to feature in the careers of more than 40 per cent of all nurses, but not a single NHS manager worked on a part-time (or job-share) basis (IHSM 1995). Similarly, in

medicine, part-time work is considered 'unsound' (Allen 1988) and part-timers are heavily segregated into certain types of – less prestigious – work. Having researched doctors' careers for many years, Isobel Allen concludes that

> The medical career structure has evolved through what has been perceived to be the best way of organising the delivery of services to patients and satisfying the manpower needs of the profession and the health service. The needs of women doctors has never been a particularly important factor in bringing about change in the way the profession is organised. (1988:85)

One of the few branches of medicine in which part-time work is more acceptable is in general practice, and many women doctors elect to work here partly because of the compromise it offers. In 1998 part-time women GPs outnumbered equivalent men by more than two to one (EOR 78, 1998). More generally, Crompton and Sanderson (1990) have observed that many professional women remain in 'practitioner niches', practising their profession, rather than moving into management of other professionals, precisely because this offers part-time possibilities. Thus, it is clear that organisational personnel procedures, which allow shorter hours in some areas of work, but not in others – specifically, not in management – contribute to the concentration of women with children into practitioner niches. Part-time work may enable women to stay in the labour market, rather than not being there at all, but it clearly does not facilitate hierarchical careers because of the way part-time posts are segregated from mainstream career hierarchies. Women professionals may be acquiring positions where they can practice expertise, but are far less likely to achieve positions of bureaucratic authority (Savage 1992).

Discussion
In sum, far from being gender neutral, it has been argued that formal organisational rules and procedures are patriarchal. It is suggested that men use organisational structures to sustain their dominance. The primary agent of power in these accounts, then, is men, and not management, as Kanter suggests. The precise configuration of this may vary from one organisation to another. However, there seems to be compelling evidence that organisational structures do indeed contribute to the construction and maintenance of gender inequalities. It is not simply that organisational imperatives have, accidentally, maintained differences between men and women of the corporation. While the issues discussed above may be presented as if they were organisational

imperatives – the only way to organise work – the evaluation above suggests that this conceals the way male interests are served by organisational structures. Formalisation of organisational procedures in the archetypal Weberian sense does not, it seems, ensure their gender neutrality. It is not simply that managers flout these formalised procedures, following their own prejudices instead, although certainly this happens:

> Exhorting managers to 'judge people on their merits', ignoring all they 'know' about the supposed capacities of women and men and the actual functioning of their organisation, is like asking someone to ride a bicycle by following the instructions in a rule-book, ignoring all the ordinary know-how. (Webb 1991:18–19)

Indeed, liberal faith in changing the formal rules and expecting managers to comply can seem a little naive in the face of evidence from organisations where this approach has been taken and failed (see discussion in Chapter 7). But more than this it seems that apparently neutral structures are in fact gendered. Thus, even where formally neutral procedures are followed to the letter, as it stands, they will not guarantee fair outcomes. Rather, it is argued, male power is embedded in even the apparently most innocuous of organisational structures.

One of the most powerful arguments in this vein, is found in Acker's recent work (1990, 1992). The particular power of bureaucracy, she argues is in its neutral appearance. This makes it acceptable and difficult to challenge. However, Acker claims that far from being neutral, bureaucratic structures are in fact premised on masculine social characteristics. She makes this argument from the initial observation that jobs and organisational hierarchies are devised independently of the people who might fill them. Indeed, as we saw earlier, this was a central feature of Weber's ideal-type bureaucracy. However, while for Weber this was central to the positive move away from traditional and charismatic forms of authority, Acker interprets it as inherently gendered. This is because the abstract structuring of jobs and hierarchies excludes any other demands which might be made on the abstract worker (by family or other responsibilities). Acker continues:

> The closest the disembodied worker comes to a real worker is the male worker whose life centres on his full-time, life-long job, while his wife or another woman takes care of his personal needs and his children... The woman worker, assumed to legitimate obligations other than those required by the job [does] not fit with the abstract job... hierarchies are gendered because they are... constructed on these underlying assumptions. (Acker 1990:149)

Thus, Acker concludes, bureaucratic organisation is deeply gendered. Gender is not a superficial layer on top of an otherwise neutral bureaucratic structure, as liberal perspectives on gender and organisational structures would suggest. Far from being an unwanted import, gender is embedded in bureaucratic organisation. Systematic, structural male power resides in bureaucratic structures. Bureaucratic structures have been designed by men, in men's interests. Every time these bureaucratic structures are invoked, male power is activated. Furthermore, it is argued that men actively maintain the structures which benefit them *as men*. From this perspective challenging the gendered structure of organisations would not be good for everyone – as Kanter asserts – but would be good for women and bad for men. Not least, as Crompton and Jones (1984) argue, the extremely high probability which male workers have of achieving promotion rests on the establishment of a group of workers who are 'unpromotable'. Only with women removed from contention can the majority of men expect to get on.

So, where do we go from here? Might it be possible to redesign bureaucratic structures in such a way that the male power embedded within them was effectively removed? Were the cooperation of those in powerful positions – mainly men – secured to achieve this, how much change would need to take place? Is it merely a case of imposing more bureaucratic mechanisms to get rid of inherent biases, for example in job specifications or biases against part-time workers? Or would an effective challenge to gendered organisational structures require a more fundamental transformation of bureaucracy?

Organisational structures as masculine discourse

Ferguson (1984) suggests that, in fact, no bureaucratic mode of organisation could be established which would significantly diminish male power or improve the experiences of women inside bureaucracies. However the structures were redesigned, women would never flourish because bureaucratic principles of organisation are far closer to 'male' ways of doing and being than they will ever be to feminine ways of doing and being. In this claim, she is drawing directly on the work of radical feminist writers such as Gilligan (1982) and Chodorow (1979), placing an emphasis not only on the structural and systemic nature of power relations between women and men but also on fundamental differences between women and men.

These points were developed early on in the second-wave women's movement which identified traditional hierarchical structures as inimical to women's liberation. Bureaucratic forms of organisation were seen as competitive and intimidating, not simply because they were dominated by men, but in and of themselves. There was a suspicion of structures and a belief that modes of organisation should 'carry the future' (Rowbotham et al 1979:30). In other words, we should organise along the lines of our utopian visions. For the early second-wave feminists this meant that 'there should be no hierarchy, no elites, no chair, no committees and even no meetings in some cases' (ibid:30). Taken to this extreme, alternative forms of organisation proved difficult to maintain, and there was a backlash with some feminists arguing that structurelessness led to more problems than traditional models of organisation, because it allowed individuals to dominate by force of personality (charisma perhaps?) alone (Freeman 1975). Nonetheless, an emphasis on ensuring full participation by rotating tasks (from tea-making to chairing meetings) and collective decision-making has remained in many women's organisations such as women's centres, local government women's committees and rape crisis organisations (Halford 1991, Brown 1992).

Ferguson draws on this line of argument in her comprehensive *Feminist Case Against Bureaucracy* (1984), integrating insights from radical feminism with both Marxist and poststructuralist analysis. Ferguson aims to unmask the 'façade of neutrality' (p. 17) which has legitimated and depoliticised bureaucratic organisation and in doing so to offer a basis for opposition to the bureaucratisation of modern life. Like Weber, and others, Ferguson links the rise of bureaucracy with the development of modernity and capitalism. Unlike Weber, she understands bureaucracy as a new form of 'disciplinary regime' replacing old feudal forms of social control. Ferguson sees a close link between the development of bureaucracy and the demands of capitalism, suggesting not only that bureaucracy offers useful administrative techniques but also that 'class relations are both captured and disguised within bureaucratic networks' (p. 40). Far from being a progressive or meritocratic form of organisation, Ferguson sees that bureaucracy enshrined the privileges of those groups which were already dominant as bureaucracy emerged, that is men, whites and property-owners. Ferguson argues that bureaucracy has 'provided a way of controlling large numbers of people rendering their behaviour stable and predictable' (p. 32), without the need to impose control through direct force or confrontation which might provoke rebellion.

Power here is understood as far more than specific rules and regulations prescribing and proscribing behaviour. Rather power is understood to be embedded within the discourse of bureaucracy. 'Bureaucracy' is presented as a truth – *the* rational way to organise, 'inevitable, necessary and/or good' (p. 62) – which serves to order people, limiting them to a finite range of acceptable roles and behaviours.

In speaking of bureaucracy as a discourse, Ferguson is clearly talking about far more than the organisational structures of hierarchy, formal rules and regulations. For instance, in drawing on Foucault her argument stresses the significance of language in enabling and constraining identities, thoughts and practices. The language of bureaucracy constitutes particular understandings, and denies others. Nonetheless, bureaucratic structures are central to Ferguson's understanding of bureaucracy:

> [S]ince individuals in their day-to-day interactions with bureaucracies tend to experience them as static and fixed authority structures, it is the established structural dimensions of bureaucracy that are most readily identified. (ibid.)

What then of gender in this argument? Ferguson begins with the contention that rather than being simply patriarchal, bureaucracy is, in fact, harmful to everyone: 'bureaucracies have a tremendous capacity to hurt people, to manipulate, twist and damage human possibility' (p. xii). However, Ferguson goes on to argue that women, and particularly feminists, have a special potential to offer a critique of bureaucracy. She suggests three interconnected justifications for this claim. First, the revelation of gender inequalities and gendered organisational relationships inside bureaucracies refutes the Weberian myth that bureaucracies are neutral or objective. Second, women are able to see the harm that bureaucracy does far more clearly than men. Ferguson explains that this is partly due to the fact that women are socialised into more 'connected' and empathetic personal relationships than men are and that they are thus more vulnerable to the loss and separation of such relationships which bureaucracy requires. Women's special vision is also partly explained by the fact that women are so marginal to bureaucracies that they can see the harm they do more clearly. This also echoes what Harding (1988), Smith (1988) and others have called 'feminist standpoint theory', whereby women are more able to 'see' inequality because of the way they are affected by it. Ferguson refers to this vision as 'a different voice, a submerged discourse' (p. 23) and, following Foucault, as 'an insurrection of subjugated knowledges' (p.155). Third, Ferguson suggests that women's sociability – especially their capacities for friendship and 'connected-ness' – offers an alternative organisational model to bureaucracy: '[I]n their role of caretakers women's experience offers grounds for envisioning a non-bureaucratic collective life' (p. 26). This position is endorsed by Brown (1991) in her study of British women's centres. Refuting biological determinism she nonetheless claims that

> women's socialisation makes them better equipped than men to perform the skills necessary for the creation of democratic and non-hierarchical organisation. (p. 192)

(See Chapter 4 for a lengthier discussion of this argument.)

Because of this, Ferguson argues, it would be a big mistake to try and establish ways of encouraging women into bureaucracies (for example, redesigning gendered organisational structures) because to do so would be to stifle women's 'true active and authentic participation in public life' (p. 83). Allowing a few women to play in the whole organisational tree won't change anything for the majority of women (Cockburn 1991) or, more importantly, realise the potential for the overthrow of bureaucracy which feminism offers.

Clearly, then, Ferguson is suggesting that everyone – men as well as women – would benefit from the undermining and destruction of bureaucracy. Far from being universally beneficial, bureaucratic power is understood to dominate both sexes. However, she is also suggesting that men are more tied into bureaucratic organisation than women. Because they are more central to bureaucracy, they have more to gain from it and are less able to see the harm which it does. Because of differences in male and female socialisation, men suffer less than women from the dehumanising demands of bureaucratic life, although this in itself should be challenged in order for all humans to realise their true potential. In some ways, Ferguson's argument could be seen as an extension of Weber's concern for the loss of more sociable ways of organising. However, her argument stands in fundamental contrast to Weberian claims about the benefits of depersonalised structures and formal rules and procedures. Far from ensuring being efficient for all and ensuring equity, Ferguson sees bureaucracies as 'political arenas in which domination, manipulation and the denial of conflict are standard operating procedures' (p. 17).

Ferguson ends by flagging a way forward from bureaucracy which emphasises the rejection of hierarchy and the reintegration of processes of thought and control at work with the actual execution of tasks. This prescription ties in closely with radical feminist thinking although, of course, Ferguson is suggesting this as a way forward for all, men as well as women. Ultimately, then, Ferguson veers away from a Foucauldian analysis which stresses that power is ever-present across all social arenas. While she uses Foucault to critique bureaucracy, unlike Foucault she offers a clear alternative in which power – as domination at least – is dissipated.

Summary and conclusions

This chapter has reviewed some very different ways of understanding organisational structures and their relation to gender. In each case, we have seen that the nature of the relation between gender and organisational structure hinges on the conceptualisation of power. For the Weberian, bureaucratic structures are progressive – at least potentially – because they serve to banish 'bad' forms of power, leaving behind only productive, democratic authority. This is essentially then a sovereign conception of power. Here power is centralised and exerted in the form of specified 'laws'. So long as individuals conform to these laws they are otherwise freed from the exercise of power. For the structuralist, organisational structures simply and inevitably reflect, mobilise and sustain the power or men (and whites and ruling classes) by keeping women (or most women) in positions of powerlessness. In this case, power is understood as domination, and understood to reside in organisational structures rather than eradicated by them. Whether this structural power can be challenged without completely dismantling the structures of bureaucracy is debatable. For Ferguson, among others, bureaucratic structures are part of a disciplinary regime which inevitably dominates, not only women but all those subjected to it.

We could say then, to put it starkly, that we are left at the end of this review with two alternative understandings of relations between gender and organisational structures. Either organisational structures have the potential to be neutral and to challenge gender discrimination; or organisational structures will always reflect unequal power relations and effectively dominate women. This seems to be a difficult choice to make. While some of us might be instinctively drawn to one position or the other, we are left with a nagging doubt that to make this choice is to deny something significant about the other position. This is partly a question of time-scale and political strategy. Take for instance the establishment of rules to bar sexist questioning in interviews. In the short term this use of rational-legal power inside bureaucracy must be a good thing for women who want wider access to organisational hierarchies. However, such changes do little to challenge the more general domination of masculinity in bureaucratic life (expectations about hours of work, what makes a good manager, and so on). Indeed, these small changes might only serve to diffuse broader challenges which women might have made had they not been allowed a tokenistic change to organisational practice. There is also the question of social differences between women. Changes which might be good for one group of women might not have any such effect on other groups. For instance, developing career break schemes or providing a workplace nursery might be very helpful for middle-class women who are in a position to build careers and pay for childcare. They would be of little use, for example, to a woman earning the minimum wage as a part-time cleaner and dependent on family and friends for childcare. Manipulating bureaucratic procedures is unlikely to do much for this woman. Finally, there is the question of gender identity. On what basis are we to conclude whether women should be enabled to be the 'same' as men (as in the Weberian view of organisational structures) or that women must be allowed to express their difference and see their difference valued? If some women, and there are many of these women, say that they want bureaucratic careers should we accept this? Or should we assume that they have simply fallen victim to patriarchal ideologies and can't see what is in their true interests?

How can we accommodate these competing positions? We want to suggest that developing an analysis of the multiple forms and exercises of power which coexist inside work organisations offers a way forward. Rather than seeing organisational structures in either liberal-Weberian terms as (potentially) bearers of neutral, rational-legal authority, or as mobilisations of male power, or as a set of discourses bearing disciplinary power, we want to suggest that all three forms of power operate simultaneously, in relation with one another. In this way it becomes possible to see how organisational structures may both empower and disempower women, as well as men. It is possible to see that in their engagement with organisational structures, women and men may be *both* agents of *and* subjects of power. And it is possible to recognise both the broader and more fixed configurations of power within work organisations and to the smaller scale exercises of power that take place on a daily basis inside organisations everywhere. As we show in Chapter 6, there is constant resistance to established formations of organisational power, and these broader configurations of power should never be seen as fixed or immutable.

3

Organisational Cultures

Introduction

It is not only the formal design of an organisation that determines the ways it is gendered. Organisations consist of a multitude of 'informal' processes through which gender relations are constructed and reproduced. In this chapter, we shift the focus from examining how power articulates through the formal aspects of bureaucracy such as rules, procedures and the ways hierarchies are structured, to look at the relationships between gender and power as they articulate through the less tangible aspects of organisational life, such as attitudes, beliefs and values, as well as organisational symbols, language and practices. Indeed, 'how things are done around here' (Deal and Kennedy 1982) is of crucial importance to understand an organisation fully, as

> it is necessary to understand the context in which it operates, the content of its cultural knowledge, and the social processes which are in operation. For organisations, like tribes, have belief systems about the rightness of certain social arrangements which motivate their actions. (Pettigrew 1979, quoted in Pemberton 1995:109)

In this chapter, we show that it is through these belief systems that power operates to construct understandings about gender performances, identities and relationships within organisations.

In the last chapter, we examined the argument that an individual's structural location in an organisation shapes their attitudes, values and behaviour. In this one, we approach the relationship from the other side, and ask to what extent the values, attitudes and behaviour which are present in the organisation determine not only an individual's structural location but also the wider experience of working within the organisation. In other words, how are men and women working within the organisation understood and valued, and how are they expected or enabled to perform? What is of real interest in this chapter are the ways power is embedded in these beliefs and attitudes and, in particular, whether the form of the relationship between culture and power has differential consequences for women and men working within organisations.

Since the early 1980s, the concept of culture has been subject to extensive analysis within the organisational literature (Liff and Cameron 1997), and studied from a wide range of competing perspectives. From her look at the mainstream literature, Smircich (1983) identifies two main approaches to understanding the concept: culture as a variable – that is, something an organisation 'has' – and culture as a root metaphor – something an organisations 'is' (Legge 1995, Liff and Cameron 1997, Pemberton 1995). The first approach, which is most common in the 'management' literature, understands culture as an organisational tool or lever which can be managed and changed: something which organisations can create and recreate in order to enhance their performance (Pemberton 1995). It may be related primarily to a pre-existing paradigm of cultural beliefs and attitudes endemic in the wider society which are imported into an organisation through its members, who then help to shape and determine the organisation. Alternatively, the culture is sometimes conceptualised as an internal phenomenon, produced by and within the organisation. Organisations consciously construct their own values, language and rituals, which are an important by-product to the production of goods and services, indeed, often a part of this performance. For example, certain mainstream management writers (for instance, Deal and Kennedy 1982, Peters and Waterman 1982) identify organisational rituals which are designed to integrate and unify the workforce, as well as ensure commitment and enthusiasm for the organisation, its policies and products. Annual golf matches, go-kart racing, after-work pub sessions, Christmas parties, company gifts to reward performance, the creation of company 'heroes' ('Employee of the Month') and the commissioning of corporate logos, are all examples of management practices which are designed to bring a certain 'spirit' or 'ethos' into the organisation, as well as to represent it to the outside world. Such practices are widely evident in UK and US organisations, both public and private sector, which may be seen to be following Peters and

Waterman's (1982) advice that companies with 'strong cultures' are high performers. In this structural perspective, therefore, culture is the mobilisation of hierarchical power, the way management can deliberately attempt to achieve a unitary organisation with collective consensus. It works not only to give employees a sense of identity and direction, but, by embracing individuals with an all-inclusive meaning system, is assumed to eradicate differences between organisational members.

The second approach identified by Smircich shifts the focus from the kind of culture an organisation may *have*, to look at the way the organisation functions *as* a culture. Culture may be seen as a metaphor for organisation (Czarniawska-Joerges 1992), since organisations also operate as mini-societies. Culture emerges through the social interaction and negotiation of organisational members (Legge 1995) to produce a system of norms and behavioural arrangements which are continually constructed and reconstructed. These beliefs and assumptions are perceived as being of a deeper level than in the first approach, and may even operate unconsciously, as 'a projection of the mind's universal unconscious infrastructure' (Legge 1995:186), defining in 'a "taken for granted" way an organisation's view of itself and its environment' (Pemberton 1995:113) As Pemberton goes on to explain:

> [T]he organisation is a subjective experience, and therefore the purpose of studying an organisation is to discover the shared cognitions and beliefs: to understand the rules that collective minds have generated and which guide action. (Ibid.)

From this approach, therefore, culture is both 'the shaper of human action and the outcome of a process of social creation and reproduction' (Legge 1995:186). However, anthropological and ethnographic studies of organisational cultures take issue with Pemberton's assumption that organisations are consensual. These have identified that organisations are frequently found to be subdivided into different groups which perform in different ways and may have different attitudes. Yet what is clear from this understanding of organisational culture is that it is not viewed as a conscious mechanism, a means by which those with power can deliberately manipulate the organisation. Rather it is seen to be a collection of interactive and productive processes emerging throughout the organisational community as a whole. Of particular interest here are the ways these processes may have a gendered basis, either in the broader organisation as a whole or within subdivided groups.

These two approaches to understanding organisational culture, while tending not to use power as an explicit concept in their analysis, can be seen to differ fundamentally over the way the relationship between culture and power is conceptualised. In the first approach, culture is an important method of power mobilisation, the dominant voice of the organisation. From our discussions of the different perspectives on power in Chapter 1, we can see that this has its roots in structural conceptions of power. In the second approach, culture is understood as more diffuse, belonging to everybody, such that there is not only one voice, but competing voices, and competing versions of reality (Legge 1995). Depending on where you stand, this approach can be seen to have connections with both liberal and poststructuralist conceptions of power. While this approach is not a direct exponent of either perspective, we will see that both can be more or less successfully used to produce a theoretical understanding of the interrelationships between gender, culture and power.

The two approaches thus present us with two broad questions. First, we saw in the last chapter how, in many western organisations, men dominate in the upper echelons of organisational structures where formal, hierarchical power is held and decisions are made. If we take a top-down view, that culture is 'set' by managers, should we see organisational culture as essentially a means by which power is exercised by men over women to maintain the traditional shape of gendered organisational structures?

The alternative understanding of culture and power generates a second question. If organisational culture is more diffuse and fragmented, do different people, or groups, at different times, with different sets of attitudes and beliefs, jostle with each other, sometimes gaining and receiving acceptance, and sometimes not? Here, power is more individualised, and unstable, not necessarily ubiquitously attached to all members of a particular group, such as men, but a possession which is altogether more fluid and fragmented, which anybody may hold.

In this chapter we explore these two broad questions. We start, in the next section, by looking at organisational culture as a means of exercising male power. While this may be very obvious and overt in some organisations, in others the ways men are able to wield power may be altogether more subtle, often belying attempts towards equal opportunities. In the following section we discuss the range of evidence which suggests that the relationships between gender and power are not as unilateral as the structuralist approach claims. We explore research that focuses on the *differences* in organisational cultures. This research attempts to demonstrate that women's and men's initiatives and responses to the exercise of culture vary, such that the equation of culture = power = structure may be challenged as being simplistic. In the final section of the chapter we conclude by returning to our discussion of organisational culture, and how best to conceptualise it. We show that, by bringing in the concepts of gender and power, the dichotomy introduced by Smircich cannot be held as distinct as was first suggested. For the organisational culture by which management may wish to direct the organisation cannot be simply achieved, individual organisational members must actively and continuously enact it. In this way, organisational culture becomes both a tool *and* a process of social interaction that works to gender work organisations. By exploring more specifically the forms of power which are involved in organisational culture, a rich and complex picture of its role as a gendering agency emerges.

Organisational cultures as male power

Clearly, each organisation is different, determined by a mix of social, political and economic factors specific to the context in which that organisation is placed. Both public and private sector organisations in Britain and North America have experienced some quite dramatic changes in management style and culture in the last twenty years. In the public sector, from a history of traditional roles and relations based on notions of public service, many organisations have been metamorphosed into highly competitive free-market enterprises. Similarly, the cultures of many private sector organisations have also been through periods of dramatic change, as the notions of competition and consumer choice have become increasingly hardened. This means that each individual organisation has its own, peculiar, culture constituted by the particular mix of recent events in their industrial or professional sector, particular historical events within the organisation itself, as well as of the actual men and women that work within it, their attitudes towards each other and their interpersonal relations (Maddock and Parkin 1993). These factors all work together in different ways to produce different cultural climates which will affect gendered relations in different ways.

However, we have also seen that in many British, Western European and American companies and public institutions it is white, middle-class men who continue to dominate decision-making positions. It is thus largely *men's* experiences and attitudes which shape the way in which things are seen to be. While differences may exist between organisations as to the extent of male dominance, research in organisational culture demonstrates overwhelmingly how it is masculinity which determines both the general culture and the gender cultures within organisations, with the result that women are subordinated not only at the structural level but also at the mediative and symbolic level, demonstrating itself in language and imagery (Hearn and Parkin 1987) as well as interpersonal behaviour, in both formal and informal contexts.

Cultural missions or 'ethos'

In the last decade, the fashion has been for most organisations to produce a description of themselves in a summary statement or 'mission'. The mission describes how the organisation perceives itself, not only in terms of its aims and objectives, but also in terms of the kind of culture that its leaders are attempting to create in order to maximise effectiveness and/or profitability. The mission statement attempts to encapsulate the 'corporate' culture or 'ethos' of the organisation, often using similar rhetoric to that also to be found in the same organisation's corporate policies and processes. From a more radical perspective, the corporate culture is that created by senior management for the lower orders to follow (Legge 1995), while a more liberal approach would encourage a more facilitative understanding of the power relations involved, seeing that the senior management of an organisation has a directive role in developing the collective conscience in a 'healthy' direction for growth (Legge 1995).

However, some organisational theorists argue that the norms and values which at present dominate the public world of work, the culture of organisations and the ways they describe themselves through mission statements and the like, reflect only the 'man's world'. Marshall (1984) suggests that organisations in Britain, Europe and the United States articulate primarily the 'male principle', that is, male forms of expression and achievement. By contrast, the 'female principle' tends to be penalised. The main characteristics of the male principle are independence, focus, clarity, discrimination, competition, individualism, activity, control of the environment and attention to parts. These reflect the profile of the effective, rational organisation (recalling Weber's concept of bureaucracy, which we looked at in Chapter 2). By contrast, the characteristics of the female principle (interdependence, patterns, being, acceptance, receptivity and perception of wholes) are judged as antithetical to the bureaucratic organisation (Marshall 1985) and notions of organisational progress. These images of male and female are used to shape organisational cultures, describe what their missions are (and are not) about, and, in the process, determine acceptable and unacceptable behaviour among their employees.

For example, organisational goals and plans, policies and corporate rhetoric frequently draw on metaphors of sport and/or the military (Rexford and Mainiero 1986, Townley 1994, White 1995). As Case elaborates,

> Clients are 'targeted' by the sales force, powerful people are referred to as 'big guns' and workers are put 'on the front lines' or 'in the trenches' to see how they react 'under fire'. (Case 1994:157)

Such metaphors draw on concepts, myths and language which emphasise the masculine values of hierarchy, competition, conflict and the survival of the fittest. The characteristics which dominate are the need for leadership, discipline, group solidarity, an emphasis on a win–lose dichotomy and a strategic, unemotional and analytic approach. Researchers in organisational communication argue that organisational metaphors such as these do not necessarily fit equally comfortably with men and women alike (Case 1994, Hegelson 1990). Owing to the difference in male and female socialisation patterns, men and women tend to develop different attitudes and attributes. For example, Hegelson (1990) claims that the kinds of games children play help to form them into very different human beings. Male children learn to put winning ahead of personal relationships or growth, to feel comfortable with rules and to use their individuality for the greater goal of the school, team or game. Females, however, learn to value cooperation and relationships: to disdain complex rules and authoritarian structures, and to disregard abstract notions like the quest for victory if they threaten harmony in the group as a whole. Women are generally encouraged in their life experiences to be intuitive, spontaneous and cooperative, rather than rational, analytical and competitive. These early differences in socialisation are constantly reinforced in relations between women and men in their adult lives, not least within organisations. This means that missions framed through sporting/military rhetoric may be more in tune with men and masculinity than women and femininity. Indeed, early guidance for women hoping to master corporate culture (Harragan 1977, Hennig and Jardim 1978) advised them to indoctrinate themselves in the military mindset and study the rules of football (Hegelson 1990). However, many women may be unwilling or unable to conduct business within these symbolic frameworks. Yet it is usually women who have to make changes, adapting to the existing norms and standards of behaviour of their male colleagues.

Communication and language

Through our discussion of the masculinity of corporate rhetoric, we have demonstrated one instance of how communication and power are intimately linked. However, power influences not only the content of communications, but also who communicates with whom, the ways in communication occurs, the degree to which other people attend to communications and the attention paid to the communications of others (Colwill 1982). Structural analyses of communication patterns within organisations support the view that they are a major means by which power is exercised to marginalise women. Not only do men attempt to exclude women from sources of power and information, but the dominance of masculinity as a *style* of communicating is ubiquitous in organisational life.

First, men have many opportunities to communicate with each other when women are not present. Participation in the sporting opportunities and facilities of an organisation, which are frequently male-oriented and dominated, allows for communication about work to occur in an all-male environment such as in the locker room, or on the golf course:

> At our sports club it's all solicitors and accountants, all the sorts of contacts you need... you see, it's a lot easier to 'do things' on a Saturday, after the match, over a few pints in an informal situation. (Collinson *et al.* 1990:145)

Clubs are not only formal, but also informal. White men, jealously guarding their power base (Newman 1995), largely control them. Success in the organisation often depends on access to these networks, where the 'real' business goes on. Maddock and Parkin (1993) describe this as an 'exclusion culture', where men build relationships with each other on the basis of common agreements and common assumptions. Male outsiders can join the group through participating in sport and talking about it, as well as talking about women and sex through jokes and sexual innuendoes to confirm their heterosexuality. Women, however, are firmly excluded:

Men still exclude women from 'drinks-in-the-pub' and evening socialising, it's difficult asking a woman because everyone assumes you must fancy her, even if all you want to do is talk about work. (Male director of Housing) (Maddock and Parkin 1993:5)

Male bonding through involvement in company sporting activities is compounded by 'the old-boy network' in which contacts made in all male environments such as school, university and through the male side of the family help each other in working life. Davidson and Burke (1994) note that many studies indicate that women are largely excluded from old-boy networks, which traditionally are composed of people who hold power in the organisation (Hennig and Jardim 1979, Kanter 1977, Fagenson 1986). While women also have opportunities to talk in men's absence, and have been successful in consciously forming their own networks, both within and between organisations, these networks do not necessarily provide access to the 'old-boy networks' where structural power is held (Davidson and Burke 1994).

Second, Hearn and Parkin note how most organisations are havens of sexist language, with 'continual assaults usually by men upon women by such words as "chairman", "manpower" "statesman", "manning levels", "spokesman" "workmanship" "master plan/file/key" "fellowship" and so on and on' (Hearn and Parkin 1987:145). The most obvious use of sexist language is found in job titles (Colwill 1982), wherein 'stable boys' and 'firemen', 'cleaning ladies' and 'shampoo "girls"' all carry the badge not only of sex-role appropriateness but also the degree of power and status in their jobs. The ubiquitous use of 'girls' to describe women of whatever age, even in their fifties, reflects the powerlessness of most women, and the refusal to accept mature women as equals (paralleling as it does the once common practice of white people calling black men 'boys'). Power differences are also reflected in 'who will be called what by whom' (Colwill 1982:121). High-status people (men) are usually addressed by their formal titles 'Mr Smith' or 'Dr Jones', whereas low-status people (women, and this may be in spite of the fact that they may also hold a senior position within the organisation) are frequently addressed by the more informal use of their first name. As Colwill explains,

[B]y the indiscriminate use of informal or familiar terms of address, the powerful are demonstrating their freedom to invade the privacy of subordinates by becoming intimate, without regard to the latter's preferences. (Colwill 1982:121).

From a structural perspective, the ways language is used to represent and situate people is one of the most powerful mechanisms of confirming power relations between groups such as men and women.

Third, power is not only is disseminated through the rather 'static' language devices of labelling and naming, but differentials are continually constructed and maintained through language processes. It is now widely accepted that women and men 'talk differently', that is, that they make different use of the language resources available to them (Coates 1995). Much of the evidence suggests that male speakers are socialised into a competitive style of discourse, while women are socialised into a more cooperative style of speech (Coates 1989, 1991, Tannen 1992). In organisations, it is the language of men, the dominant group, which has become the norm: Coates suggests this is because of the split in public and private spheres, whereby, since the nineteenth century, women have been largely excluded from the public world of work. Male discourse thus tends to be information-focused and adversarial in style, favouring linguistic strategies which foreground power and status differences (Coates 1995). By contrast, women's talk in the private sphere is interaction-focused, favouring language that emphasises the creation and maintenance of good relations and cooperation. Thus the same linguistic strategies, of questions, directives and turn-taking may be used to different effect. Questions may be used to bring others into the conversation, to ensure that the conversation continues and to check that what is said is acceptable. Directives are frequently prefaced by the word 'let's', thus stressing cooperation and connection. Further, different models for turn-taking apply, whereby conversation is often simultaneous, with questions and comments being made while another person is speaking, signalling active listening and helping to produce a joint text (Coates 1995). However, this means that, linguistically, women may be at a double disadvantage in the public domain: first, because they may be less 'skilful' at using the adversarial, information-focused style expected in such contexts; second, because the more cooperative discourse styles in which they are fluent are negatively valued in such contexts. Even when women are able to acquire the required style, they may still find themselves at a disadvantage, because when they perform the more assertive, more masculine style of discourse, they are perceived as 'aggressive', 'strident' and confrontational (Coates 1995).

Language in the public domain thus works both to construct and maintain power relations. High-status people (usually men) talk not only more often, but for longer periods of time (Eakins and Eakins

1979). In group situations such as board meetings and interactions with subordinates, they are able to control the topic of discourse, through the use of questions, directives, dominance in turn-taking, and interruptions. Choice of questions may do the ideological work of setting the agenda, as well as constraining the responses of others. Directives and imperatives help to maintain a universe where senior members of an organisation, such as professionals and managers, are all-powerful. Interruption may be used as a strategy through which the powerful participants in a discourse gain the floor and control the topic of conversation, as well as claiming original ideas as theirs. As West and Zimmerman (1983) describe it, interruptions are a way of 'doing power'.

It is not only formal language situations that are gendered, however. Organisational humour may also serve to keep women and men 'in their place'. Collinson (1988) noted how heavy sexual references and jokes are accepted as a natural form of shopfloor life (Collinson 1988: 196). Cunnison 's (1989) study of joking in a school staff-room found that 'gender joking' was common, usually initiated by men. Such jokes referred mostly to women's appearance, and conventional ideas about gender and femininity. The function of this kind of humour was to draw attention to the fact that women teachers are *women*, a category which is stereotypically assumed to have less commitment to the job and lesser competence. Jokes served to reinforce and reaffirm this view and, in the process, work to maintain male power. The fact that women are frequently the butt of humour within organisations reinforces deep assumptions that their presence within them is on limited terms.

Finally, language is not only a verbal tool. Body language is also a way through which men may dominate women. This language may be exaggerated: in meetings, men will lean back in their chairs, stretch out their arms and legs, rocking backwards and forwards, drawing attention to their bodies and detracting from other people. Or it may be more subtle – a hand on the back, 'guiding' a woman along, or leaning over her while talking.

Imagery

Structural male power may also be reaffirmed through the types of imagery that are used within an organisation. Imagery operates in a way that is comparable to language, though less easily defined (Hearn and Parkin 1987). Gendered imagery may be used in organisational literature and publications, as well as in what is hung on the walls or displayed in common areas such as staffrooms or waiting rooms. Glossy booklets advertising the company may have photographs of men and women employees in stereotypical roles, and in poses indicative of power relations: for example, the male manager standing looking over the female secretary's shoulder as she types, perhaps pointing with his index finger to her work, in a posture which indicates that of 'correction'. Paintings in conference rooms may be of female nudes. More extremely, pin-ups and 'girly' calendars may be pasted up in full view.

Imagery is also transmitted through staff uniforms, dress codes and name badges. For example, if women are asked to wear a 'sexy' uniform, in occupations such as club waitress or barmaid (Adkins 1995), then it is clear that the performance of '(hetero)sexiness' is part of the job. In some private hospitals, nurses uniforms incorporate aspects of femininity such as frilly, lace caps and pink belts (Halford and Leonard, forthcoming). All of these symbolic aspects of communication may be judged to be in some way representative of the gendered power relations within the organisation (Cockburn 1991).

Space

Further, the management of space and movement may also reflect and foster a male authority. As Colwill notes succinctly, 'Space is power, and the powerful are accorded more of it' (Colwill 1982:127). Senior people have bigger desks and bigger rooms. Further, 'the boss may freely walk into lesser [sic] employees' offices and desk areas, but the subordinates don't have the same privilege of entering the boss's office' (Henley 1977:31, quoted in Hearn and Parkin 1987:135). As organisational structures are gendered, so are organisational spaces. The (usually male) boss will have his own room, while the (usually female) secretaries may have to share with four others.

Personal space is also a reflection of power, or lack of it. Women have been found to be accorded less personal space when being addressed than men: both males and females stand closer to women when talking to them (Willis 1966).

Home and work

The way the worlds of work and home are conceptualised within an organisation's culture is also a means by which male power may structure gender relations. For historical reasons, home and work are commonly seen as two separate spheres (Kanter 1977b), both in physical, spatio-temporal terms as well as in terms of attitudes and behaviour. As we have discussed above, work has long been conceptualised as the public realm of wage labour, and is socially valued as a rational world of economic production. Home, on the other hand, is identified as the private territory, a non-political, 'natural', affiliative, irrational yet nurturing and restorative world which focuses on social and biological reproduction (Nippert-Eng 1995). These dichotomous perceptions are underpinned by the fact that historically, by and large, men have been the primary wage earners from their jobs in the public realm, while women have been primarily responsible for looking after the home and being responsible for the children. This latter responsibility has remained unchanged for most women, in spite of the fact that 71 per cent (EOC 1996) also work in the public world at the same time. This means that for most women, at some time in their lives, 'the truth is that the combining of child-care, husband-care and housework with a demanding paid job *is* very difficult indeed' (Cockburn 1991:86). Often a man

> comes home and he's got a wife who puts a meal in front of him, makes sure the children are in bed or kept quiet. If you're a woman you have to come home, stop off for the shopping, see to the children, cook the meal. Obviously you're going to be at a disadvantage. It's structured for men. (Cockburn 1991:86)

Most women carry a disproportionate share of domestic responsibilities: Recent survey information from *Social Trends* (1998:217) finds that men spend an average of forty minutes each day on cooking and routine housework, compared with women, for whom it occupies up to two and a half hours of each day's activities (Speakman and Marchington 1999). Working women are more likely to have to find time during their business hours to take a sick member of the family to the doctor, visit the school and so on.

However, many organisations have cultures that deny that men and women participate in home life under different conditions. Few organisations provide on-site day-care, and work hours are usually not restructured to allow family members' needs to be met. Many working women therefore operate at a competitive disadvantage with comparable men. If organisations do recognise that women carry more responsibility at home, then it is common for these facts to be turned around and used as the bases for prejudice against them. Thus, rather than acting as guidelines for real policy changes and effective shifts in organisational culture, the set of values about home and work plays a key part in restricting the entry of women into the labour force (Mills 1988). Female entrants may be filtered into a narrow range of occupations that mirror assumed domestic roles and the skills of carers and nurturers (such as nurses and teachers), cleaners and food preparers. Even if a woman is celibate or childless, she is still seen and represented as one of the maternal sex (Cockburn 1991). Further, in terms of recruitment and promotion prospects, women may be judged in terms of their private and domestic lives rather than their work ones. For young women, the question may be whether they are likely to get married or have children whereas older women may be assessed on their childcare arrangements. Married and partnered women are assumed to be less mobile, and unable to move.

A consequence of this may be that women may feel pressure to hide or deny their personal and domestic lives, in an effort not to be judged by them. This silence reflects what Hochschild (1989) has termed 'the cultural cover-up', promoting the idea that it is perfectly feasible to easily combine a career with having children. Any traces of stress or need for compromise are 'kept underground', with children and domestic pressures rarely given as reasons why deadlines may not be met or meetings unattended (Leonard and Malina 1994).

Nippert-Eng conceptualises the myriad ways in which 'home' and 'work' are conceptualised as a continuum, ranging from 'integration' to 'segmentation' (1996). For some men, their more powerful positions may give them the freedom to acknowledge other aspects of their lives and they may be able to integrate the home and work worlds. For many women, however, their lower status makes them more vulnerable, and the pressure may be on for them to attempt to push their two worlds into two very separate compartments. This attempt to dichotomise may, of course, be an impossible one: the public and private domains cannot be easily separated. What happens at work affects the family, and what happens in the family affects work (Martin 1992). For both women and men, the concerns of the private domain are inextricably intertwined with life at work, yet most organisations have working cultures which remain doggedly averse to admitting this. They are based on the assumption that all parents, irrespective of gender, have full-time support at home.

The work–home, public–private divide can thus be regarded as a useful way to explore further the divisions of gender and gender within organisational cultures. In particular, this is men's power to dominate women's lives (Parkin 1993). Women are positioned and controlled at work through discourses about the woman–man, home–work relationship that may or may not have a relationship with the reality of their lives. Indeed, Evetts (1994) notes how both working fathers and mothers are torn between the conflicting demands of their jobs and the desire to see more of their families. Further, in Halford *et al.*'s (1997) study of different organisational sectors, women and men when asked to evaluate the personal significance of a range of non-work activities revealed that gender differences are less marked than differences between the sectors. Bank workers of both sexes appeared to be less work-oriented and more home-oriented than were local government workers and nurses. However, contrary to the cultural assumptions discussed above, men in all sectors placed a slightly higher or similar emphasis to women on the value of spending time with their children, while women were equally as likely to place a high value on work. In contrast to these empirical findings, few organisations regard work–family issues as universal, and not just as a woman's concern.

White cultures and sociabilities

It would appear that for many women working in cultures such as these is highly stressful. This stress may be augmented by discrimination not only of her gender but also of other aspects of her identity as well. For organisational culture is not only male-dominated but *white* male-dominated. Fernandez (1981) has argued that since black people have been relative latecomers to white-collar organisations in Europe and North America, organisational life was already established as 'white'. Since 'white' culture had become the norm, whites had come to assume 'that the white culture is the only functional one for the business world, and that other cultures are incompatible with white culture' (Fernandez 1980:50–1). Thus, it is argued, whites were almost automatically assumed to hold the right organisational values, while blacks were assumed to hold different values which, furthermore, would clash with pre-existing norms, causing friction and disruption (Davis and Watson 1982). In consequence, as blacks came to enter white organisations, they encountered: 'foreign social space, with unfamiliar protocol, with habits, markers, values and styles of thinking that until very recently were very new to them' (Davis and Watson 1982:1).

This marginalisation may be far more exaggerated for black women, whose sex and race makes them 'double latecomers' and who are even more likely to find themselves 'the only one' in their office or team. Nkomo cites one black woman's comment that corporate life was like 'an uncharted journey through rough psychological waters' (1988:138), while Carroll sums up the experience thus:

> There is no-one with whom to share experiences and gain support, no-one with whom to identify, no-one on whom a black woman can model herself. It takes a great deal of psychological strength just to 'get through the day', the endless meetings and lunches in which one is always 'different'. This feeling is much like the exhaustion a foreigner speaking a foreign tongue feels at the end of the day. (1982:120)

Much of the literature documents the imperative of 'learning to speak' the language of white corporations (for example, Fernandez 1981, Davis and Watson 1982, Bell 1990). This metaphor extends beyond the verbal: '[I]n order to fit in one has to assume a new identity; negotiate a truce between the old one and the required self' (Davis and Watson 1982:10). While it is acknowledged that whites too may have to undergo some process of accommodation on entering such organisations, Davis and Watson (1982) argue that their 'whiteness' offers an easy identification with, and smooth transition into, corporate life. By contrast, accommodation to corporate life is far more difficult for blacks since 'black life is further than white life from what might be called the cultural norm' (Davis and Watson 1982:10). Thus fitting in to the organisational cultural norm means becoming as white as possible. One black manager summed this up: 'They want you to be like them. They want you to suppress certain aspects of your racial identity – your life style, sense of humour, way of dressing – existential things that are part of your racial heritage, I can do it. I can "behave"' (ibid.: 38).

Being able to behave, to fit into prevailing white norms, may become more important for black staff than any other skills or attributes they have. However, even when black people do 'behave', it may be impossible for some people not to see race and ethnicity first. Leggon (1980) claims that blacks, and especially black women, in management and professional posts are 'status-discrepant', meaning that they don't fit the (white) stereotype and as a consequence are judged on factors other than their professional and/or technical skills. Similarly, the black women managers interviewed by Liff and Dale (1994) reported being constantly made to feel aware of their sex and race and never being seen as 'just a manager'. Thus, ascribed status (race and/or sex) is placed above achieved status (professional). In this context, 'You can be as smart as hell but if you don't sound like a white man [sic], white men will judge you to be unintelligent' (Davis and Watson 1982:95). Ethnicity cross cuts gender here, with black men and black women from different ethnic groups identifying distinct forms of difference and marginalisation from the white, male norm. Cheng (1997), for instance, describes how Asian American men are marginalised in organisational cultures that privilege a hegemonic, white, macho masculinity. Where Asian men present a quieter, gentler and less assuming 'Confucian masculinity' (p. 197) they are penalised for not performing in a way deemed appropriate for their biological sex, and therefore lose out in the career race. As a white selector explained: 'We don't pick nerds. Its not that they're Asians. We don't want nerds, we want real managers' (ibid.:196).

While formal qualifications may improve blacks' chances of acceptance into white corporations, these are never enough. There is evidence that black women in particular need higher qualifications than white women to be taken seriously (King 1995) *but* that even then the need to develop a 'bi-cultural competency' (Fernandez 1981: 50, also Bell 1990, Davidson 1997) remains crucial.

While most researchers agree that there is a racist imperative for black organisational members to adopt white identities and sociabilities, and report a certain degree of 'success' in this respect, they are also quick to point to the costs of such adaptation. In particular, there is emphasis on the way blacks working in white corporations may become 'caught between two worlds' (Bell 1990). Becoming part of a white organisation may alienate individuals from their past, their roots, their families and communities. Yet at the same time there may be inadequate recompense in the new, white environment (Davis and Watson 1982, Bell 1990, Denton 1990). Similarly, some blacks may feel guilty at their success in white corporations and/or at the compromises that they have made to get on (Davis and Watson 1982). This estrangement may be particularly severe for black women, caught between the conflicting demands of home and work (like many white women) and between the demands of the black community and mainstream white culture (like many black men) (Bell 1990, Davidson 1997, Denton 1990).

As a black woman manager interviewed by Denton (1990) explains, 'As I move up in my profession I get feedback from my family and friends not to be so "close" to whites. I was feeling torn apart for a while' (p. 455); and another, interviewed by Davidson (1997), concludes: 'I sometimes feel that there are two of me – a side which I have to show at work with the white culture which is very professional; then there's the personal side of me which I reveal outside work, which is much more ethnic' (p. 35). Indeed, there is some evidence that some blacks reject white corporations precisely because of these tensions (Essed 1991).

Organisational culture is thus not only male but white. Within this white culture, blacks are understood as different: whites assume blacks to be different and blacks too see themselves in distinction from dominant white norms. Black women thus experience a double marginalisation, by virtue of their race and/or ethnicity and through their femininity in a male dominated culture. This may mean that they are forced to sacrifice the racial and/or ethnic part of their identities in favour of what is 'normal' in the dominant culture (Bell *et al*. 1993). As Bell points out, this suppression of identity can happen at the superficial level of dress, hairstyle, and language patterns and at much more substantive levels of social, personal and political values (Bell 1990, 1993). At both levels, the personal cost is high.

Traditional cultures

So far, our discussion of organisational culture and gender has demonstrated that, in many organisations, the differences between women and men are well defined. In their research on public sector organisations however, Maddock and Parkin (1993) and Newman (1995) found that different patterns of gender relations exist in different organisations. They suggest typologies that provide useful models to understand the different kinds of culture, gender and power that may exist and coexist within and between organisations. For example, at one end of the continuum are 'traditional' cultures. In these, structural gender divisions reflect the most traditional views about appropriate male and female roles and positions. These are accompanied by strong degrees of role distance and expected deference between (high-status) male and (low-status) female jobs, such as is demonstrated in the relations between medical consultant and nurse, manager and secretary. Thus the gender basis of this culture goes far beyond the sexual division of labour: it also builds on sets of gendered and sexualised meanings operating within the workplace, which set up 'invisible' hierarchies between male and female roles, and the men and women who occupy them. Women in traditional regimes are offered quasi-familial roles and identities around a core of male hierarchies and privileges. A women may act as 'mother' (concerned with staff welfare), 'aunt' (the older, often single woman, allowed senior status, but little real power), 'wife' (the supportive assistant) or 'daughter' (allowed a few privileges, but no real power). Sometimes a woman may be admitted to the ranks of the 'lads' as a 'fun-loving sister' or tomboy. Women who attempt to take on a role outside of these categories, for example, 'sexy', or 'feminist', are perceived as problematic. Black and working-class women are rarely admitted to the 'family' at all, but are kept in an organisational subclass in occupations such as catering, cleaning, word-processing and printing. 'Class, race and generation, then, underpin the hierarchy of female roles in the traditional regime of public-sector bureaucracies' (Newman 1995:16). There are differences within traditional cultures. At their most extreme, they are akin to the 'Barrack Yard' (Maddock and Parkin 1993), a bullying and vicious culture, where subordinates are shouted at and rarely listened to. The possession of power is automatically expected to deliver respect. As women (together with manual workers and black people), rarely have senior status within such organisations, they are rendered invisible. Further along the continuum, male power in traditionalist regimes may be exercised through a web of politeness and civility, where relations between men and women seem, on the face of it, to be based on mutual respect and an assumption of 'difference'. This is the 'Gentleman's Club' (Maddock and Parkin 1993). However this culture is still based on traditional understandings of gender: politeness and courtesy from their male managers can be very disempowering for women, working to keep them firmly in established 'feminine' roles. These exclusive cultures thus rely on women understanding what they have to lose if they attempt to seek less traditional work or roles, and more decision-making power.

However, as we show in the following section, while many traditional cultures still exist in organisations, these are by no means the only cultural forms.

Discussion

This discussion of organisational culture has revealed many instances of the ways culture and male power are intertwined. 'Doing culture' is also a way of 'doing power'. Through the mobilisation of both the explicit cultural 'image' or 'ethos' of the organisation and the ordinary, everyday cultural practices of an organisation, differences between men and women are constantly constructed, augmenting the authority and status of the former group at the expense of the latter. Thus it would appear that, far from being 'corporate', a tool created by senior (male) management to bind all organisational members together and help them work effectively, organisational culture can be a divisive mechanism, consisting of values, attitudes and behaviour which reflect and construct masculinity and male power. Thus men, as a social group, tend to experience organisational culture more easily than women, and certainly enjoy more of its benefits.

However, in our discussion of the literature so far, ambiguity within the gender groups or, indeed, other categories of difference is largely denied. Each group is seen to share a large degree of consensus in terms of their attitudes and beliefs, as well as to share a similar relationship to power. Men and women are represented and understood as easily understandable and recognisably different categories, which construct, experience and receive organisational culture and power in ways common to their gender. While a largely structural picture of power emerges, with the dominant group (white, middle-class, male) subordinating anyone who does not fit in (black, working-class, female), we can also see evidence to support the more liberal conception of episodic agency, whereby individual men intentionally use their power to achieve definable ends.

Of course, culture and power are usually exercised within organisations against a background of change. Organisations are continuously changing, in part as a result of deliberate management strategies and in part as they are embedded in the wider political, economic and social context of change. For example, in the last twenty years, dramatic changes in management style and culture have affected most organisations in the western world, metamorphosing them from cultures based on traditional roles and relationships of power and authority with both their employees and their customers and clients, into highly competitive free-market enterprises. Changes in organisational cultures on this scale have in some cases had a consequent effect on the gendered cultures operating within these organisations. However, rather than an organisation experiencing a dramatic and wholesale change, what may result is a complex mix of coexisting cultures, some more traditional, others reflecting gradual changes in relations between men and women. For example, from their research in contemporary public sector organisations, Maddock and Parkin (1993) and Newman (1995) found them to be typically characterised by a mix of cultural forms. Each is based on a complex mix of administrative, professional and gender discourses, delivering its own language, imagery, values, relationships and ways of doing things. Thus, within some organisations, not only can culture be seen as a seamless mobilisation of male power over women, but also different *kinds* of gendered cultures can be seen to coexist. Here, individual women and men may use and experience the power of organisational culture to gender in very different ways.

Thus it may be that within many organisations the simple formulas of men = powerful, women = powerless become complicated by the process of change. In the next section, we turn to look at research evidence that argues that organisations can be seen to be along a continuum. For example, research which looks at recent changes in the public sector demonstrates the different cultural forms appearing in organisations as they attempt to become ever more competitive. These are opening up new definitions of women's roles and positions at work and a new relationship with power. Some of this research adopts an approach which recognises the complexity of organisational cultures, with their particular, and individual, mix of gendered attitudes, values and behaviours and thus this provides alternative ways of understanding the relationships between gender and power. Possibilities may exist for individual women actively to modify, challenge or resist conforming to the dominant, traditional gender–power relations. Such an approach opens up understandings of power as something altogether more diffuse, belonging to particular individuals, irrespective of their gender or organisational structural location.

Organisational change, culture and power

We have noted above that in the last decade a climate of cultural change has reshaped the face of organisations. Across organisations in both the public and private sectors, a spirit of 'new enterprise' stemming from the 'Thatcher years' has encouraged the development of 'competitive' cultures (du Gay 1996, Halford and Leonard 1999, Newman 1995). This 'encouragement' to make sweeping change has, more often than not, been imposed onto organisations through government initiatives and legislation (in the public sector) and through the appointment of new board directors and managers (in the private). In both sectors many organisations have found themselves being dramatically restructured, with changes in culture being consequential. These have also affected the gendered cultures operating within these organisations, although the form that these take depends on the ways the broader organisation responds to initiatives to restructure.

'New Managerialism'

One assumption that has long received consensus among organisations attempting change is that it is through the appointment of new managers with a different and 'effective' management style that change can most successfully be delivered. Typically, the requisite management style for such jobs is seen to be that which has been described as 'new managerialism: a style of management which emphasises innovation, creativity (especially with finance) and empowerment (Exworthy and Halford 1999). 'New' managers tend to be 'highly motivated, resourceful, and able to shift the frame of reference beyond established norms and procedures' (Exworthy and Halford 1999:6). At their crudest, these characteristics have been assumed to display themselves best through 'macho' or 'cowboy' styles of management (Newman 1995). A hard edge is also seen to be desirable, with successful change managers seen as needing to be 'go-getting, insurgent, and ruthless, tough on both competitors and [their] own staff' (Newman 1995:17).

Competitive cultures typically advocate the setting of performance and budget targets. These put pressure on managers, such that they have no desire to block or obstruct employees who can work eighty hours a week, and deliver on time. New managers are driven by extreme competitiveness, and this may lead to discrimination against those who cannot work at the same pace or challenge economic criteria. In the hardest cultures, if an employee cannot keep up then they may be, at worst, sacked or demoted, or at best, suffer considerable loss of earnings where salaries are heavily performance-weighted.

Superficially, this appears not to be a gendered culture, for women are allowed to take part as long as they can demonstrate that they can deliver on the same terms as men: thus it is what you do, not who you are; judgements are made on performance, not ascriptive sex. Indeed, the last ten years have been marked by high-flying women entering and 'making it' in most organisations in increasing numbers. For women with children there is a pressure to be a 'superwoman', juggling career and children, yet still achieving impressive performance targets (in the United Kingdom, Nicola Horlick, a six-figure-salaried banker with five children is a notable example). Indeed, many women managers gain the reputation of being as ruthless as any man. Their presence challenges the old patriarchal power relations, as Newman explains:

> Many of the old patriarchs and benevolent paternal figures are dethroned (made redundant) or depowered (through restructurings which break up

some of the old fiefdoms and power bases). In competitive cultures power lies where the action is – where people do business. Informal hierarchies develop around the jobs that are seen to be most 'sexy' – those linked to dynamic, thrusting entrepreneurialism. (Newman 1995:16–17)

Although women are very much a part of competitive cultures, to a certain extent they must be 'new' women. The masculinity of new managerialism

> does not share the women's-place-is-in-the-home mentality of the old guard. These men expect to find women in the public sphere. Nominally at least they welcome women into this exciting new world because their presence adds sexual spice to the working day. (Cockburn 1991:156–7)

Although not explicitly gendered, cultures within 'competitive' organ- isations are still not easy for women. However, power is more fluid than in traditional cultures, and there are fewer rules about how it should be exercised (Newman 1995). It operates in a personal and elusive manner, where individuals may gain power in quite strategic ways. For example, many of the arguments presented in the section above on organisational cultures as male power have supported a top- down, structural relationship between communication, gender and power. However, research is appearing which suggests that, rather than being 'less skilful' victims in an oppressive communication system within which they have little control, women are challenging and confronting masculine tactics with techniques of their own.

For example, McDowell's research in international finance demon- strates how women are deliberately and consciously using their femin- inity as a different method to 'sell' to clients. As one respondent explains:

> It's all about developing relationships and, as I say, there's different ways to do that. So the thing I could never do is ehrm, is uhm, you know, take people to a strip show and I don't usually get tickets for rugby and football matches which a lot of people are after. But on the other hand, uhhm, you can use your personality, and use your charm, the fact that they might like to be taken out, erhm, you know, by a... a pleasant girl, errhm, you know, it's different and as a girl, if you've got that, you might as well use it. (McDowell 1997:176)

Another corporate financier agrees:

> As long as you are competent you can use being a woman to your advantage. It might be easier to gain a client and his confidence. I worked for clients briefly because someone was off on holiday, and they demanded me back because they just love having a girl on the account. (p. 198)

Another woman in McDowell's research spoke very clearly about what she termed 'tricks and methods of manipulation'

> It's a strength being a female and you should use it to your best advantage. You get a chance to speak maybe when others don't; you can dress for a certain meeting in a way that will instantly change the atmosphere slightly or I mean you start to learn that there are things you can do that manipulate things. You can influence things by being more female or less female. (Ibid.)

McDowell argues that this description of being 'more female or less female' is a clear recognition of the significance of a fluid gender performance in the workplace. The following quotation demonstrates that this can be a wholly conscious performance:

> If you walk in the door and you're properly dressed, and you've got a smile on and you just a little bit like, you know, you're reasonably put together, uhm, you know, that instantly takes them back a tiny bit because they, they usually expect a woman to look slightly like the back end of a bus. There is a sort of perception that some women in business are very aggressive and harsh, and so the trick is not to be. It's all tactics'. (Ibid.)

Similarly, drawing on research in the professions (Fisher 1991, West 1990, Nelson 1988, Coates (1995) demonstrates that some women in the public sphere are deliberately resisting the pressure to conform to 'androcentric' discourse norms in daily interactions such as board meetings and interactions with clients. They are employing their own, more cooperative speech style, which makes greater use of questions, turn-taking and directives. Maddock and Parkin (1993) also give examples of women who have developed their own tactics to match men's domineering body language in meetings:

> I spray myself with perfumes in meetings and wear low cut dresses and generally flaunt myself. (public relations officer)

> I've learnt to wear bright colours and generally be loud, otherwise you just disappear'. (college assistant principal) (Maddock and Parkin 1993:5)

Indeed, dress and appearance is a major means by which women can play with their femininity in order to communicate a changing set of images of themselves:

> It depends who I'm going to be seeing. Sometimes I'll choose the 'executive bimbo' look; at other times, like today, when I've got to make a cold call, it's easiest if I look as if I'll blend into the background. I think this [a plain but very smart tailored blue dress] looks tremendously, you know, professional.

> No statement about me at all. 'Don't look at me, look at these papers I'm talking to you about.' But I wear high heels too, so I'm six feet tall when I stand up. And I think that commands some small sense of 'well, I'd probably better listen to her, at least for a little while. I do dress quite consciously because you've got to have some fun in life, and sometimes wearing a leather skirt to work is just fun because you know they can't cope with it. (Manager, Bluebros) (McDowell 1997:199)

Furthermore, as more women move into the professions, they have set up networks in order to share knowledge and information, as well as support. A 'sense of empowerment', gained through mechanisms and techniques such as these, may mean that women are able to operate more effectively in their own work organisations. However, what these examples also demonstrate is that, although exceptional women may be permitted entry to the power bases of organisations, joining is highly conditional on an ability to play with and challenge the dominant assumptions and practices.

> At one moment you must be daughterly and decorous; at another tough and pushy. To succeed, you have to join in the competitive ethos, but you have to retain your womanly characteristics and remain 'nice' while doing so. (Newman 1995:18)

Even so, some women sometimes attract the attention and/or derision of other men and women, owing to their 'unnatural' behaviour. As Newman claims, 'those that fall, fall hard; and the media are always more than gleefully ready to pick the bones' (Newman 1995:17). The case of the same Nicola Horlick who was mentioned above, who was spectacularly sacked in full view of the British media in 1996, would seem to substantiate this. It would appear therefore that the possession of power is transitory and potentially unstable: the opportunity to 'dethrone' powerful women is often pounced upon.

Transformational change

The macho style of new managerialism has not been the only response to the pressures to change organisational cultures however. An alternative model has emerged which is based on the idea of 'transformational' change (Newman 1995), focusing not so much on short-term competitive strength but on building larger changes in the longer term. The goal is to build up a strong and visionary culture that recognises the value of empowering people to achieve effective change. New ways of doing things are looked for, a development that in some cases has opened up new spaces for women. There is an increasing emphasis on the so-called, 'feminine' qualities of good communication and demo-cratic approaches, and the old styles of traditional or macho manage-ment are often eschewed in favour of an alternative 'feminine' management style, which specialises in listening to both clients and staff. (This is discussed more fully in Chapter 4.) At the same time, the emphasis on empowerment at all levels means, literally, that people throughout the organisational structure are being encouraged to take on more responsibility. Ways are sought such that people may become more involved in the decisions which directly affect their working lives. At its best, this means that many women are able to feel more powerful at work:

> It seems to offer women the opportunity to become more active partners in the reshaping of cultures and in the delivery of new styles of interface between the organisation and its customers. Their communication and collaborative skills may become more valued as organisations recognise the need to build relationships with partners, stakeholders and communities. (Newman 1995:18)

On the one hand, this is all good news for women and some men. The emphasis on valuing human resources at all levels means that women's traditionally defined contribution to the organisation may be chal-lenged. Further, 'organisational change may lead to better training and development opportunities for women staff and a more sympa-thetic climate for "female values" and ways of working' (ibid.). Cer-tainly there are examples of even quite traditional organisations seeking to make changes in this direction: in 1999 a review was ordered by the government of the opt-out of equal opportunity laws by defence organisations and, as if to show good will, in June 1999, Patricia Purves was made brigadier in the British army, the highest-ranking female officer ever.

However, on the other hand, these changes may be based at the rhetorical level only: few are seriously prepared to challenge the male power base by making cultural changes which would fundamentally change the ways organisational power is held and performed. For, although transformational organisations may espouse gender equality, many are in the large part essentially gender and racially blind, assum-ing that there are no differences between the lives and experiences of women and men. The 'level-playing-field' approach assumes that every-one can excel if they try. Such a denial of difference ignores three important factors. First are the domestic responsibilities and the social realities of most women over the age of 35, as well as the obstacles and difficulties that affect the choices that women can make. By excluding any acknowledgement of child-or parent-related caring roles, the cul-ture is in fact a discriminatory one. It encourages women to aspire to superwoman status: the perfect mother, as well as the perfect career. 'Those who deny the difference that a person's gender makes to their lives are like ostriches, hoping traditional power models will go away, yet without challenging the status quo' (Maddock and Parkin 1993:6). The result is that the prospective 'pool' of 'new' managers is limited more often than not to the childless and highly mobile. Second, gender and 'racial' inequalities of power operate beneath the surface, and these remain even if workgroups may seem consensual and to be based on equality. Women may operate with contradictory sets of meanings, on the one hand invited to contribute as equals, on the other having to remember their real place. A consequence of this is that women may take on more than they are actually paid for, as the junior members of a team in which responsibility is supposedly shared equally. 'This may be good for the career development of some women, but is exploitative of many' (Newman 1995:19).

Third, the achievement of transformational change has often been associated with transformational leaders. These leaders are expected to have certain characteristics: the emphasis is often on inspiration and vision, with leaders operating at affective as well as cognitive levels. 'This has resonances with the mythic and heroic imagery of charis-matic leadership, derived from military or political models' (Newman 1995:19). As we explored in Chapter 2, although Weber claimed the rational-legal authority embedded in bureaucracy would outlaw cha-rismatic power, personal characteristics can and do lead to powerful positions within organisations. However, such 'heroes' are more likely to be men, as such characteristics are often more admired in men than women. 'Leaders, we learn, are born, not made: and they are nearly always born male' (Newman 1995:19). The fact that transformational leaders are associated more with masculinity than femininity (an issue which we discuss more fully in Chapter 4) means that women are less likely to be promoted to top jobs, in spite of a culture of supposed gender equality.

Even when the particular qualities looked for are supposedly more 'feminine' ones, or even 'feminist', male leaders may be favoured. In some organisations, especially those which have well-developed equal opportunities policies, a 'new breed of man' has developed: men who are well versed in feminism, think of themselves as non-sexist, and often gain leadership positions on the strength of this platform. Maddock and Parkin (1993) call these men 'the Feminist Pretenders'. However, although they pay lip service to equality programmes, in practice these men do little to promote or develop women, black people or other minority groups. They learn the language, and use it to their own advantage. Maddock and Parkin (1993) argue that in some gender cultures men and women may attempt to out-do each other over the correct way to deal with equality issues, and hierarchies of oppression can develop where a person's status is determined by their position on the ladder (female, black, gay, working-class etc.). The result is that new forms of power and oppression develop, and individuals who do not conform to the 'alternative' stereotypes, such as the assertive feminist, or black activist, are belittled and patronised. Men may advise women on how to liberate themselves, which many women may find even 'more irritating than traditional bullies' (Maddock and Parkin 1993:7).

However, what our discussion of transformational culture reveals is that the opportunities for power are diversified throughout the organisation. In many cases, power is still retained by men, either owing to their place at the top of organisational structures or just by virtue of the fact of their gender. Yet opportunities also exist for women, who may use changing cultural rhetoric and the fashion for alternative and more pluralist models of organisation to gain both personal and organisational power, in which their voice may be heard and rewards may accrue. However, the ability to gain power may rest on an understanding of the different cultural attitudes which may prevail within an organisation at the same time: few organisations have lost their traditional cultures completely, and these underpin and inform subsequent developments and changes. As Newman comments:

> Women, then, have to live out the contradictions between these cultures, in a climate which is rife with mixed messages resulting from the interplay between old and new regimes, and between the gender and racial stereotypes underpinning each. (Newman 1995:18).

Complex cultures

Women have thus to negotiate their work identities around this interplay of cultural forms. They have to position themselves in relation to the pre-existing narratives of gender relations and, in doing so, they either reaffirm or reinvent the cultural context. Clearly, some women have more opportunities and resources for doing this than others. Each woman is different – differentiated at the very least by class, race, ethnicity, regionality, age, sexuality, motherhood and other caring responsibilities, and physical ability, as well as other disjunctions of interest and experience. The negotiative process between culture and the individual, with all her differences, may mean therefore that different experiences and positionings may result. Thus organisations may be full of women with very different experiences and relationships with power. An example of this is provided by the research of Gherardi (1996) on women in Italian organisations. She found that women constructed themselves and their situations in different ways. Her descriptions of the experiences of different women in different cultures, often with references to the individual's personal and private circumstances, helps to give a picture of the ambiguities which pervade people's working lives. For example, Giovanna, a married woman with two children in her early thirties, was welcomed by her all-male colleagues and given sensitive understanding about her childcare commitments. However, after several years of working there, she still felt that she was treated as a 'guest'. Complex feelings resulted: dissatisfaction at never being fully integrated, mixed with feelings of ungratefulness at colleagues who thought they were being 'nice' to her. In the case of Fiorella, an extremely successful manager who rose smoothly to the top at a young age, there is again a complex mixture of feelings and experience. On the one hand her promotion can be seen as evidence of non-discrimination, yet, on the other, she found that she was rendered invisible, treated politely, yet counting for nothing. 'I realised that I had been pushed to one side, even though my expertise was publicly praised' (Fiorella in Gherardi 1996:193). Again her feelings are ambiguous: 'I am sorry that I felt so resentful, but being ignored is horrible' (ibid.) Rita, on appointment to a managerial position, found a cooperative atmosphere and was welcomed warmly. However, after several years, she was told that everyone expected her to pass on to head office, as if her 'holiday' with them was over. As Gherardi (1996) explains, this narrative illustrates how reciprocal positioning can coexist in a sort of ostensible dialogue: the boss positions herself as democratic and her subordinates as willing partners in the same game. 'Yet as these latter play the game they are waiting for the holiday maker to go home' (Gherardi 1996:194).

The polite treatment from colleagues was not Fiammetta's experience. She was unexpectedly promoted to a director's post at a stage in her career which was really only clerical, very much to her own, and everybody else's, surprise. However, once in post, she encountered open hostility. 'They greeted me like a bad smell' (Fiammetta in Gherardi 1996:194): she was positioned as 'the enemy within'. She reproached herself for being extremely ingenuous, for not having suspected earlier what she later discovered. Angelina's experience was also one of hostility. Working in forestry, in a job that was often manual and traditionally male, she was injured at work. She suspected it happened because of her workmates' negligence. After the accident 'I felt as distant from them as they said they felt close to me' (Angelina in Gherardi 1996:198).

In all these examples, we get little sense of a cohesive, women's subculture that may be drawn upon to give strength in a situation of hostility. Rather, women seem to muddle along in isolation, often in a state of some confusion, trying to decipher what is happening. While some of the women in her study saw the cultures in which they were working as largely friendly, describing their positions as 'guest', 'holidaymaker' or 'newcomer', others described themselves as being in a hostile context, feeling themselves positioned as a 'snake in the grass' or an 'intruder'. Often women go through several interpretations of their situation as their relationship with an organisation changes over time. In particular, instances of discrimination may be very unclear, as is demonstrated in the friendly–guest culture. Although the climate may be overtly friendly, by being constantly treated as a guest, one is not accepted as either regular or long-term. While all the cultures in Gherardi's study presented particular difficulties for women which were in many ways disempowering, the metaphors they use also emphasise mobility and movement, suggesting possibilities for, and sometimes resulting in, change and contestation.

Women thus interpret cultures, and perhaps resist or modify them, in many different ways. Such possibilities for contestation are echoed in Leonard's (1998) study of women lecturers in a further education organisation undergoing structural and cultural change. Her study revealed that women took up different positions within the organisational culture according to how they interpreted it. While some positioned themselves as being 'very different' to the 'macho' management style, constructing and adopting an alternative, 'feminine' style, others preferred to confront the masculine dominance of management more politically, as a trade unionist or on the platform of equal opportunities. Still others withdrew from the dominant cultural norms of the organisation, to construct their own alternative value systems and modes of behaviour. What was clear was that there was not one pattern of response: individuals might choose to attempt to resist or transform the different mobilisations of power within organisational cultures, according to their own sense of personal identity, personal circumstances and political direction (Shoenberger 1994).

Discussion

Our discussion of the complex nature of organisational culture has to a certain extent problematised the concepts of gender, power and also identity. Clearly the group 'women' in organisational life is configured by many differences within and between the individuals who loosely constitute it. Not all members of this group have similar experiences, or react to the interplay within gender, power and their identities in the same way. The diversity that lies within their personal lives mediates their organisational lives and produces a myriad of different responses to organisational culture. This makes it difficult to talk about people as being merely members of a group. As Martin explains in her discussion of racial identities:

> Class and gender differences among blacks, for example, challenge assumptions of homogeneity within a group of blacks. For example, the reactions of a black women raised in poverty in the south, first in her family to earn a college degree, may well have little similarity to the responses of a college-educated black man raised in a prosperous suburb. (1992:136)

Further, people may belong to more than one group at once, leading to a sense of being 'pulled' between several competing groups, none of which captures all aspects of the person's identity. Bell (1990) describes the bi- or tri-cultural pulls experienced by some upwardly mobile black women, who may work in an organisation dominated by white men, feel limited affinities with white women, and no longer fit comfortably in the black communities where they were raised (Martin 1992). This may mean that in actual fact the salience of particular subcultural memberships, such as 'being a woman', 'may wax and wane, as issues surface, get resolved, or become forgotten in the flux of events' (p. 136). This said, however, what is also demonstrated from these descriptions of the different kinds of gendered cultures which may exist within organisations, is that women and men's identities are in part defined and constructed by the organisational context in which they find themselves. Baudrillard (1981) explains that 'we are terminals of multiple networks': organisations are jostling with competing relations and attitudes that situate people in different positions. We have demonstrated how gender is a key criterion by which people are defined and situated in organisations: masculinity and femininity are both concepts and categories which are mapped onto people as they enter organisations. Frequently, they they find that a strong gendered culture pre-exists, which may be very difficult to challenge and change. Even though mobility and challenge may be possible through the formal hierarchy, 'true' acceptance may remain elusive, as prejudiced attitudes that pervade everyday interpersonal communication refuse to be shifted.

Further, some women may, of course, collude with or fail to resist these stereotypes and prejudices that undermine their position. There are various explanations for this, which draw on different understandings of power. From a structuralist perspective, women's self-esteem and survival may be so closely connected to traditional norms that they do not see change to be necessary. Many people see their place as naturally ordained, and therefore do not challenge men's right to manage. Alternatively, women who are working in a culture heavily dominated by men, perhaps on their own or with very few other women, may find it difficult to negotiate on their own terms. Although they might be desirous of change, the men they work with may not be, and may position women workers in ways that render them powerless. For many women, the stress involved in trying to achieve change may to be simply too much for them to wish to handle, so they carry on in traditional roles as the easy way out.

From a poststructuralist perspective, the performance of stereotypes must be looked at deconstructively. It may be that in individual situations, personal power may be generated from the very animation of what, on the face of it, may appear to be repressive roles. For example, in Pringle's (1989) study of secretaries, she found that some (female) secretaries were able to play on their own sexualisation to wield a substantial degree of personal power over their (male or female) bosses.

Summary and conclusions

In this chapter, we have explored the relationships between gender, power and organisational culture from two different standpoints. First, we have examined the evidence that suggests that the mobilisation of organisational culture in large western organisations is also, inherently, the mobilisation of patriarchal power. Commonly, the *types* of culture adopted exemplify a particular version of masculinity, and encourage employees, irrespective of their sex, to perform behaviours that are assertive, individualistic, task-oriented, 'rational' and even 'macho'. The conclusion drawn is that joining in with this culture therefore demands a process of acceptance and accommodation which is differentiated along gendered divisions, and necessarily results in marginalising women. This conclusion relies on the assumption that men and women have different values, priorities and ways of behaving. This means that such behaviours *do* come more easily to men, because of their socialisation and experiences, and that women *do not* possess these qualities, and thus find the system more difficult. Men are thus able to rely on their life experiences to work in their favour, while women's experiences mean that they have to operate in an 'alien' world. Difference within the sexes remains unacknowledged: a strong degree of consensus is assumed to exist between men on the right ways to organise, while all women are assumed to find the resultant culture hostile and alienating.

The research produced within this approach seems to provide strong evidence to support the view, introduced at the beginning of the chapter, that culture is a powerful tool by which an organisation is gender-structured. Our discussions have shown how, through subjective interpretations, patterns and forms of social interaction, the creation of symbols, images and forms of consciousness (Acker 1992), organisational structures are enacted, and become 'embodied systems of social relations' (Halford *et al.* 1997). It is clear from our discussion that far from allowing a natural, inevitable of preordained state of affairs, men, at worst, work very hard within organisational cultures to establish and maintain their positions of power and dominance over women, or, at best, merely coast along, making the most of the 'unearned' privileges of being a man. Men can be seen to foster solidarity at a cultural level, using it, at the hardest end of the approach, to 'sexualize, threaten, marginalise and control women' (Cockburn 1991:215).

However, the demonstration of the way divisions occur within organisations along gendered lines provided by the research evidence we have discussed would seem to make it difficult to understand culture merely as an organisational tool, something an organisation *has*. If the corporate philosophy is in fact one of 'corporate patriarchy' (Green and Cassell 1996), then this has a powerful ideological impact on relations *within* the organisation. If the corporate philosophy itself is anti-integrationist, then so will be the organisation. It would therefore seem that this approach to understanding organisational culture collapses into the second approach (that organisations *are* cultures) when seen through the framework of male power. Although the 'organisations are cultures' approach starts from an assumption that organisational members share a set of basic assumptions, beliefs and behaviours which operate unconsciously in a basic, taken-for-granted fashion, there is a growing recognition that, in many organisations, these basic assumptions and internal processes are gendered, imposed on some by others, such that organisations become shot through with internal divisions – not only along the axis of gender, but also by other social groupings such as race, ethnicity, age, class, sexuality and physical ability. However, different coexisting cultural groups may *all* be located within a corporate patriarchy, so characteristic of bureaucracies (Alvesson and Billing 1992, Green and Cassell 1996). Men are thus generally found to be 'culturally active' in creating an environment in which 'women don't flourish' (Cockburn 1991), using a variety of exclusionary practices to make their gender work in their favour. The structural approach to understanding power thus has resonance with both approaches to culture, and, indeed, brings them together. The point is that not only is masculinity wielded as a powerful tool to marginalise and discriminate against women, but organisational cultures are also masculine in style. To understand culture merely as an admired set of ideas, and a reflection of particular versions of masculinity, does not allow for an account to be made of the daily processes in which men use their power, to work to define women. It is clear therefore that culture can not be held as distinct as Smircich's (1983) original dichotomy suggests. The explicit organisational culture by which management wishes to direct the organisation cannot be achieved without being actively and continuously enacted, lived out or 'animated' (Halford and Savage 1995) by organisational members.

So far, our theorisations of gender, culture and organisation seem to have left behind the traditional, liberal approach to understanding power. However, the point being made is also that individual men wield power over individual women on a daily, observable basis. Further than that, their *non-action* in failing to transform organisational cultures into more women-friendly spaces, for example, cultures which recognise their domestic responsibilties, is also an exercise of power (Bachrach and Baratz 1963). Thus the liberal understanding of power can be seen to have resonance too. However, whereas the liberal approach to organisation typically assumes that either culture is an integrative and unifying mechanism for the organisation, or, alternatively, that an organisation is a harmonious and consensual culture, our discussion identifies gender as a key point of structuration. Different groups or 'subcultures' within the organisation have very different values, beliefs and ways of doing things. The fact that men have more power than women within organisational structures and hierarchies means that they can influence organisational culture and use it to perpetuate the system in which they benefit. By seeing organisations through the lens of a gendered hierarchy, structural power is placed at the centre of analysis.

However, from our second approach to understanding gender, culture and power, this kind of dichotomous thinking might be seen as rather oversimplified, leading even to the misrepresentation of the attributes and viewpoints of women and men inside work organisations. For our discussion of differentiated power has revealed that different women may respond to gendered cultures in different ways. But difference and ambiguity may not stop there: at times the *same* woman might feel the consequences of her marginal position very sorely, whereas at other times things might not seem to be too bad. Within this poststructuralist approach to gender and power, organisations are understood to be cross-cut with multiple sets of meanings and lines of cultural identification, the individual to be fractured by different aspects of identity. Ambiguities constantly arise as contradictory sets of meanings or prescriptions for action intersect. Alongside this, power is conceptualised as altogether more fluid. Power is not seen as an 'entity', possessed by men alone, but rather, different sorts of power are thought to be mobilised by different sorts of people in different kinds of ways. Women may find a variety of strategies through which to mobilise power and improve their marginalised position. As Martin argues 'taken together, these factors create an organisational world characterised by distance rather than closeness, obscurity rather than clarity, disorder rather than order, uncontrollability rather than predictability' (Martin 1992:132).

To conclude, this consideration of the relationship between gender, culture and organisation has extended our understandings of how power is mobilised within organisations to situate women in distinctive and largely marginalised positions. We have shown how power may be mobilised through culture, making it work to support the design of an organisation and to maintain the structural relations within it. Organisational culture thus acts to gender organisational life (Davies 1996). As individuals move into these gendered cultures, they undertake considerable internal mental work (Acker 1992) in order to assimilate the organisation's gendered structure of work, opportunity and gender appropriate behaviours and attitudes. Organisation is thus bound up with the ways in which relations between individuals are interpreted and performed, and the ways in which individual identities are enacted. Social interaction may merely reflect the gender relations as defined in the structural hierarchy, or it may intensify them, and by so doing undermine women's positions in decision-making positions. Gender is thus produced within organisations, as part of its concrete work (Acker 1992). However, we have also seen that we cannot assume gendered identities, relations or feelings simply by reference to any individual's structural location and that individuals are not passive subjects in the gendering of organisational life. Culture also provides opportunities for individual people to resist the dominant power relations, by drawing on alternative sets of value and belief systems and ways of doing things. Women working within organisational cultures also engage in 'internal mental work', of course (Green and Cassell 1996). This may include constructing their own understandings of organisational structures and cultures, and making their own decisions on where and how to position themselves as they learn how to manage the world of the organisation (Sheppard 1989, Morely 1994). Thus, it may be inaccurate to see women as a cohesive and unified group within an organisation, as different women draw on different sources of power to modify their position within the organisation's structure and culture.

4

Gender and Management in Organisations

Introduction

Our examination of organisational structures and cultures in the previous chapters has documented the very different experiences of women and men working in contemporary organisations, and begun to reveal the centrality of power – in multiple forms – to the constitution of these experiences. In particular, we have seen that organisations have been constructed in ways which favour men in terms of status and reward, such that men have continually dominated senior positions, while women have been relatively excluded from the management tier. However, in recent years women have increasingly started to 'make it' as managers and leaders in many organisations in most industrialised countries. The changing social, political and economic climate of the 1960s and 1970s meant that women started to enter management in more significant numbers, such that at the turn of the millennium it can no longer be seen as the exclusive male club it was for so many decades (Davidson and Cooper 1992).

Yet the amount of literature, both academic and journalistic, which has accompanied the arrival of women into management would seem to indicate that this gradual transformation has been received as 'problematic'. Both theoretically and practically, 'woman' and 'manager' are often constructed as a binary opposition, a clashing combination of concepts which need some justification and explanation. This sense of opposition takes a variety of forms. When women first started to enter management they were perceived as so different (and almost irrelevant) to the established masculinity of management that, while their entry was bound to raise all sorts of minor organisational head-aches, they were of little real concern. However, as numbers increased, two questions started to emerge. These are questions which have remained dominant in subsequent interest in the issue, and they are, essentially, questions not only about gender but also about power. It is the relationship between gender, power and management which we explore in this chapter.

The first question has its roots in both liberal and structuralist traditions. It asks, why are there so few women managers, compared with men? In other words, who and what is preventing women from becoming managers in equal numbers to men? How is power being exercised to marginalise women and keep them located primarily at the lower end of the organisational tier? Our investigation of organisa-tional structures and cultures in Chapters 2 and 3 has gone a long way to answering this question. We have seen how the structural patterns of organisational design, the range of organisational rules and procedures as well as sexist attitudes about women and men, and masculinity and femininity work, more or less openly, to maintain male power. In the next section we examine the research which ana-lyses specifically how these aspects intensify for women as they attempt to rise through organisations and challenge the (male) possession of managerial power.

Clearly, however, this is not the only side of the story. While the research evidence presented in the next section seems fairly unrelent-ing, we also know that women *are* making it into management, and, in some sectors, in quite significant numbers. In the subsequent section which follows, we turn to explore the issues raised by this development through our second question. This question asks, what are the differ-ences between women and men managers? Initially the interest in this issue revolved around male–female difference. Much of the research sought to establish whether women and men offered different attrib-utes and brought different skills to the management process. Two distinct arguments developed. First, developing the liberal model of differential socialisation, feminist organisational sociologists asked why women's qualities could not be recognised and accommodated within management hierarchies. In other words, this approach demanded that officially sanctioned management power should be shared between men and women. Second, taking an altogether more radical line, it was argued that women offer a complete and better alternative to masculine ways of managing. This is a direct challenge to male power: women are positioned as the 'new' managers, and put forward as preferable replacements. The conclusions of this radical approach are diverse, however. Blurring the boundaries between liberal and radical, some writers recommend that the way forward is for men and women to join forces, bringing their different but equally valued skills to management. Others remain within a radical or structural understanding of power, proposing that the extant hierarchy is overturned, and that men's dominant position is taken by women. Still others recognise that the chances of this happening are slim, and thus recommend that women disassociate with men's organisations altogether, establishing their own, separate ones.

More recently, influenced by post-structuralism, the work on difference, gender and management has shifted to produce a broader understanding of the concept of difference. Research within this approach focuses less on the categorical differences between women and men, and more on the myriad and complex nature of difference. Multiple differences are understood to occur and intersect not only between the genders but within them. Thus women managers may differ significantly from each other, intersected as they are by multiple features such as race, ethnicity, class, regionality, age, sexuality, family responsibilities and so on. Similarly, men managers also differ from each other, in terms both of style and of their relationship with, and exercise of, power. Much of the research within this approach thus takes yet another conceptualisation of power, seeing it not so much as a necessary attachment to certain group members but more as a transitory possession held by certain (any) individuals at certain moments in time.

In the final section of the chapter, we conclude that, while the literature on gender and management makes little mention of power in any explicit sense, this is the critical concept which underpins it. In fact, what gives the literature its sense of urgency for many is that what is really being discussed is whether a significant challenge is being made to the male domination of organisational power. In many senses, the discussion about management is a politicisation of the relationships between gender, power and organisation.

Women managers and male power

The figures

The numerical distribution within the ranks of management is one of the most obvious and visible differences between women and men in work organisations in practically every country in the globe. For example, in the UK, women constituted 45 per cent of the 1990s workforce (Labour Force Survey 1995). However, the Institute of Managment has reported that the percentage of women managers was only 15.2 per cent (though this figure represents a significant rise in a few years: in 1994 the figure was as low as 9.5 per cent; (EOR 1994 b, 1997a) These jobs are likely to be in occupations which are traditionally associated with women, such as catering and retailing, and service sector organisations such as local government, education, the National Health Service (NHS), training, personnel and professional services. A survey of 100 large Confederation of British Industry (CBI) employers (Hansard Society Commission 1990) revealed that only 6.7 per cent of senior managers were women, and that only 3 per cent of the companies sampled had women on their main boards as executive directors. By 1999, the number of women directors on the boards of the 200 largest companies listed by *The Times*, still accounted for only 5 per cent (EOR 1998a) . Even in the organisations where women are employed in significant proportions, they are grossly under represented in senior management. In the Civil Service, for example, which comprises 66 per cent female staff, mainly at lower clerical grades, in 1998 only 9 per cent of principal grades were occupied by women, with only 4 per cent in higher positions (EOR 1998b). In primary education, 40 per cent of head teachers were female, but in universities, only 3 per cent of professors, and 2 per cent of vice-chancellors and principals were women. In the NHS, although 90 per cent of nurses were women, only 55 per cent of chief nursing officers were women. Indeed, 78 per cent of the NHS workforce were women, yet only 4 per cent were general managers (Alimo-Metcalfe 1993).

These findings are further countered by the fact that more people generally now occupy management service positions. According to Alban-Metcalfe and Nicholson in 1984 and Nicholson and West in 1988, higher-status managers in 'generalist' positions were still more likely to be male; moreover, empirical evidence shows that by 1997 those few women who had climbed the ladder of success and reached top positions still earned only a fraction of the salaries of their male counterparts (EOR 1997a).

The UK picture is reflected in other countries. In the United States, by 1991 women's rate of participation in management had grown to 11.4 per cent, but only 3 per cent of these could be classified as senior management positions (US Department of Labor 1991). US figures have revealed that the position is even worse for ethnic minority women. Recent figures (1991) have shown that in the USA only 4 per cent of black women were working in management posts, compared with 25 per cent of white women (Bell *et al.* 1993; see also Morrison and Von Glinow 1990). Figures for the UK at the same time show less dramatic differences, with 11 per cent of all white women working as employers or managers, compared with 9 per cent of all non-white women (OPCS 1991). However, the 1991 census also revealed significant differences between ethnic groups. For instance, as many as 16 per cent of Chinese women were working as employers or managers compared with only 5 per cent of Bangladeshi women, although it is worth noting that 56 per cent of Chinese women in this category registered themselves as employers in small establishments. This compares with only 17 per cent of the white female managers or employers, indicating once again the importance of the so-called ethnic economy. Looking just at large corporations and public bodies, 3.2 per cent of white women were working as managers or employers in these organisations, compared with only 1.8 per cent of Chinese women but, significantly as many as 3.1 per cent of Afro-Caribbean women.

The figures for Europe are varied, with the Nordic countries demonstrating further advancement towards equal opportunities. For example, in Finland, 18 per cent of managers in large companies are women, while they form 46 per cent of managers of small companies (Hänninen-Salmelin and Petäjäniemi 1994). In France, the figures vary according to occupational sectors, and range for example, from a low of 6.8 per cent of the managers in manufacturing and construction being women to a high of 62 per cent of managers in communication being female (Alexandre 1990 quoted in Serdjenian 1994) Indeed, in the majority of functions, the figures are well over 20 per cent. In Ireland, the figure of women managers is 17.4 per cent (Davidson and Cooper 1992). In many other European countries, the figures are more traditional. In the former West Germany, for example, only 5.9 per cent of top managers and 7.8 per cent of managers at the next level being women. Only 0.7 per cent of managing board members in public companies are women (Antal and Krebsbach-Gnath 1994). While the figures for the former East Germany are higher – estimated at around 30 per cent – they are less impressive against the 91 per cent of women of working age in employment (Antal and Krebsbach-Gnath 1994). In Southern Europe, the figures tend to reflect the fact that women have traditionally been regarded as less career-orientated. For example, in Greece the figure is estimated to be 8 per cent, in Italy it is 3 per cent whereas in Spain it is 5 per cent (Davidson and Cooper 1992).

Clearly, then, far fewer women make it to the management tiers of organisations than men, and even fewer make it to the very top levels of organisations. It is, it has been said, as if a 'glass ceiling' exists within organisations, which curtails women's progress up through the organisational structures. That is, a set of invisible yet very formidable factors operate within the organisation to 'make a shambles of evaluation and promotion systems' (Devanna 1987:470). This means that women, and also men of colour, are limited in their careers. In the remaining part of this section we turn to explore these factors.

Sex role stereotyping

One of the most popular explanations for the last twenty years for the paucity of women managers has been that of 'sex role stereotyping'. Sex role stereotyping works to define our understanding of women and men, and masculinity and femininity, by the creation of traditional and often idealised notions of what each sex are like and do (Marshall 1995). Through this process, connections are made between gender and appropriateness in a whole range of contexts, including work, organisation and management. Primarily, research within this tradition argues that male managers, male workers and some female workers tend to hold a 'masculinised' model of the good manager (Baack *et al.* 1993, Loden 1985, Marshall 1984, 1985, O'Leary 1974, O'Leary and Ryan 1994, Schein 1973, 1975, 1978, 1989, Schein and Mueller 1990, Sheppard 1989). 'Masculine' characteristics such as self-reliance, independence, analysis, aggressiveness and domination are associated with the successful manager, while 'feminine' characteristics such as cooperation, acceptance, emotion, spiritual and artistic interests and caring are judged to be irrelevant or even damaging to effective management.

> The model of the successful manager in our culture is a masculine one. The good manager is aggressive, competitive, firm and just. He is not feminine, he is not soft and yielding or dependent or intuitive in a womanly sense. The very expression of emotion is widely viewed as a feminine weakness that would interfere with effective business processes. (O'Leary 1974)

1.   This is a widely used metaphor: see, for example, Davidson 1991, Davidson and Cooper 1992, Morely 1994, Morrison 1992 Rigg and Sparrow 1994, *Women in Management Review and Abstracts* vol. 6, no. 5 1991.)

In other words, the situation is one of 'think manager, think male' (Schein 1973, 1975); whereas the profiles of male and manager overlap, this is not so for females. In a similar study originally conducted in the US in 1974, O'Leary found that employee attitudes reflect a prevailing Western cultural norm that women should not have authority over men of equivalent age and social class. Her study revealed a set of attitudes commonly held towards women managers, such as that they are given preferential treatment and premature advancement owing to the influence of pressure groups rather than on their own merits. Once in managerial posts, their presence is believed to make social interactions difficult, they are seen as less able to cope with crises than men, as undependable, as requiring an inordinate amount of sick leave owing to menstruation and pregnancy, and their employment is believed to jeopardise the institution of the family.

Recently, Schein and her colleagues (Brenner *et al.* 1989) replicated their study, in order to determine whether there have been any changes in middle managers' perceptions of women and men bosses in the ensuing passage of time. The results indicated that associations between sex role stereotypes and requisite management characteristics have not diminished in male managers' ratings, while women managers rated the degree of resemblance between 'man' and 'manager' as identical to 'woman' and 'manager'. Women managers see some of the traits necessary for successful managerial performance as more likely to be held by women, and some of them as more likely to be held by men (O'Leary and Ryan 1994). Yet the fact remains that men's attitudes were remarkably similar to those of the earlier sample. Even more depressing are the two most recent studies using Schein's descriptive index with US, British and German management students (Schein and Mueller 1990), the results of which reveal that males in all three countries perceive middle managers as possessing the characteristics, attitudes and temperaments more commonly ascribed to men in general than to women in general.

In spite of the difficulties, the figures above reveal that some women *are* appointed as managers. Once in post, however, there is evidence that the woman manager will still be affected by these prejudiced attitudes and gender stereotypes, which may prevent her from rising to the very top. We saw in Chapter 2 that in many organisations, the woman manager is a token (Kanter 1977), meaning that she is often the only woman in the management group. She may have been appointed so as to support claims of equality of opportunity, or female managerial competence (Tanton 1994) rather than because of any real belief of her competence. Tokenism often intensifies for blacks who are promoted within white organisations. Similarly, this may be a reflection of a company's desire to appear progressive or morally decent by promoting a few visible tokens without tackling any of the more pervasive forms of organisational racism. Tokenism often leads to stereotyping, as people are thought to be appointed more for what they are, rather than what they can do. The result is that characteristics will be distorted and misperceived, as the token is placed in a familiar context from which she may be understood. Through this process, women may be encapsulated into a small range of limited roles, usually ones which benefit men, which they are forced to play.

For example, Kanter (1977) describes four minority roles which she sees as developing in organisations. First is the 'mother' role. This is the role of comforter and sympathiser to the men in the work group, the one to whom they bring their problems, often family-related troubles rather than ones to do with work. This is a comparatively safe role, not necessarily vulnerable to sexual pursuit, nor is she likely to be the source of competition or jealousy. The mother must be available to everybody. However, it is a problematic role, as the mother is more likely to become renowned for her emotional rather than professional skills.

Second is the 'seductress'. This is a more fraught role, as it introduces an element of sexual competition: while 'the mother can have many sons, it is more difficult for the sexually attractive to have many swains' (Kanter 1977:234) . This role may be conscious or unconsciously adopted, but the consequences are usually problematic. If she is assumed to be sharing her attention too widely, she 'risks the debasement of the whore' (Kanter 1977:234). If she restricts her attention to any man in particular, she arouses resentment and suspicion, and will, in all probability, be ultimately hounded out. This is because the seductress is often able to form an alliance with very senior men within organisations, a position which might be resented by other male employees. Women who take this role, and, as we say, this may be quite unconscious or unwilling, are never short of attention, but this is of the sexual rather than the professional kind. Her competence and ability are thus masked by her sexuality.

Third is the role of the 'pet'. The pet is adopted by the male group as a 'cute amusing little thing and symbolically taken along on group events as mascot' (Kanter 1977:235). Pets often have a great sense of humour and can be 'one of the boys' – fun to be with while never really being regarded as equal. For example:

One woman reported that when she was alone in a group of men and spoke at length on an issue, comments to her by men after the meeting often referred to her speech-making ability rather than the content of what she said (e.g. 'You talk so fluently') whereas comments the men made to each other were almost invariably content-or issue-oriented. (Kanter 1977:235)

In other words there is 'a kind of look-what-she-did-and-she-is-only-a-woman attitude' (Kanter 1977:235) prevailing, which tends to encourage self-effacing girlish responses, and which in turn prevents them from realising their own power and competence.

The final role is that of the 'iron maiden'. Women who fail to fall into the first three roles and, in fact, overtly resist behaviours such as flirtation which may trap them into a certain sort of relationship, are often labelled as tough, feminist, or hard as iron (in Britain, the Conservative prime minister from 1979 to 1980, Margaret Thatcher, was universally termed 'The Iron Lady'). Indeed, these women often become stereotyped as tougher than they really are, and 'trapped in a more militant stance than they might otherwise take' (Kanter 1977:236). Whereas women encapsulated in the other roles do, at least receive some sort of attention from their male colleagues, iron maidens are left to flounder on their own when they have a problem, and are then attacked for not handling it well.

Kanter argues that token women managers have few options in their response to this kind of role encapsulation. They may accept a stereotypical role, which could limit their participation in situations and lead to programmed responses from men. If they try and fight it, they risk being classified as iron maidens and face rejection by the group. The strategy of trying not to exhibit any of the stereotypical characteristics takes considerable effort and may cause much stress.

Many people in organisations hold not only sexist stereotypes but also racist ones. Research in this area reveals that there is a general underestimation of black workers and an assumption that blacks are less intelligent, less competent and inherently low achievers. Combined with the claims made in Chapter 3 about the clash of black values with white organisational culture, blacks are thus often ruled out of contention for more senior posts, especially management. The few black managers who do exist are seen as exceptional, having achieved their status against the norm. Unlike whites; '[b]lacks must "prove themselves" in situations where white managers are deemed to be capable' (Davis and Watson 1982:169).

Sex-specific stereotypes are less well documented in the literature on race and organisation, although Dumas (1980) provides a notable exception and elsewhere there are some tantalising hints at how the stereotypes debated in black feminist writing more generally might exist within organisational discourse (for example, see Liff and Dale 1994).

We have already described (in Chapter 2) the specifically racist and sexist incorporation of black workers into the labour market and into white-collar organisations. Underlying this process there were clearly racially specific contructions of femininity whereby the notion of white femininity as weak, dependent and passive was contrasted with constructions of the black woman as strong, hard working, dominant and promiscuous (Hill-Collins 1990, Essed 1991). While the roots of this conception may lie in slavery, colonialism and imperialism, the constant recycling and reconstruction of these historical memories remain a central part of contemporary constructions of race, gender or class (Ware 1992; see also Spaights and Whitaker 1985). Black feminist writers have elaborated several components to white constructions of black femininity. Of particular relevance here are the 'matriarch', the 'mammy' and the 'whore'.

Dumas (1980) concentrates on the significance of the 'matriarch' and the 'mammy' in her analysis of black women in organisational leadership positions. The image of the matriarch draws on assumptions about the comparatively large numbers of black women (compared with white women) heading families and households without the permanent presence of a male partner. This 'woman' is constructed as dominant, powerful, aggressive, emasculating/castrating and unable to supervise her children properly because of being out at work. In other words, 'unfeminine' in dominant white terms, and an omen of what goes wrong when men are not in charge of their families (Hill-Collins 1990). By contrast, the 'mammy' constructs black woman as faithful, obedient, loving, nurturing, ever willing to put herself at the disposal of those around her (Hill-Collins 1990, Dumas 1980). This second image lies closer to the (white) feminine ideal, but constructed through reference to tasks performed under slavery and domestic work it retains a racial specificity which marks it out from the 'good mother' image, so central to constructions of white femininity in organisational life as elsewhere (Kanter 1977, but see also Cockburn 1991, Halford, Savage and Witz 1996).

Dumas (1980) argues that the dominance of these stereotypes limit the roles open to black women inside white organisations, because, as we have already seen, black women are judged less on their professional or technical competencies than their ascribed sexual and racial characteristics, Dumas argues that black women have little choice other than to occupy the specifically black and female subject positions offered by the matriarch and the mammy. Clearly, the mammy may have more to offer than the matriarch, since it does at least have some positive (if circumscribed) dimensions. But the women interviewed by Dumas found that they were all too often stuck in the middle of conflicts which they were supposed to solve drawing on their supposedly unlimited personal resources as mammies. All this was in addition to the performing of the tasks they were actually employed to do. Dumas found that the only resistance open to women in this position was to refuse to take on the mammy role, a step which led to their representation as cold, inflexible and authoritarian, or what Dumas calls the 'wicked malevolent mammy' (p. 210). Thus resistance flips over into the alternative image of the matriarch, the bad mother, refusing to supply her natural, bounteous capacities and generates even more problems for the black woman to deal with.

The third image which dominates black feminist writing about the construction of black femininity is that of 'the whore'. This is an image we explore more fully in the next chapter. In brief, a different level of sexuality is commonly assumed for all blacks compared with whites, such that blacks are regarded as being much more sexually active. While more passive than constructions of black male sexuality, black female sexuality is nonetheless constructed as passionate, responsive and active, in contrast to white femininity which is seen as pious, pure and almost asexual. This hypersexuality attributed to black women does not constitute any advantage in gaining access to posts, especially those in management and leadership, where women's sexuality is generally regarded with suspicion, and as being inappropriate.

Clearly, the gender and race stereotypes discussed here have a clear cumulative effect on women's careers within white male organisations. It is to this discussion we now turn.

Effects of sex role stereotyping on careers

Research on the more tangible factors involved in building a management career, such as organisational recruitment and selection procedures, assessment and promotion decisions, networking and mentorship, leaves us in no doubt that these stereotypes flourish in organisational cultures. First, when it comes to recruitment, if the stereotypical view of the woman boss is as someone who has inappropriate qualities and characteristics, and for whom no one, man or woman, wants to work (Bowman *et al.* 1965, Feber *et al.* 1979, Kahn and Crosby 1985, Sutton and Moore 1985, O'Leary and Ryan 1994), then a woman is less likely to be appointed to the position of manager. We saw in Chapter 2 how Kanter's (1977) study revealed the careful containment of power and privilege by (male) managers to the 'right sort of person'. Social similarity tends to become extremely important for managers, who try and replicate themselves in new appointments to management positions. Kanter termed this process 'homosocial reproduction', explaining that, although it provides some reassurance in the face of uncertainty about performance measurement in high reward, high-prestige positions, it also means that 'management positions become easily closed to people who are different' (Kanter 1977a: 63).

Second, when it comes to assessing candidates for promotion to management, judgements are also very much wrapped up with the daily life and dominant cultural attitudes of the organisation. Decisions draw on accepted understandings about which characteristics and attributes are valued and desired as appropriate for management, and which are devalued or regarded as inappropriate. As we saw in Chapter 3, parallels are often made between management and a certain sort of masculinity, whereas femininity is more often associated with traditionally 'female' roles (of which seniority in business is not one). Alimo-Metcalfe (1994) has provided the following elaborated typology of qualities seen to be desirable for management, which clearly demonstrates this dichotomy (Alimo-Metcalfe 1994a:29):

Valued	*Devalued*
objective	subjective
rational	irrational
expert	untrained
abstract	case-by-case
dehumanised	humane
detached	involved
impersonal	personal
unemotional	emotional
authoritarian	nurturant
unequal	equal
graceless	with grace
unsympathetic	sympathetic
untouched	moved

The prevalence of the association of these attributes with gender, not only within work organisations but also in the wider culture, means that a ready-made discourse exists within which decisions are made, largely uncontested. Clearly, opportunities exist for these prejudices to permeate all stages of the assessment and promotion processes. Male power is thus embedded in the decision-making procedures about who gets into management, and the numerical paucity of women in some occupational sectors means that often there is little chance of challenge to this (ab)use of power.

This essentialist reading of human nature means that women managers face an intensified set of performance pressures. They have a stark choice of options. The first is that they adopt the set of 'valued' (masculine) characteristics, and manage 'like men'. This strategy is not often liked, as a respondent in Renshaw's research on women managers in the Pacific islands summed up as follows: '[A] woman being a success is often seen as someone who is deviant – too intelligent, too masculine, too religious' (Renshaw 1988:133). Similarly, an interviewee in McDowell's comparable research into British banking explained: '[A]n aggressive male dealer – well, that's how dealers are; an aggressive woman – it's not natural' (McDowell 1997:175). Alternatively, they must go it alone, and manage according to their expected (female) gender characteristics, while proving that they can still be effective. This can be a difficult job, because if women do perform better, then they may be resented by their male peers (Cockburn 199; Halford *et al.* 1997). Alternatively, they may be liked while the going is good, but shot down when it is not:

> As a woman it's quite easy to get your foot in the door because you are different but if you are good, as a woman, you will get on well, but if you are bad, and a woman, you will have a far worse time. Men don't suffer female fools gladly in this business. (McDowell 1995:177)

These pressures are likely to be intensified for black organisational members (Davidson 1997), linked not only to the racist judgements made about the competence of black workers (Greenhaus *et al.* 1990) but also, it seems, to a sense that black workers are judged as representatives of their 'race'. The black women managers interviewed by Liff and Dale (1994) reported feeling pressure that any failure on their part would count against black people in the future: 'It's important that I perform well so that black people aren't seen as poor performers' (ibid.: 190). Similarly, a black male manager paraphrased the message he was getting from his boss: 'Be a credit to your people. Don't take a coffee break. Don't take lunch. Don't get sick. Don't go on vacation – work' (Davis and Watson 1982:27).

However, notwithstanding the racism and inequity in these pressures to perform, Davis and Watson (1982) argue that they constitute a 'Catch-22', since, as with women, if black workers do perform better than whites they may be resented and systematically undermined. It follows that the combined impact on black women will be especially severe.

Women and black workers may be promoted to 'special' management positions which are linked directly to their gender and race – such as advisors on equal opportunities, or on ethnic market, or community relations – but not linked directly into mainstream organisational career paths. For black managers, even where such ethnic 'specialisation' does not exist, evidence is offered to show that they are marginalised into the least prestigous positions, which offer little hope for further advancement into the most senior organisational echelons. For example, Davis and Watson (1982) found black managers sidetracked onto secondary career tracks in personnel and public affairs, while Dumas (1980) claims that the few black women who do make it into leadership roles are limited to leading other black women and/or children, not whites or men. A tokenistic status is also seen to derive from affirmative action and equal-opportunity programmes inside work organisations. While these initiatives do no more than begin to correct the white biases and racist disadvantages experienced by black people, their existence is often interpreted as giving black people an unfair chance and offering promotion to those who don't deserve it. Thus, a 'discounting process' operates whereby blacks in senior positions are assumed to be no more than tokens of liberal commitment by the organisation rather than good at their jobs (Heilman *et al.* 1992, Liff and Dale 1994). This only adds to the stigmatisation and presumed incompetence of black managers (Heilman *et al.* 1992).

Third, as we saw in Chapter 3, not only is the formal organisation dominated by men, but so is the informal organisation. In the previous chapter, we discussed how the patterns of communication and socialising are also often almost exclusively male. This means that women, as well as members of minority ethnic groups (Ibarra 1993), are often excluded from the chance to form important work relationships, such as with mentors and sponsors, or to develop networks. However, these informal relationships with more senior managers are seen to be the key to career success: 'You've got to have exposure. There are a lot of technically talented people around who don't have exposure and they'll go nowhere ... exposure is like 80%' (white male manager interviewed by Cianni and Romberger 1995:357).

This exclusion is certainly not a question of choice on the part of marginalised groups but a structural constraint arising from their marginalised position inside organisations. Persaud *et al.* (1990) found male managers were twice as likely to watch and engage in sports and discuss current events with male subordinates, and three times as likely to engage in non-work-related conversations. Indeed, in a 1987 survey of US women in management the 'old-boy network' was one of the three most cited forms of professional discrimination against executive women (Northcraft and Gutek 1993); 'It's tough. The ways I am excluded are very subtle ... before meetings or during the break, I am often left by myself whilst the men chat with each other' (Watts 1989:32 in Northcraft and Gutek 1993:224).

According to Ibarra (1993), the stereotypes and characteristics ascribed to both women and minority groups mean that they are seen as less *useful* to white men and therefore more likely to be shunned in the construction of their networks. White men tend to seek out other white men. Where cross-sex or cross-race relationships do exist, Ibarra claims, they are fraught with tensions. In response, Ibarra discovered, women and minority groups seek out same-race or same-sex networks to provide support in this exclusionary context. Denton (1980) argues that these personal networks offer essential support, especially to black women dealing with the bi-cultural stresses which develop from engaging with white organisational life. But however effective these personal networks are in dealing with the specific stresses of being female and/or black in white male organisations, they cannot offer the same career support as participation in the white male networks.

Similar points are made in discussions of mentor relationships at work. Cianni and Romberger (1995) found that women and minority groups had fewer opportunities to cultivate mentor-type relationships with senior managers. This was partly because they were excluded from informal networks, as described above, and lacked information about what events and activities were important for career development. One black male manager, initially at a loss to explain his slow progress compared with his white contemporaries, illustrates this point:

I woke up and realised what was going on, everybody belonged to the same golf club...I had no idea you had to belong somewhere in order to get ahead or just be known to someone else. (Cianni and Romberger 1995: 358)

Other black and female managers described feeling uncomfortable in predominantly white male social settings. Cianni and Romberger (1995) report that Asian managers of both sexes felt this particularly acutely:

There's also a thing of the ethnic background that precludes you from certain events...you may not want to go because that's not part of your tradition...Basically Asians are not party goers. They're fairly quiet, as a race as a whole...They'll stay in the background...and this is a time when you have to be outgoing and really swallow hard and go up to that VP and introduce yourself.' (Asian male manager interviewed by Cianni and Romberger 1995: 359 see also Davidson 1997: 43).

Such problems were compounded for black women, as Cianni and Romberger describe different axes of exclusion by sex adding to those of race. In sum, most writers conclude, limited access to white male informal networks and to mentoring relationships with white men mean that women and minority groups suffer multiple disadvantages in developing organisational careers.

   The result of these barriers and pressures is for many women in management positions, particularly senior management, to experience a fair degree of loneliness at work (Alban-Metcalfe 1984; Davidson and Cooper 1983, Asplund 1988, Marshall 1984, Powell 1988). Tanton (1994) notes how the experience of loneliness at work can raise a number of further uncomfortable roles or issues for women. Women may be constrained to adopt a distinctive type of performance, or become labelled as a particular type of person. She outlines a number of key roles: a 'boundary marker' (Marshall 1984, Scase and Goffee 1989): 'she treads the way men may wish not to go'; 'extra-visible manager' (Kanter 1977, O'Leary and Johnson 1991): 'if she puts a foot wrong, she will be noticed'; 'traitor' (O'Leary 1988): criticised by other women; martyr: 'I have to go on otherwise I'll let my other women colleagues down'; 'one of the boys' (Marshall 1984, Tanton 1992): 'I don't have any problems, I'm just like a man'; 'conformist' (Ferguson 1984): 'the price of success in a bureaucratic world' or 'unrecognised explorer' (Tanton 1994): 'I have to go where no other women have been, but there is little success when I get there.' All of these roles are likely to marginalise the woman manager from the larger group, as well as make her feel uncomfortable and isolated in her work situation.

Fourth, as well as lacking access to important informal relationships and networks, women managers may also lag behind their male counterparts when it comes to the provision of education and training, often essential to the building of a successful management career. Indeed, dissatisfaction with training and/or inadequate training has been shown to be a common complaint from female managers (Davidson and Cooper 1992). One of the reasons for this dissatisfaction is that the problems discussed above may be merely exacerbated on training courses, if women are very much in the minority. For example, Vinnicombe and Colwill (1995) note that management trainers are almost exclusively men who bring their conventional male attitudes and values to their teaching. Thus materials are often sexist, with few case-studies of senior women managers, and many of the theories and principles based on research using only men. There are few opportunities to discuss the gender and power issues relating to working women such as sex role stereotyping, sexual harassment, internal politics and dual career families. Further, Davidson and Cooper (1992) found that some management trainers have a tendency to assign female managers particular roles on a management course (such as Kanter's mother, seductress, pet or iron maiden types which we discussed earlier) which only work to restrict their learning and experience. The female manager's ability to take risks and develop valuable ways of learning new skills may be further reduced by the presence of overwhelming numbers of men, who may have certain expectations about a woman's role, as well as by the possible underlying sexual overtones (Davidson and Cooper 1992).

As a response to these difficulties, many organisations and management training centres now offer 'women-only' management training programmes. However, these are seen to be somewhat controversial, by both women and men, who argue that in the long run they may prove to be detrimental. First, the creation of such courses could be seen to suggest that women are deficient in ways men are not, and as such need more training; second, some may feel that women are receiving more favourable treatment, and this may work to increase the alienation and tension between women and men managers (Harlan and Weiss 1980, Davidson and Cooper 1992). In spite of this, many women welcome the provision of gender-specific training, arguing that women share very similar problems within organisations, such as suffering sex discrimination, lacking senior role models or mentors, or having to act as role models themselves. Colwill and Vinnicombe (1991) found that in all-female groups women are more likely to admit faults and to identify needs and areas where they feel inadequate.

Stress

Clearly, the pressures women managers face when attempting to build a management career will mean that organisational life may be extremely stressful for many women. Indeed, Alimo-Metcalfe (1987) found in her research on women managers that women feel considerably less relaxed at work than do men. The reasons they gave recall many of the aspects we have discussed so far in this chapter, but two given particular emphasis were the lack of due recognition for one's qualifications, experience and potential, and the lack of access to important information or important people in the organisation. Women felt that they were regarded with resentment or suspicion by male colleagues, and there was a strong sense of women feeling that they were highly visible and thus having to prove to others that they are as good as the men. This was often received as being expected to behave like a man, which for some respondents felt entirely 'unnatural'. Further, some expressed a sense of alienation in an environment where the emphasis was on competition, withholding information, and aggression (see also Davidson and Cooper 1983, 1992, Cooper and Davidson 1984). The increased stress felt by women managers often results in pressures on their health and a greater dependence on stimulants such as coffee and smoking (Davidson and Cooper 1992).

The frustrations felt by women managers working in male-dominated organisations led them typically to construct a variety of 'coping strategies' (Alban-Metcalfe 1984, Leonard 1998) such as relying on factors and support groups outside work for social and psychological support. For many, the family, church or music (Alban-Metcalfe 1984, Leonard 1998) become an important source of solace. Other women resolve to concentrate almost exclusively on those bits of the job they enjoy and interact with other managers as little as possible (Leonard 1998). The starkest choice is to leave the organisation altogether. Marshall (1995) studied sixteen senior managers who had left, or wanted to leave their organisations, and found that, although no generalised patterns emerged, the main reasons given were the male-dominated organisational culture, the lack of opportunities or untenable nature of the job, organisational conflicts and lack of recognition, stress and tiredness. Some women managers felt that the organisation had completely taken over their sense of personal identity, and wanted to rediscover what else they could do or be. Marshall terms reasons such as wanting a change, not liking what they had become, and fostering other relationships with husband and/or children 'identity development factors', and for many they were a means of reasserting personal power over 'male-dominated' organisational power.

While domestic lives may be a source of alternative strength for many women, they may also be yet another source of stress. The task of balancing home and work is intensified for women managers, who may have very large responsibilities to carry and long working hours to put in.

Balancing work and home

In the last chapter, our discussion of home and work demonstrated how women cope with the major share of domestic and family duties (Vinnicombe and Colwill 1995). There are many studies which identify the problems that women managers particularly face in attempting to balance a satisfying career with domestic responsibilities (see for example, Alban-Metcalfe and Nicholson 1984, Cooper and Davidson 1984, Davidson and Cooper 1987, 1992, Leonard and Malina 1994, Scase and Goffee 1989, Valdez and Gutek 1987). The main domestic responsibilities rest on the (working) woman and mother, regardless of whether she has a partner or not, and regardless of the seniority of her position. It is hardly surprising therefore that women managers are less likely to be married than men managers (for example 60.9 per cent as compared to 93.3 per cent of men managers (Alban-Metcalfe and Nicholson 1984), more likely to be childless, or, if they do have children, to have fewer of them (Cooper and Davidson 1984) and to delay having them until their thirties (Davidson and Cooper 1987). Twice as many women managers are divorced or separated (Cooper and Davidson 1984).

For many women managers who do attempt to combine family and home, therefore, the day is constructed as a 'double shift': one at work, and one at home. It is perhaps not surprising that such women often feel tired, stressed and guilty, owing to the conflict inherent in their attempts to fulfil the roles of both homemaker and career person simultaneously (Davidson and Cooper 1992, Parasuraman and Greenhaus 1993). In one study, 47 per cent of married women managers maintained that being married had proved a disadvantage to them in terms of their career development and advancement (Davidson and Cooper 1983). For example, there is evidence that some women avoid family tension and competitive feelings in their partners by moving to lower-status jobs (Davidson and Cooper 1992) or by making compromises that limit their career success (Valdez and Gutek 1987, Hochschild 1989, Sekaran 1986). However there is also evidence that this is not exclusive to women: many men do not move jobs or seek promotion for family reasons either (Halford *et al.* 1997).

Summary and discussion

In this section, we have considered research which explores, first, the barriers facing women who aspire to be managers, and, second, the experience of being a manager once in post. We have seen not only how it is made disproportionately difficult for women to reach management positions, but also that their experience once they reach this level may be disproportionately problematic and uncomfortable. Liberal explanations concentrate on how the possession of stereotypes among predominantly male managers leads to the mobilisation of prejudiced attitudes, such that women are perceived as being merely the embodiment of a cluster of 'feminine' attributes rather than suitable management material. Through the mobilisation of these stereotypes, men block the passage of women to managerial positions. Stereotyping can also be conceptualised as part of a structural process, therefore, whereby men as a group use their power to restrict women's entry into management. Women's deliberate exclusion from social activities, their consequent limited access to mentorship, education and training, and their prime responsibility for childcare are all material factors which make men and women's positions and experiences quite different. Of course, it is impossible to separate out these different aspects and hold any of them as fully accountable: the factors which construct the gendering of management are clearly multi-layered, with men using power in both episodic and systematic ways.

This view is supported by Schwartz (1989), who argues that the structural metaphor of the glass ceiling is a misleading one. A more appropriate metaphor, she argues, is the kind of cross-sectional diagram used in geology. This allows us to see that both liberal and structural approaches to power and gender have explanatory value. From a liberal perspective, the barriers to women's leadership occur when potentially counter-productive layers of influence on women; namely maternity, tradition and socialisation, meet management strata pervaded by the largely unconscious preconceptions, stereotypes and expectations of men and their views on women's relationship with the family. From a structural perspective, men mobilise power more consciously through recruitment, promotion and family duties to maintain their power base at the top of organisations. Thus it is interesting to note that the evidence shows that although the problem of juggling work and home demands is a significant one for many women, this may not have as much influence on advancement as other barriers (Morrison 1992). Tashjian (1990) points out that despite the common belief that women leave their companies because of conflicts between family and career, professional women leave mainly because they see limited career prospects for themselves, a finding which we saw was supported by Marshall's research (1995). The stress of constantly battling in a hostile environment is what, finally, pushes women to quit.

Certainly, what is underlined by this evidence is the political and gendered nature of management. Traditionally, men have dominated management positions, and, in spite of liberal pushes for an opening up of opportunities, it would seem that they are not going to cede their positions easily. By constructing the discourses of management and masculinity as virtually inseparable, women are placed in an antithetical position to power. To enter the inner sanctum on male terms would appear to be very difficult indeed. When it comes to the crunch, therefore, challenges to this structural basis of power have not been very significant. For this reason, some writers have argued that progress can only be achieved by challenging the very definition of what management itself means, and contesting what the manager should look like or be doing. They argue that if an organisation's understanding of what successful management includes is fundamentally reconceptualised, then alternatives to the traditional masculinist model may also be seen as acceptable. Consequently, debates have focused on the precise nature of these gender differences and the extent to which men might be able to accommodate alternative feminine styles of management. Do women offer an alternative 'feminine' style or styles which are equally effective in the management of organisations? Can men also manage differently?

Management and the question of difference

Difference in women's and men's management styles

Research which explores the question of difference between the ways women and men manage has its roots in two strands of feminist theorising: liberal and radical. First, as we have discussed above, liberal feminists concentrate particularly on sex roles and childhood socialisation patterns, to explain how and why men and women manage in different but equally valuable ways. For example, Rosener (1990) argues that their unique socialisation leads women to develop a non-traditional, 'feminine' leadership style which is well suited to some work organisations and can increase an organisation's chances of surviving in an uncertain world. Whereas men tend to work through a 'transactional' leadership style, that is, viewing job performance as a series of transactions with subordinates, and exchanging rewards for services rendered or punishment for inadequate performance; women tend to use a 'transformational' style, getting subordinates to transform their own self-interest into the interest of the group through concern for a broader goal. More specifically, this more interactive style means that women encourage participation, share power and information, enhance other people's self-worth and get others excited about their work. Women are thus making their way to the top not by adopting the style and habits that have proved successful for men but by drawing on the skills and attitudes they developed from their shared experience as women: 'As it turns out, the behaviours that were natural and/or socially acceptable for them have been highly successful in at least some managerial settings' (Rosener 1990:124).

Hegelson (1990) also agrees that women and men operate in different ways when in managerial positions. She uses the image of a web in women's conception of structure: women tend to place themselves in the middle of things: companies, office spaces, human relationships, not at the top as men do. Inseparable from this sense is women's notion of being connected to those around them, bound as if by invisible strands or threads. This is reflected in the management structures they create, and the way they organise meetings.

In the previous section of this chapter, we saw how the perceptions of women by, in particular, male managers, relied on stereotypical assumptions about women's sex roles. As male managers tend to be the people who recruit and promote, these prejudiced perceptions lead to the creation of a barrier (perhaps a subtle one) to women's advancement. In contrast, the present approach rests on an assumption that men and women *are* socialised according to different principles, namely those of masculinity and femininity, and *do* possess different traits. But the key point liberal feminists would emphasise here is that the sexes differ not because of any innate biological or psychological difference but rather because of sex role orientation. However, there is an increasing recognition that the gap between the stereotypical view of what men and women are like and the actual possession of traits is wide. Korabik (1990) draws on the work of Bem (1974) to show that not all males are socialised to have more masculine attributes, nor all females feminine ones, but that many people are 'androgynous', possessing both masculine and feminine traits. This view is supported by the leadership literature, which offers many exceptions to the task role being filled exclusively by males or to the social-emotional role being the primary province of females (Korabik 1981, 1990, Korabik and Ayman 1987). As Korabik concludes:

> The results of these studies clearly support the contention that biological sex is not an important factor in determining leadership style. The demonstration that socialisation rather than biology is responsible for leadership style means that females should not be excluded from positions which require instrumental ability merely on the basis of their biological sex.The realisation that men and women can be equally proficient in task oriented roles should result in more leadership positions being opened up for women. (Korabik 1990:287)

Writers such as Korabik (1990), Sargent and Stupak (1989) and DeMatteo (1994) argue that the fact that people possess both masculine and feminine traits provides a useful way forward for managers and leaders. They claim that organisations in the West are facing a critical shift in cultural values from the vertical, agentic, masculinist, values of individualism and action to the horizontal, feminine values of 'communion' or relationships. This new value set requires each person to have a blend of values, competence and compassion, action and introspection:

> They should combine the so-called feminine approach, which focuses on collaboration, caring and socialised power, with the more traditional 'masculine' approach which focuses on analysing problems, exercising unilateral power, negotiating, competing, and gaining credit for one's impact. The androgynous manager integrates and incorporates and employs both types of behaviours. He or she is both dominant and flexible, and combines independence and power with nurturing and intimacy (Sargent and Stupak 1989:32).

Managers of both sexes should thus work at developing this 'andro-gynous blend of competencies, for this is 'the style required for effect-ive leadership in organisation(s) in the years ahead' (Sargent 1989:30).

This approach sees that both masculine and feminine leadership qualities have an important role to offer the organisation of the late twentieth century, ensuring a management team of both balance and vision. In this model, power would become to be shared equally between the sexes. However, some critics point out that the androgyn-ous ideal is intrinsically sexist, and that male power is embedded in the very concept of androgyny. For example, some findings show that it is the masculine attributes of androgyny that are correlated with self-esteem and adjustment. The qualities that are actually endorsed in organisations do not reflect the ideals of femininity as well as mascu-linity:Basil (1972) found these to be decisiveness, consistency, objectiv-ity, emotional stability and analytical ability. While the concept of androgyny ignores issues of power and social structure in its promise of social change through individual psychological transformation (Grant 1988), it may in fact lead to a reconfirmation of the traditional power relations.

Other studies within the liberal perspective are even less clear-sighted about the distinctive contribution of feminine principles, and the ana-lysis of power in sexual politics became somewhat diffused (Grant 1988) in the late 1980s. In some accounts, the emphasis moved to how women could be resocialised to compete on an equal basis with men. Women were seen to have psychological characteristics or indi-vidual attributes which were blamed as being responsible for limiting their employment opportunities. These were variously referred to as the 'fear of success' (Horner 1972); the 'imposter phenomenon'; or the 'feminine modesty' effect; all being attributed to poor self-image or fear of power (Dowling 1988, Orser 1994).

Research such as this, all of which adopted a 'blame-the-victim' approach, led to the emergence of writing and workshops which aimed themselves at changing and developing women. 'The Assertive Woman', 'Women and Success', 'Dressing for Success', and 'Women-in-Management' were all titles of seminars and self-help groups, all of which stressed women's need to conform to the existing 'masculinised' corporate culture (Orser 1994), rather than to challenge it. It was this feature which led some radical feminist researchers to react against such developments by attempting to launch a backlash, in order to confront the power relations within organisational management more explicitly.

Radical approaches

Accordingly, a second approach, which focuses more explicitly and politically on *the feminine* and privileges women's alternative skills, has gained prominence. Inspired by the radical feminist aim to move away from concerns with issues of equality towards a more uncompromising position of difference (see, for example, Chodorow 1979, Dinnerstein 1977, Gilligan 1982), research within this approach seeks to demonstrate that yes, women are different from men, and that this difference should be celebrated within organisations by enabling women to do what they do best. In other words, women's experience, traditional values and ways of behaving, feeling and thinking should be valued by organisations and rewarded with promotion to management. This 'woman-centred' perspective thus celebrates and exonerates female difference, instead of suggesting that 'women imitate male agentic features with an androgynous sprinkling of communal qualities' (Grant 1988:58). For example, Loden's (1985) *Feminine Leadership or How to Succeed in Business Without Being One of the Boys* represents an explicit reaction to both advice that aimed at neutralising gender and that which encouraged women to be more assertive and strategic (Brandser 1996).

Loden (1985) argues that the traditional, male, 'heroic' leadership style has become obsolete in contemporary organisations, which now highlight the qualities of communication, participation and team-building as being essential for effectiveness. This change opens up leadership positions to women, who offer a unique feminine style, based on the feminine values of empathy, attachment, nurturing and care. This is behaviour which 'comes naturally' for women, as a result of their different experiences.

Grant (1988) agrees that women have developed special female qualities which they can bring to organisational life. She argues that

> women have an extensive involvement in the processes of our society: an involvement that derives from their greater participation in the reproduction process and their early experience of family life; both of these activities, so different from the activities of men, lead to the development of different psychic structures. Thus women may indeed be the most radical force available in bringing about organisational change... women must learn to value their own experiences, believe in their own values, and listen to their own inner voices and the voices of other women if indeed they are to speak 'in a different voice' in organisations for which they work. (pp. 62–3)

An important difference between women and men is their relationship with power. Grant argues further that women 'clearly experience, use and view power in a fashion different from that of men' (Grant 1988:60). Women tend to equate power with giving and caring, and see that strength comes from nurturance, while men equate power with aggression and assertion. For women, even those working in very agentic professions, communal qualities are emphasised.

For Marshall (1984, 1985), the difference in women's experiences and approaches comes from their 'heritage of resources' (Marshall 1984:77). She identifies 'five dimensions of womanhood' – fundamental aspects of women's identity which offer a new agenda for organisations. These are, first, 'perceptions of the world', that is, attention to relationships; second, 'emotional grounding', that is, women's close relationships to emotions; third, 'nurturing', or servicing the basic life-maintaining needs of society generally, and of families in particular; fourth, 'continuity' or maintaining relationships, a quality which requires patience, resilience, endurance and personal transformation. Finally, 'core femaleness': that is, the 'wild spirit of womanhood', 'wild, intractable, untamed knowing: capable of deep-rooted laughter, strong and wise' (Marshall 1984:81). Marshall suggests looking again at the traditional images of women in history and mythology that have been lost or devalued, yet which portray women as competent. These offer new images and 'new riddles' for women exploring their own purposes and identity:

> *Luna*, moon, has a sense of natural rhythm, tactfulness and timing, and the capacity for empathy...*Lila*, playfulness, in touch with the sense, attuned with beauty, pleasure and enjoyment, shy and girlish, or sensually alluring...*Pallas Athena*, the inspiration for career women able to fight for their own needs and human dignity and causes...*Medusa*, the abyss of transformation, the seemingly chaotic riddle (Marshall 1985:176).

Marshall sees the development of the female principle as part of a general review of values in Western society, and of particular relevance to what is going on in organisations. By learning to listen to others and recognising the value of different experiences, people may be able to live with less discord between their public and private identities. The needs women become aware of through this process will not always mesh well with organisations as they are, but have great significance for organisations as they could be.

Discussion

The radical feminist approach seeks to challenge the traditional view of the manager and what it is to manage quite fundamentally. Women managers, it is claimed, are substantially different from men managers. One of the principal changes is the understanding of the manager's relationship to power. Calas *et al.* (1991) note that:

> [U]nder this view the manager becomes less visible. The manager role has less saliency in relation to employees because the purpose for managing changes. Man-as-agent of control becomes woman-as-connector of the whole, defining a different mode of engagement with other people, the workplace and the wider environment. Her 'relational self' seeks connections and balance with various environmental dimensions, fostering openness and receptivity. There is more interest in ecological balance/harmony than in mastery. Her power is *power-with* rather than *power-over* [our italics] others. (pp. 11–12)

While one of the most significant aims of the radical feminist work on management is to challenge the male dominance of power at the upper tiers of the organisation, it seeks to do so by suggesting a fundamental change in the manager's relationship to power and use of it. The principal aim is to shift from a structural (ab)use of power to an altogether more pluralist and facilitative conception. Women's power lies in the ability to give it to others: to facilitate others to achieve. Thus, on one level, the radical approach is not about women seizing power, but setting up alternative styles of management which enable power to flow more naturally through the organisation.

The view that women manage and use power in ways that are different from and perhaps preferable to those used by men has been received somewhat sceptically in other quarters, both feminist and non-feminist, however. Research looking at how women manage in organisations which they set up themselves, as well as how they manage in large corporations, has given only partial support for the difference view, or, in certain cases, shown that the differences between men and women are almost non-existent.

First, studies by Brown (1992), and Ianello (1992), which focus on women-only and feminist organisations, both demonstrate that when women set up and establish their own organisations, such as women's and community centres, these are frequently non-hierarchical in structure with power diffused among the participants rather than wielded in a top-down manner. However – interestingly – these organisations have not been found to be as unproblematic as the above arguments would tend to predict. Competing values and attitudes within the organisation, patchy enthusiasm for participation and interactions with the outside environment all mean that in reality, fully enacted non-hierarchical organisations are rare and limited in time (Brown

1992). It would appear that 'the construction of a non-hierarchical organisation is not, as some have claimed, a naturally occurring outcome of human social activity' (Brown 1992:192). Although Brown acknowledges that it may be reasonable to argue that women's socialisation and experiences makes them better equipped to lead in non-hierarchical ways, 'this should not be promoted to the status of an alternative determinism' (ibid.).

Second, Powell (1990), looking at male and female managers in large corporations, strongly rejects the idea the idea that female and male managers differ. He conducted an extensive review of the research on sex differences (Powell 1988), in particular that which focuses on task-oriented and people-oriented behaviour (for example, Rosener 1990, Grant 1988). Powell argues that his 'meta-analysis' of research studies does not support the view that men tend towards the former, and women the latter. Male and female leaders exhibit similar amounts of task-oriented and people-oriented behaviour, regardless of the type of study. Further, female managers are found to be as least as motivated and committed as their male counterparts, and no difference was found in subordinates' responses to actual managers. 'Overall, the pattern of research results on sex differences in managerial behaviour favours the "no differences" view' (Powell 1990:70).

Powell's findings based in the United States are largely echoed in other countries. In Britain, Alimo-Metcalfe (1987, see also Alban-Metcalfe and West 1991) has carried out extensive research on women and men managers, comparing them biographically and in terms of the ways they see themselves (their 'self-concepts'). Gender was found to be a significant variable biographically (age, educational qualifications, marital status and having children), whereas with respect to perceptions of themselves there was a 'remarkable similarity' (1987:213) among the men and women. Women and men perceived themselves as equally ambitious, controlling, forceful, creative, trusting, optimistic, happy and content, and had the same dislike of uncertainty. The only differences were that women felt more tense and perceived themselves as more intellectual than men did: women were also less likely to keep their feelings to themselves than men. Similarly, Bourantas and Papalexandris (1991) show that in the context of Greek organisations, neither leadership styles nor subordinates' satisfaction with supervision differ between male and female managers.

In spite of the results of this evidence, it can still be seen that one of the predominant preoccupations in the research and theory on gender and management is the question of difference between men and women. Although the ontological explanations vary, women and men, femininity and masculinity are conceptualised as being different: as binary oppositional categories, who may be readily and relatively unproblematically understood. As an extension to this ontological position, power is also conceptualised as differentiated by gender. While men are typically conceptualised as autocratic, women are seen as democratic. While men are seen to draw on their structural power to maintain their position and share it with other, similar men, women are described as using their power to increase the power of the whole organisational community: a facilitative conception, as opposed to a dispositional one.

Through this challenge to men's dominance in the management levels of organisations, it would however appear that the radical approach does not give up on structural conceptions of power altogether. For many, the political aim is to reverse the structural patterns of gender relations, and place women centre stage. Although, from this position, it is argued that they will have a different relationship with power, and consequently their subordinates within the organisation, a clear structural challenge is seen to be an important part of the journey to get to this point.

Both gender and power are thus conceptualised rather unambiguously in the liberal, structural and radical approaches we have discussed so far. However, we have seen in Chapter 1 that one of the developments made in gender theory in the last decade has been the emergent problematisation of essentialist notions of gender, and the acknowledgement that difference may occur across all sorts of categories and boundaries. Clearly, there are many ways of managing and organisational theory has endeavoured to identify these. However, we have seen above that any consistent connection of these with gender is hard to establish: it may be that there are as many differences within the categories 'women managers' and 'men managers' as there are between them. It is to this discussion we now turn.

Differences within gendered management categories

Although research taking this poststructuralist approach is by no means extensive, there is evidence to support the argument that gender is altogether a much more nuanced category than has been suggested in the literature we have discussed so far. For example, Collinson and Hearn (1994) argue that the category 'men managers' is too crude, and that *various* masculinities are central to the exercise of gendered power in organisations. Not only do these masculinities shape managerial practices, but also managerial practices can impact on the emergence of various masculinities in the workplace. In particular they identify five discourses and practices of masculinity that appear to remain pervasive and dominant in organisations: authoritarianism, paternalism, entrepreneurialism, informalism, and careerism. These are particularly interrelated with different managerial styles.

Authoritarianism is typically but not exclusively related to those in positions of seniority. It is characterised by an intolerance of dissent or difference, a rejection of dialogue and debate and a preference for coercive power relations based on dictatorial control and unquestioning obedience. Based on bullying and the creation of fear in subordinates, authoritarianism celebrates a brutal and aggressive masculinity. Hostility is aimed at those who fail to comply with this aggressive masculinity, such as women and minority men.

By contrast, in paternalism, men eschew coercion and seek to exercise power by emphasising the moral basis of cooperation, the protective nature of their authority, the importance of personal trust relations and the need for employees both to invest voluntarily in their work task and to identify with the company. It is a specifically masculine discourse of control, which draws on the familial metaphor of the 'rule of the father' who is authoritative, benevolent, self-disciplined and wise. By investing in paternalism, male managers seek to differentiate themselves from women and identify with other men. Older men in particular are likely to be paternalistic towards their younger male colleagues. So long as women conform to conventional notions of female identity, they will experience little hostility.

Third, entrepreneurialism articulates a hard-nosed and highly competitive approach to business and organisation. Here economic efficiency and managerial control are elevated at the expense of all other criteria. These men managers identify with other men who are as competitive as themselves and willing to work at a similar pace. The requirements of this style exclude some men who supposedly are not 'man enough' or predatory enough to be satisfactory and most women, whose employment, particularly in senior positions, is often seen as incompatible with entrepreneurial concerns. In fact women generally are probably seen as incompatible with entrepreneurialism, as domestic commitments and pregnancy are often treated as taboo, being seen to challenge and even undermine everyday business practices. Differences between men within this discourse are likely to be articulated along the axis of age, often with younger men being more comfortable with this model.

Fourth, men often try to build informal workplace relationships with one another on the basis of shared masculine interests and common values. Groups develop which serve to differentiate their members from other men and from women. Typically the informal currency between the men at various hierarchical levels will concentrate on humour, sport, cars, sex, women and drinking alcohol. At the extreme, these informal and aggressive dynamics may result in sexual harassment, the reduction of women to sexual objects, and the undermining and sexualising of managerial women.

Collinson and Hearn (1994) note that the four discourses discussed above seem to reflect and reinforce a simultaneous sense of unity and differentiation for men in organisations. However these are also quite fragile, precarious and shifting, primarily because more individualistic and competitive concerns also characterise men. Thus the fifth discourse is that of careerism. In the case of middle-class masculinities, competition for career progress comes to be synonymous with conventional masculinity. This expresses itself by a primary orientation to work, often at the expense of domestic commitments, and an excessive concern with self-promotion. There is a widespread preoccupation with hierarchical advance: upward mobility is a key objective in the search to secure a stable masculine identity.

Collinson and Hearn (1994) conclude by noting that these differences, divisions and conflicts between men and multiple masculinities in organisations are particularly acute within the managerial function. In fact, they may quickly turn into sources of conflict, which may be related to structural struggles for organisational power and influence, and/or they may be shaped by the identity preoccupations of individual managers concerned with self-differentiation, self-elevation and the negation of others. In either case, multiple masculinities may well shape the motives, processes and outcomes of these intra-managerial conflicts for organisational power, status and identity.

While Collinson and Hearn have summarised the different masculinities – that is, the different choices of performance that may exist for the male manager – a variety of femininities may also exist for women managers as we enter the millenium. For example, in an interesting variation on Kanter's (1977) work on the roles available for women managers, Rowe (1999) elucidates five types of successful and contemporary female manager. Although the connection with Kanter's work is clear, Rowe works from an altogether different understanding of power. Whereas Kanter's emphasis is on the stereotyping process which prevails in male-dominated organisations, forcing women into a narrow and limited set of role behaviours, Rowe offers us the flip-side, seeing these behaviours less as roles, but as *strategies*, deliberate and calculated performances which are very powerful. As Rowe explains, 'feminine wiles are a wonderful way of getting things done in a friendly manner, and they can help you go far. It's good to be a woman in the 90s' (Rowe 1999:102).

The first of Rowe's strategies is 'The Friendly One'. This relies on a sensitivity to other people's moods and needs, working out how to make the most of a situation, and adopting an overtly friendly approach. As Claire, an example of this approach explains:

> People often say after they first meet me that they feel like they've known me for ages. That's because I make a real effort to listen to them. I try to make people feel comfortable – often I'll curl my feet up on the chair to create a relaxed atmosphere. And I never power dress: I always wear baggy trousers, a T-shirt, fleece and trainers. I don't want to intimidate people. I have to be a chameleon, changing to fit in ... which is something women are better at. It's not two-faced, it's simply getting the best out of people. I never push my opinion on others either, I just make sympathetic noises. I want them to go away thinking I really liked them (Claire, in Rowe 1999:105).

The second strategy is 'The Girly One'. This is to adopt rather sweet, childlike behaviour in order to get one's way, a strategy which seemingly diminishes personal power, yet is all about achievement and winning through in the end. Rhona explains:

> I'm very ambitious. I used to wear shoulder pads and be aggressive, partly because I'm blonde and wanted to be taken seriously. Now I find it more effective to be feminine. I'll wear a flirty skirt and cardigan in board meetings to create a 'aren't I sweet?' image. Although I'm not childlike, I'll sometimes give that impression – particularly with female clients – so that I don't come across as domineering. (Rhona, ibid.)

Third is 'The Motherly One'. Not unlike Kanter's 'mother' role, this is a performance deliberately adopted in order to make use of the kind of strategies a mother uses to get things done, and to ensure everyone cooperates with each other. Thus this approach draws on a combination of praise and encouragement, listening, gentle scolding where appropriate, and even bribery, as Nichola explains:

> Once a week we have a meeting first thing and I always walk in with a jolly attitude. A bit of encouragement improves the atmosphere and women are

good at defusing difficult situations. Once in a gridlocked meeting, two men were fuming with anger, so I just said, 'Come on guys, let's sort this out' in a motherly way and they relaxed. As a boss I try to be approachable. A lot of men don't like admitting they've got a problem and I think people are more likely to open up to a female boss: just as they often prefer to go to their mums for help. Like many mothers, I also resort to bribes – taking staff out for a drink always works wonders. I always try to look attractive and well groomed, but I'd hate to appear threatening. (Nichola, ibid.)

'The Flirty One' is not ashamed of using her sexual charms to get her own way. 'If a bit of harmless flirting or a coy look gets people on your side, why not do it?' (Jo in Rowe 1999:106). This is a strategy which works well not only with men, but also with women. 'If someone doesn't think they can do something, I'll flutter my eyelashes and say, "I know you can do this" and after that they'll try harder' (Jo, ibid.). However, the flirty one is careful to keep control of the situation: 'I smile a lot, but if anyone comes on to me, I make it clear I'm not interested' (Jo, ibid.).

Finally there is 'The Tough One'. This is the most overtly powerful performance, one which uses authority with confidence and eschews revealing any form of personal weakness. The purpose is to instill fear in others, rather than display it oneself. Lucy, a partner in a large firm of solicitors and the first female president of the Newcastle Law Society, explains:

I don't bully my staff, but I'm a no-nonsense person. If people know you expect the best, they'll try harder. Gaining your staff's respect is more important than being their friend. ... To win over the judges there's a fine line between being assertive and aggressive. If I think I'm going too far, I'll pause and smile sweetly. I usually wear sombre, uncluttered navy or black skirts. Recently I had to speak at a huge conference and I wore a red suit to make me feel more confident. When I'm nervous at a meeting I'll go to the loo, put some lipstick on and come out looking self-assured. I never show my fear or insecurities as that would be perceived as weak (Lucy, ibid.)

Rowe's work puts a new spin on Kanter's notion of 'ready-made' gendered identities constructed by the organisation, into which there are pressures to fit. These women are altogether more agentic about the role performances they give, constructing themselves quite deliberately, often drawing on a combination of gendered managerial styles which they see as quite distinct from their identities in other contexts. This approach suggests, therefore, that an individual's management style is a nuanced performance constructed from *inter alia* multiple gendered identities.

Discussion

In this section, we have focussed not so much on the barriers facing women managers but on the manager role itself. This focus started from an exploration of the relationship between gender, power and management, asking: has management become so embedded with a particular version of masculinity, such that to perform one, is necessarily to perform the other? The softer liberal approach to this question is that women are not represented in management to any great extent because they do not possess the required characteristics to make good managers: that is, they have been socialised to be relationship-centred, caring, passive, emotional, intuitive, and group-oriented, all of which are antithetical to the attributes desired in a manager. Further, they may lack the self-confidence to believe that they could be managers, and thus do not enter the race. The conclusions drawn from this approach is that women in organisations need to exert themselves on to the management stage. One suggestion is that women can be empowered through specialist assertiveness training to develop the necessary confidence and set of characteristics which enable them to gain power and use it effectively; another is that male managers need to receive training in assessment procedures such that they learn to recognise the stereotypes under which they may be operating.

A harder version of the liberal approach, while agreeing with the way women are understood and represented, suggests that change ought to be more organisational than personal. Men need to recognise the value of other, more feminine characteristics and attributes. Ultimately, this approach recommends the emergence of the so-called 'androgynous' manager. DeMatteo (1994) explains that adopting an androgynous style does not mean that men and women managers will come to behave exactly alike:

> [W]hen the door is opened and we are all free to select beyond sex role stereotypes, a whole new range of behaviours will be possible, and each of us will be free to choose our own blend. (Sargent 1981:60 quoted in DeMatteo 1994:26)

In this way, men and women can draw on a range of skills and move beyond stereotyped behaviours. This, it is argued, will make them more versatile and able to adapt to the changing needs of the environment.

As a recommendation for change however, this approach has been found to be problematic. Firstly, as we discussed above, it was found that in reality, androgynous skills were actually closer to masculine ones than feminine ones. Secondly, not all managers will be capable of change (DeMatteo 1994), especially when current organisational structures favour more masculine attributes. Thirdly, from a structural perspective this approach can be criticised as failing to address adequately the concept and nature of gender and power. Studies have shown how men have been able to resist initiatives designed to equalise gender opportunities very effectively (Cockburn 1991). Thus, although a culture may be put into place which would seem to enable a change to occur in who gets managerial posts, in reality it may be that structures of power are maintained and men are (still) assumed to be better 'androgynous' managers than women.

Another recommendation has been to devise a new, more 'feminine' management structure to replace the traditional model of hierarchy. For example, as we saw earlier in the chapter. Hegelson (1990) describes women managers who have devised 'circular' systems, where positions are represented as circles, which are then arranged as a series of expanding orbits. Management is positioned at the centre: the image is one of a spider's web, and the style is defined as 'the web of inclusion'. The web is different from the hierarchy in that the top is no longer the preferred place to be. Rather, it is the middle, which far from the old view of being stuck with nowhere to go, is seen to be the centre of activity. As Hegelson argues, 'it is more natural to reach out than down' (Hegelson 1990:27). This boundary-less structure is imagined as being easier to communicate within, and women are seen to have a better chance of achieving equal status with men.

Although this new image of organisational structures has received a lot of support in feminist quarters, it, too, has been criticised as not adequately addressing the question of power. As we discuss more fully in Chapter 6, explicit structures, systems and reforms are frequently undermined by hierarchy, bureaucracy, patriarchy or the participation of men (Blum and Smith 1988, Cockburn 1991, Ferguson 1984, Halford 1992). Further, women managers rarely manage men. As we saw in chapter 2, they are frequently recruited and hired to manage other women and, like the women they manage, they are crowded into lower and middle hierarchical levels (Kanter 1977a). As such they may be able to implement innovatory sub-structures within the larger organisational context, while the broader power structure remains intact.

A second, radical approach points to the valuable and very different contribution that women, *as women*, are able to make to organisations. Many researchers argue that women manage in different, more 'feminine' ways. Women' s socialisation, their shared experiences and their feminine attributes all predispose them to lead in ways which are more effective and humane. Organisations should be fundamentally changed to reflect this preferable management model. However, as Billing (1994) has argued, the contention that women have shared experiences is in itself problematic.

> First, it is difficult to imagine that the experiences of women are common; second, if they were, they would hardly lead to a unitary critique of the predominant way of organising, or to a unified preference for an alternative organising. (p. 181)

The problem lies in the way experience is seen to be fixed, true and a guide to action, as well as a producer of human nature (Leonard 1995). What is not taken into account is the possibility of competing gender identities or competing interpretations of experience. Instead, essentialist notions of 'woman' and feminine values are turned into an ideology about female management. This argument seeks (perhaps in a rather evangelical way) to persuade the male managers who at present dominate organisations that it may be in their best interests to learn to manage, and be managed, in more 'feminine' ways. And there is some evidence that they have succeeded, although some feminist critics note that this strategy, far from enabling women to become more powerful, has merely locked them into behaving in stereotypical gendered ways to boost the profits of the male power elite.

Sheppard's research (1989) illustrates the constraints embedded in a 'feminine' management approach. In her study of Canadian women managers, she found that they employed 'strategies of gender management' (1989:155) through which they tried to stay 'feminine enough' so as not to challenge prevailing sex role conventions and 'businesslike enough' so as to be seen as credible organisational members. All too often, being too feminine means being seen as unbusinesslike, and therefore to act in this way may undermine the power of a women manager's position. Thus the consequences of the 'difference' argument may not be as emancipatory as is hoped. Further, as Powell (1990) argues:

> [w]omen are at risk when corporations assume that they have a monopoly on human resource skills. The risk is that they will be placed exclusively in managerial jobs that particularly call for social sensitivity and interpersonal skills in dealing with individuals and special interest groups ... these jobs are typically staff functions, peripheral to the more powerful line functions ... Corporations that rely on Grant's (1988, see above) assertions about women's special abilities could very well perpetuate this trend. (p. 72)

On the other hand, some writers have embraced the core set of 'feminine' management attributes and skills with alacrity, arguing that they offer the way forward for organisations in an uncertain world. Tom Peters, for example, has proclaimed that the 'new organisation' is one of networks, fluid relationships, process and teamwork (Peters 1990). What were once labelled women's weaknesses and cited as reasons they were ill suited for top jobs are suddenly the very traits male executives are expected to wear on their sleeves (Calas and Smircich 1993). Fierman describes women as the 'new Japanese' (Fierman 1990:115): people from whom Western organisations have a lot to learn. However, this may not be as optimistic a stance as it might appear. The focus on global competition, productivity and profitability merely retains traditional assumptions about the goals of organisations and directs the energies of managerial women toward the benefit of the currently dominant stakeholders (Calas and Smircich 1993). As Calas and Smircich put it rather cynically, 'Difference becomes simply another way of competing with Toyota' (p. 14): the 'different' is still in service to 'the same'.

Thus, arguments which rely on women's difference from men, while attempting to open up management power structures and carve a place for women, may in fact work only to disempower them. But this rather seems to leave women managers in a stalemate position: they are unable to act *like* men, for men will always be preferred, and, it seems, they are unable to act differently to men as this difference may be their downfall.

From a poststructuralist approach, this problematic position arises from the fact that the liberal and radical–structural approaches take an over dependent focus on the attributes of gender, creating simplified, binary categories, and implying that a hierarchical relationship exists between men and women, with one gender (usually men, but in some feminist versions, women) dominant and superior and the other subordinate and inferior. This hierarchical relationship has been contested somewhat by work which seeks to explore the differences between men and women. To claim that all men manage in one masculine style, and that all women manage in an alternative, feminine style is, it is argued, to oversimplify all of the concepts of gender, power and management. Individual men may manage in very different ways: some will be macho-male, wielding power in traditional ways; others will be more feminine, and may themselves be subject to more dominant colleagues, either male or female. In other words, this approach to management complicates both gender and power, in an attempt to resist making definitive or categorical statements about men and women managers.

Conclusions

It would thus appear that while it is undeniable that women in increasing numbers are becoming managers and making it into the upper echelons of organisations, the terms of their acceptance are problematic. Management is, by and large, understood as a highly gendered activity, and when women become managers they become *'women managers'*. In turn, their assumed difference, whether this is understood to be a result of societal, organisational or gender factors, seems to mean that they are usually less powerful than their male colleagues. Either they have to leap far more hurdles than men in order to become managers, with a resultant wear and tear on their mental health and private lives, or they feel constrained to 'perform' gender (Butler 1990): whether this be particular versions of masculinity or femininity. In all probability they have to cope with both of these processes.

It is clear, therefore, that a complex relationship exists between gender, power and management. Although women managers are ostensibly, and by definition, powerful, research from both structural and liberal perspectives have demonstrated that there are many factors contributing to an onslaught against this power. First, it is made very difficult for women to gain access to those managerial positions where the greatest officially sanctioned organisational power is held. They are more likely to be given 'minority' issues such as personnel, public relations, equal opportunities and so on, where their influence may be limited. Second, once in post, their performance may be restricted by the expectations and beliefs of not only their male but also their female colleagues, who see that the category of 'women managers' should animate the role according to rather limited descriptions.

Although working from different understandings of the nature of power and gender, liberal and structural approaches collude in focusing on the masculinity of management power. The case that men managers work to exclude women from gaining access to or enjoying power is made repeatedly and convincingly. However, the problem with this approach is that 'women, as a group, are represented as powerless victims, unable to influence or decisively affect the companies in which they work [Gerson 1985]' (Bell and Nkomo 1992:238).

The dynamic interaction between the individual and the organisation is ignored, which means that

> we lose critical knowledge about the power women bring into the workplace, the ways in which women's and men's roles are evolving in managerial positions, and whether organisational structures are adapting to increasing numbers of women. (p. 238)

In fact, it may be that to talk about 'women managers' is too limiting to enable us to understand the full range of complexities involved in issues to do with gender, power and management. For example, the relative paucity of information about non-white women managers means that the image of gender uniformity is reinforced and differences between women are minimised. In reality, of course, interpretations of 'the manager' are cut through with race and class differences, and the idea that the experiences of white, middle-class women managers are congruent with the experiences of women of colour and/or the working class has yet to be justified (Bell and Nkomo 1992) . Indeed, as Calas and Smircich argue, it may be that theories constructed to emancipate 'women' only work to minimise diversity within organisations:

> One cannot fail to observe that the values represented by the feminine in management literature are those of white, formally educated middle to upper class American women, and that it is *their* mothering style, family values and relationships to children that are represented in the 'authority through connection' metaphors. (p. 75)

Calas and Smircich note that the increasingly international nature of many contemporary organisations means that a whole range of new international management positions have opened up. Thus one of the consequences of the utilisation of woman-centred discourses may be simply to extend the established power structure by moving the values of those who are at present 'second best' – that is, white women – into the less-desirable, vacated domestic managerial spaces through an illusory promise of opportunity and change. Rather than increasing diversity at management levels, it is thus strictly managed and reserved for the selected few: namely, the white middle class. In this way the larger economic and political establishment remains predominantly immune from the wide variety of challenges that may be launched from a fuller recognition of difference.

Bell and Nkomo (1992) recommend that we need to rethink our approach to investigating and theorising the experiences of women managers and the organisations in which they work. Individuals have different histories, different biographies and different identities, all of which influence their attitudes and behaviour at work. At present in much women-and-management theory certain aspects of identity are relegated to invisibility. Race, ethnicity and class are integral to the concept of identity and are not, for many women, 'lower down the hierarchy' than gender. They all have significant and far reaching consequences in women's lives (Bell and Nkomo 1992; see also Spelman 1988, Hill-Collins 1990).

To conclude, this consideration of gender and management has demonstrated that the concept of power is integral to our understanding of the multiplicity and complexity of that relationship. We have shown how the management stratum within organisations is a highly contested location from the perspective of gender: power is exercised to restrict entry to it, and to define the manner of performances from those within it. However, it may be that to see all women as subjects of male power is to deny the complexity of factors which determine an individual situation, and the ability that many women managers have to use power to challenge traditional organisational structures and cultures should also be recognised.

5

Sexuality and Organisation

Introduction

On the face of it, sex and sexuality might appear to have little to do with most people's working lives. After all, what goes on in the privacy of the bedroom or nightclub, in realms separate from to the daily routine of work, would not seem to affect the interactions of the organisation. Indeed, we saw in Chapter 2 how the bureaucratic organisation has been viewed predominantly as sex-less: Weber's model of the 'ideal type' of bureaucratic organisation emphasises its rational and objective character. This would seem to imply that sexual displays and liaisons are deemed to be inappropriate and counterproductive to the purposes of the organisation. Since the late 1980s however, organisational researchers from a range of perspectives have been to keen to point out that, far from being removed from organisational life, sexuality in fact 'permeates the workplace' (Gutek and Dunwoody 1987:256), pervading it at every level. For some organisational theorists, sexuality, or more particularly, heterosexuality, is seen to be the primary means by which both people and organisations are gendered, and through which power is exercised. Further, whatever the form in which sexuality is made explicit, this gendering process hinges on power inequality: sexuality acts to differentiate and discriminate. The purpose of this chapter, therefore, is to consider the place of sexuality in the gendering of organisations, and, in particular, to consider the ways sexuality is bound up with power in gendered organisations.

A range of theoretical explanations have been drawn upon to account for the relationships between sexuality and organisation (see below). However, these must be seen alongside the more common-sense approach to understandings of sexuality, which tends to dominate popular understandings of sexuality in organisations, or elsewhere. This draws on a biological understanding of sexuality which insists that women and men have distinct and essentially complementary sexualities. Men are seen to possess an active, constant and aggressive sex drive while women are seen to possess a more passive sexuality, which is awakened through the 'enjoyable' processes of male attention or woo-ing. Each sex is assumed to find the sexuality of the other ('the opposite') attractive and hence assumptions about the naturalness and inevitability of heterosexuality underpin this approach. Because of this, it is thought that whenever and wherever men and women work together in an organisation, physical attractions and intimate relation-ships between the sexes will inevitably occur. Organisations are seen to be a 'natural breeding ground' for romantic involvements, as 'Sexual feelings are a natural phenomenon ... When people walk through the office door, their sexual feelings are not extinguished' (Quinn and Lees 1984:36–7). By putting people in close proximity with each other, the interactions necessary for establishing intimate relationships are not only created (Anderson and Hunsaker 1985:57) but are bound to occur. Quinn (1977) found that 62 per cent of his respondents had had at least one romantic involvement with another colleague within their organisation in which they worked.

Within this biological model, the issue of power is seen to be unprob-lematic. For those who assume that men possess a stronger sex drive, it is also seen to be inevitable that men will have a 'natural' propensity to aggress sexually against women. However, such powerful exertions of sexuality are seen as biological fact rather than discriminatory intent, and as such provide no grounds for particular concern (Tangri *et al.* 1982). For those who assume that women and men have equally strong sex drives, it is seen that power may be a stimulator of intimacy, for an influential position can make a person appear more attractive than he or she would be otherwise. (Quinn and Lees 1984). 'As one young woman succinctly expressed it, "I can't help it; I think power is sexy"' (p. 37). However, here again power is not understood to be problematic, it is merely an aphrodisiac.

According to Gutek (1985, 1989), the biological, or natural model is the one most frequently held by organisational employees. In her research of workers in California (Gutek 1985), most of the respondents viewed sexual behaviour at work as benign or even positive. Thus relationships within organisations are viewed in terms of 'courtships' or 'office romances' rather than as sexually harassing or discriminating. The fact that when such relationships end it is usually the woman who has to leave the organisation is merely a reflection of the fact that women do not hold such important jobs within organisations, and this is therefore viewed as far from catastrophic, although it might be rather a shame (Driscoll and Bova 1980). Further, if a situation does develop into a sexually harassing one, then this is due to personal and individual deficiencies: either the women's own deficiency in handling an approach, or the deficiency of individual men in controlling their natural drives (Nieva and Gutek 1981, Stockdale 1991).

It was through the growth of feminist ideas which started in the 1970s that the biological model came to be criticised on several grounds. First, the assumption that people become involved with each other sexually, or interact with each other in a sexual or flirtatious way, because it gives them pleasure, or because they are responding to natural and biological sex drives which are present within all of us, (although these might be stronger in men) was challenged. This, it was argued, is a conceptualisation of sexual behaviour which is essentially personal and individual, rather than the result of social and/or structural factors, such as organisational hierarchy or culture or work roles. As such, what this conceptualisation fails to address is the *integral* relationship between sexuality and social structure – whether at a broad social level, for example in terms of gender, race or class, or at the more specific organisational level. For example, different groups within organisations possess different amounts of power, and with the possession of power comes the ability to manipulate people in a variety of ways, the sexual being one of these. The ability to initiate and/or conduct a sexual relationship is not equally distributed throughout the organisational power structure, nor is the ability to resist such a relationship, which may well be seen as an imposition one has to bear in order to safeguard one's position.

This latter point leads into a second criticism. The biological model argues that what is sometimes called sexual harassment is merely sexual attraction (Stockdale 1991). Thus, although the existence of such behaviour is admitted, it is seen to be neither sexist nor discriminatory, largely unintentional and as not having harmful consequences. Any humiliation, embarrassment and suffering that many women experience as a result of such behaviour (Stanko 1985) is dismissed as over-reaction or an unusual occurrence of aberrant behaviour. In contrast to this view, a number of key feminists since the late 1970s and 1980s have pointed out that sexual harassment is one of the principal means by which men exert their power over women, a 'practice that has kept working women both individually and collectively locked into a position of economic inferiority' (Farley 1978:xvi). Consequently, since the late 1970s and 1980s, an active group of feminist thinkers, many with a background in radical and structural perspectives, have fought to bring the issue of 'sexual harassment' into public and legal recognition. Indeed, many would agree that they have succeeded in raising it to be one of the most important political and organisational issues of the last twenty years.

In this chapter, we thus start our discussion of the relationships between sexuality, power and organisation with a focus on sexual harassment. We show how this issue has challenged our understanding of organisational life on both theoretical and legislative grounds. First, it has succeeded in bringing about a recognition and acknowledgement of the predominantly structured nature of the gendered relations and conditions of harassment: that is, the fact that such behaviour is usually male, and that the 'victims' are usually women. To ignore this factor, it is argued, is to trivialise the understanding of the relationship between power, gender and sexuality. Indeed, sexual harassment is an issue which is very much about the use and abuse of power, although the ways in which this power is to be conceptualised and understood have been the subject of changing debates between the radical and structural feminists and, more recently, those taking more discursive approaches. Sexual harassment is thus an issue which attracts a range of theoretical perspectives and analyses. These are explored fully at the end of the next section.

Second, through the construction of a common and acceptable definition of sexual harassment, people experiencing harassment in organisations have been given something to work from, in order to challenge its occurrence through legislation. However, the difficulties found to exist in achieving any kind of consensus with a definition and the relatively low rates of industrial action on this platform demonstrate further the variety of perspectives which now converge in this issue.

Through the issue of sexual harassment, feminist thinkers have thus sought to redefine the way gender relations within organisations are understood. From the first, they have emphasised the crucial relationship between male power and the ways women are constructed within organisations. From this beginning, the focus of interest on the place of sexuality within organisations has widened, and other researchers have also used radical and structural approaches to explore the range of ways in which sexuality can be seen as a mobilisation of male power. In the following section, therefore, we extend the discussion of sexual harassment, which is usually assumed to apply in specific contexts, to explore the pervasiveness of (hetero)sexuality within organisational life. By exploring the aspects of communication, careers and mentorship, self-presentation and relationships within organisations, we show that sexuality – or, rather, a particular heterosexualised version of sexuality – inflects organisational life at all levels, a fact which has specific and gendered consequences for men and women. One of these consequences is to render homosexuality and lesbianism within organisations 'problematic', and in the next section we consider the ways gay men and lesbian women are forced to 'manage' their sexuality in organisations.

Following this, we return to consider other theoretical approaches to understanding the nature of the relationships between gender, sexuality and power. Research is appearing which seeks to counter the understanding of the direction of the power flow between men and women as being one-way. By demonstrating the relationship that sexuality has with pleasure, the representation of women as merely sexual victims within organisations has been challenged. In fact, it is argued, the complex nature of the relationship between sexuality, pleasure and power may open up possibilities for women to empower themselves within organisations. Finally, in the last section our discussion explores how the different approaches to sexuality and organisation raise some fundamental questions about power, and the nature of power in the relationship between gender and organisation.

Sexual harassment

As we mention above, sexual harassment is the concept through which the issue of sexuality in the workplace first became visible as an issue for public attention (Gutek 1985). In many ways it has remained so. For example, in the final years of the second millennium, serious allegations were made by various women against US President Bill Clinton, a situation given a great deal of air time across the globe. The consensus of interest is clear; however, understanding of the issue is far from consensual. Vigorous debates revolve around defining what is or what is not sexual harassment, and what should be done about dealing with its existence. In this section, we discuss how different thinkers take different approaches to conceptualising what constitutes sexual harassment, why it occurs and who does it to whom.

Definitions

It may, at first, seem somewhat surprising that no universally accepted definition (Aggarwal 1987) of sexual harassment exists, considering the amount of time and interest that has been put into this issue. However, the lack of a formal definition is a reflection of one of the problems that has emerged through the push to get sexual harassment recognised as a proper, work-related grievance. For sexual harassment is understood in many different ways: not only does the action itself mean different things different people, but so are the root causes of the behaviour conceptualised in different ways.

The phrase 'sexual harassment' itself first appeared in the mid-1970s, used by North American feminists (Kitzinger and Thomas 1995) from a radical background. They used it to refer to male coercion (Farley 1978, MacKinnon 1979) of women through sexual behaviour, often backed up by the superior status and associated bureaucratic power of men in organisational hierarchies. In the UK, awareness and public recognition that sexual harassment at work was an important problem for women in particular also developed, as a result of women working within the trade union movement; particularly within unions with large numbers of women representatives such as teaching and local government. These women tended to approach the issue from a more structural perspective, reflecting their direct engagement in the world of paid work.

Both groups of feminist writers were keen to define, expose and analyse the extent of sexual harassment. They have both taken a specifically gendered approach, identifying that there are fundamental differences in the experiences of women and men within organisations, both as initiators and receivers of sexual behaviour and as possessors of organisational power and status. However, differences exist between the two approaches, which mainly involve where to place the blame for the source of the behaviour. First, the radical feminist approach contextualised sexual harassment specifically as a basic mechanism of patriarchal society. Two key works, which appeared in the United States at the end of the 1970s (Farley 1978 and MacKinnon 1979), established a framework within which to conceptualise both gender and power, which has remained extremely influential. As Farley explains,

Sexual harassment is best described as unsolicited, non-reciprocal male behaviour that asserts a woman's sex role over her function as worker. It can be any or all of the following: staring at, commenting upon, or touching a woman's body; requests for acquiescence in sexual behaviour, repeated non-reciprocated propositions for dates; demands for sexual intercourse; and rape. These forms of male behaviour frequently rely on superior male status in the culture, sheer numbers, or the threat of higher rank at work to exact compliance or levy penalties for refusal (1978:15).

Whilst MacKinnon takes a more specific look at the legal questions posed in cases of sexual harassment, arguing that this behaviour constitutes unlawful discrimination within the meaning of the Equal Protection Clause (a legislative measure designed to maintain parity between men and women at work, similar in nature to the Equal Opportunities Act 1975 in the UK), she also directly sets the problem in the context of the inferior position of women. Thus

sexual harassment, most broadly defined, refers to the unwanted imposition of sexual requirements in the context of a relationship of unequal power . . . - American society legitimises male sexual dominance of women and employers' control of workers (1979:).

Working from a more structural perspective, Hadjifotiou (1983), in the UK, sees sexual harassment as both a gender *and* a workplace issue. It is, she agrees, a practice almost exclusively practised by men directed at women, unsolicited and unreciprocated, which is principally about asserting a woman's sex role over her function as a worker. As such, it seriously restricts women's employment opportunities and undermines their value and status as workers. This definition is important, as it broadens the issue beyond that of a problem between individuals to encompass the idea that sexual harassment is experienced by women simply because they are women (Hadjifotiou 1983:8), and further that it has specific deleterious economic consequences. In other words, receiving sexual harassment from men is part of the female condition, a key structural mechanism by which men use their power to establish and confirm their dominant economic status over women.

Sexual harassment can thus be seen as a metaphor for gender relations and sexuality in the wider society (Stanko 1988). Stanko argues that sexual harassment is a significant factor in women's experiences of working, and that it constitutes a particularly problematic form of sexual discrimination in employment, as it brings together the larger 'issues of maleness, femaleness, sexual and economic power and social control' with often 'mundane, seemingly ordinary work situations' (p. 81). The key to Stanko's definition is that the attention is unwanted, yet it is backed up by male power to hire and fire (Schur 1984). Through this behaviour, a woman is no longer made to feel like an employee or a colleague, but is immediately transformed, and made to feel like a sexual object. The value of her work is now brought into question, not only by the harasser but also by the harassed herself, and a consequent drop in job performance or even resignation may be the result (Al-Khalifa 1988).

The radical and structural approaches both understand sexual harassment as something that (typically) men do to women as a way of exerting their superior power. The analysis of the forms of this behaviour range from highly specific lists of harassing behaviours to the more radical, yet subjective approach of 'any unwanted behaviour' (for example, Wise and Stanley 1987, Thomas and Kitzinger 1994). However, the problem with any definition lies in the matter of interpretation: in many people's actual or real experiences of sexual harassment there are considerable elements of ambiguity and uncertainty about meaning and intent. Thus 'any incident labelled "sexual harassment" by one person may well be construed differently by others' (Thomas and Kitzinger 1994:154). It has thus proved remarkably difficult for any real consensus over definitions to be reached, for, of course, any externally generated definition ignores how the individuals themselves define the problem, influenced as these situations are by an idiosyncratic, and often shifting, range of personal factors. While for some the definitions are too rigid, for others they are not clear enough (Brant and Too 1994). These ambivalences and ambiguities have led some writers to question whether the radical and structural approaches to defining and understanding sexual harassment are sophisticated enough to conceptualise the multiple nature of the processes involved. We return to this discussion at the end of the section.

The extent of sexual harassment

The issue of definition is of course fundamental to discussions of sexual harassment at work and estimates of its incidence (Stockdale 1991). Problems of defining sexual harassment are likely to mean that it may be difficult to pinpoint very accurately the extent of sexual harassment in the workplace and, as we will discuss more fully at the end of this section, this is exacerbated by the fact that many women do not identify their own experience as sexual harassment (Thomas and Kitzinger 1994). However, in spite of this, there has been a very great range of surveys documenting the incidence of sexual harassment and testifying to its frequency and pervasiveness. In the US and Canada, incidence of sexual harassment towards women at work ranges from early estimates of between 70 and 90 per cent (see, for example, Farley 1978) to later estimates of between 25 and 50 per cent (Canadian Human Rights Commision 1984, Gutek 1985, US Merit Systems Protection Board 1981) with certain organisations such as universities being identified as particularly prone to high levels of harassing behaviours from male members of staff (see Fitzgerald *et al.* 1988, Garrett-Gooding and Senter 1989, Paludi 1987, Somers 1982). In the UK the figures are similar: in the Industrial Society's 1993 study, 50 per cent of women reported experiences of sexual harassment (IDS 1993). All in all, the figures are in 'stark contrast to the reported incidence rate of 2 per cent among men' (Stockdale 1991:54).

This difference in experience of women and men is reflected in a gendered identification of which kind of actions or situations constitute sexual harassment (Adams *et al.* 1983, Collins and Blodgett 1981, Gutek 1985, Stockdale 1991, Thomas and Kitzinger 1994, Kitzinger and Thomas 1995). Men are generally less ready to identify behaviour or contexts as harassing: in particular, sexual teasing, looks or gestures are unlikely to be defined as such, while sexual touching shows the largest gender gap (Gutek 1985). However, differences within the sexes are substantial (Gutek 1985, Powell 1986), as individuals, whether men or women, vary widely in their personal definitions and identifications of which situations and which people are problematic. 'So while complimentary comments and suggestive remarks constitute harassment for some individuals, for others they do not' (Stockdale 1991:55). Differences also exist within the same person: behaviour which may be felt as sexual harassment from one colleague may not be perceived as such from another.

However, we can be certain that for many women, and some men, sexual harassment at work is a real and constant problem. In spite of this, the fact is that there is, to a very large extent, a 'silence' about incidences of sexual harassment within organisations. Very few women actually fight or complain about sexual harassment. In a recent US survey (MSPB 1994) a mere 6 per cent of those survey respondents who reported experiencing sexual harassment had taken formal action (Thomas and Kitzinger 1997).

From radical and structural perspectives, this silence is a reflection of the powerlessness of most women's positions within organisations. Often located in highly 'flexible' positions, their lack of organisational power means that they may be highly vulnerable, and may lack either the personal or economic power to take the case further. Researchers working from more poststructuralist perspectives explain that this 'silence' may be to some extent a reflection of the ambiguities which surround this issue. They claim that it is difficult to be conclusive about either definition or incidence. For some people, it may be hard to isolate sexual harassment from other forms of harassment. As noted above, 'factors like ethnicity, sexuality, age and religious belief coexist alongside gender and complicate it in the context of sexual harassment' (Brant and Too 1994: 24 and see contributions by Kitzinger, Raitt, Hunt and Bhattacharaya in the same collection). This approach stresses that it is also important not to take too narrow a definition of sexual harassment as something which, ubiquitously, men do to women. As Epstein (1997) points out, the harassment of gay men and of those perceived to be gay or effeminate is often ignored. Clearly, this is an issue shot through with complexity and ambiguity.

Our discussion of incidence has thus reached a similar state of impasse as our discussion of definition: it seems that sexual harassment is many different things for many different people. For this reason, some writers have argued that the radical and structural approaches which attempt to define and quantify the incidence of sexual harassment appear rather 'incomplete': there are many subtleties which are left out of such discussions (Epstein 1997, Kitzinger and Thomas 1995).

Discussion

We have so far shown that although significant steps have been achieved by feminists working from both radical and structural perspectives to confront the issue of sexual harassment within organisations, there are still considerable barriers which prevent people from making any real challenges to its incidence. It would appear that this is due partly to the discourse within which sexual harassment has been defined and understood: that is, the terms in which sexual harassment is described do not always reflect how people involved in such situations would or might want to describe their own experiences, and this may prevent them from taking things further. As we noted above, it may be that the very clarity of this discourse has rendered it problematic: the ambiguities, confusion and messiness of many people's experiences may mean that they find it difficult to define and describe them within the terms established within this framework.

From a structural perspective, the radical focus on the power relations between men and women does not tackle sufficiently the organisational context of power. Sexual harassers are frequently in hierarchical positions of power over the harassed, making it doubly difficult for a challenge to be made. Even though sexual harassment policies attempt to establish accessible and non-punitive procedures to deal with situations, the combination of structural power and gender power are still daunting, and may encourage women to remain silent. Further, if we approach the issue from a more poststructuralist perspective, we see that, for some, the experience of 'being a victim' is not as clear-cut as these radical accounts would tend to suggest. Women's 'silence' is not always a reflection of being powerless, but may be something they practice as a form of resistance to patriarchy (Cairns 1997).

Some of the more recent research on sexual harassment has thus concentrated on these very aspects by taking an approach which attempts to look particularly at the language in which sexual harassment is framed. Such discursive approaches not only look closely at the formal language through which the issue is encoded, such as in the law and organisational policy, but also the ways people working in organisations define and articulate their understanding of sexual harassment. While not all these approaches are poststructuralist, some drawing on discourse analysis to reach more structural conclusions, they do widen the debate by focusing on the ways experience of sexual harassment is socially constructed and discursively negotiated by individuals. The aim is not so much to produce a universal definition of sexual harassment from which to commence research and categorise the essence of the experience, but rather to shift the focus to see how organisational members themselves construct the experience.

Taking a poststructuralist approach, Brant and Too (1994) focus specifically on the ways sexual harassment is encoded in theoretical and organisational writing on the subject. Their concern is that fixed definitions can lead to rigid analysis, putting imaginative limits on understanding. 'Even expressions which wear well can settle into unthinking familiarity – for instance, the terms "victims" and "survivors" portray people who have been harassed as having been overwhelmed or transformed utterly' (Brant and Too 1994:9). Their aim is to question the rhetorical devices used in discussions about sexual harassment, 'to set the scene for the production of a more sensitive and responsive language' (ibid.).

Epstein (1997) suggests that the term 'sexual harassment' itself is constraining, and does not necessarily correspond to people's experiences of harassment. While these may be sexist, they may not be so overtly or obviously sexual in content or form, or people may not wish to define them as such. She suggests the term 'sexist harassment' to describe oppressive behaviour. However, Epstein (1997) also suggests that the relationship of power is not simply one in which men oppress women, but that gendered power relations are constructed through sexist harassment in ways which are complex and fluid. For example, it would be a mistake to assume that the sexist harassment of black women would take exactly the same forms as that of white women, for there are particularly racialised constructions of black women's sexuality and their gender-appropriate behaviour which impact upon the forms of sexist harassment they might experience. Of course, the terms 'black' and 'white' are not monolithic, and harassment is cut through with multiple constructions of colour and/or ethnicity and associated sexualities. For instance, as we saw in Chapter 4, it is argued that a different level of sexuality is assumed for all blacks compared with whites, and indeed attempts to pathologise sexuality as the main axis of difference between black and white can be traced back over at least a century (Gilman 1985, Essed 1991). Quite different sexualities are associated with white British/WASP, white 'Latin', Afro-Caribbean and South-East Asian people of colour, but the central component of this difference is alleged to be the inherent insatiability of blacks, which takes specifically gendered forms. While black men are commonly assumed to be sexually aggressive, black women are characterised as sexually available (*ibid.*). These constructions can be unearthed in contemporary writing about race, gender and organisation. Davis and Watson's (1982) study of American corporate life offers a good example of the construction of the black man as sexual predator and white male fear of losing 'their' women (that is, white women). A black woman described what happened when a black male manager appointed a young, white, blond woman as his secretary (an occupation defined, however erroneously, through notions of sexual availability):

You should have seen how all the white men in the section watched him – like hawks. Every time he came out of his office to speak to her some of them would stop what they were doing and listen, and God! you should see them squirming when she went into his office and closed the door. They tried everything... They tried to talk her into quitting. They used to make jokes about it to make the entire thing ugly. Pretty soon the girl did quit and the black guy got transferred. (p. 115)

While constructions of black female sexuality are more passive than those of black male sexuality, they are nonetheless understood as passionate, responsive and active in contrast to white femininity, which is seen as pious, pure and almost asexual. Black women are assumed to be always ready and willing for sex to take place and hence sex with black women is thus constructed by white men as more adventurous and enjoyable (Essed 1991). Black women come to be dismissed as sluts, always 'for sale' and this positioning can be used to justify harassment, sexual exploitation and sexual assaults. Thus black women become 'fair game for all men' (Hill-Collins 1990:54) and, hooks argues, rape becomes 'a rite and a right of white man' (1990:57). Black women's bodies are, hooks claims, 'the playing fields where racism and sexism converge(d)' (ibid.).

In an organisational context, this image of the 'black whore' can be used to legitimate sexual harassment and to undermine any subsequent complaints or action taken (Davis and Watson 1982). Similar legitimations exist for lesbians and gays. Experiences of harassment of lesbian and gay people of colour are shaped by both racist and heterosexist assumptions (Epstein 1997) which place them as 'abnormally' interested in sex, and therefore determined by it. For disabled people, the assumptions take a somewhat different form. Disabled people are not supposed to be sexual, but any sexual desire which does exist is invariably assumed to be heterosexual. While the denial of sexuality to disabled people might thus appear to rule out harassment, this very denial can be experienced as harassing in itself (ibid.).

Epstein's (1997) analysis of the different forms of harassment demonstrate that sexuality and gender are constructed through a complexity of social and power relations. Her key point is that there is not one, univocal form of heterosexist harassment but, rather, that the forms of harassment experienced shape and are shaped by the particular social locations of those who are harassed and, indeed, their harassers.

Kitzinger and Thomas's (1995) approach is also to look closely at what is assumed and what is obscured in discussions of sexual harassment, by taking a discourse analysis approach. They found important differences between the ways women and men understand sexual harassment, although there was a pervasive tendency for both men and women to deny any definition of their experiences as sexual harassment. For women, the reasons were that many disliked the connotation of 'victim', and that they did not want to define behaviour as harassment too quickly, as this would draw attention to its pervasiveness ('it happens all the time'). An essential part of the definition of sexual harassment for the women workers in their study was *power* – sexual harassment was seen to be a way of 'doing power'. Men, too, denied the existence of much sexual harassment, preferring to interpret overtly sexual behaviour as a normal aspect of relations between the sexes. They tended to see the behaviour as more about sex than about power: 'it's not taking no for an answer' as Fred explains in their study (p.42).

This latter conclusion is somewhat contradicted however by Epstein's (1997) findings. In her study, the men admitted that they had harassed women earlier in their lives, describing a pressure to be heterosexual in a particular way ('behaving like men'), which involved the harassment of women. In other words, for some men the harassment of women is a way of 'doing masculinity', of constructing and confirming themselves as both masculine and heterosexual. Sexual harassment is a *performance* of heterosexuality, rather than a need for sex.

This discussion of the literature on sexual harassment has shown how the different perspectives on gender, power and organisation have produced quite different understandings and definitions about the issue. Whereas the radical approach sees that sexual harassment is a primary means by which men mobilise their power to oppress women, the structural approach sees it as a means through which men are able to subordinate women in order to maintain their superiority in the workplace. The ways the language about sexual harassment is expressed in both of these approaches leaves little place for the concept of women's agency. Poststructuralist approaches, in contrast, through the focus on the language by which people describe their experiences, demonstrate the ambiguities which are often present in situations of sexual harassment. These ambiguities may mean that people find it difficult to match their own experiences with the prevailing legal or official language by which they are supposed to describe them. Further, the resistance shown by some women to defining their experiences of harassment too quickly as 'sexual harassment' may also be about confirming themselves as powerful and 'able to cope' with a situation.

These approaches which concentrate on language have thus also drawn attention to the complexity of power relations showing how other popular discourses about race, sexuality, age and physical ability cut across the man–woman binary. However, what is common to all the theoretical approaches is that difference is a central feature. We have seen how harassment works through difference, using it to construct hierarchies, and, as such, organisations are centrally implicated in using sex and sexualising processes as a means through which power can be mobilised, and hierarchical gender relations can be maintained.

The confusion which accompanies attempts to define exactly what sexual harassment is has led some organisational theorists to question whether 'sexual harassment' should remain the dominant paradigm within which to analyse sexuality and sexual behaviour at work, and writing has appeared which takes a broader approach to looking at the issue of sexuality within organisations. This work suggests that harassment is rather 'an intensification of the conditions under which women are employed' (Brewis and Kerfoot 1994:9–10), an aspect of 'a wider set of individual and collective male "power plays" designed for or having the effect of making life uncomfortable for women and keeping them in their proper subordinate place' (Thompson and Ackroyd 1994:2). We turn to consider this wider set of behaviour in the next section.

The pervasiveness of (hetero) sexuality within organisational life

Hearn and Parkin (1987) argue that when you 'enter most organisations (and) you enter a world of sexuality' (Hearn and Parkin 1987:3). An ever-growing body of work agrees with them, rectifying the 'booming silence' which hitherto existed on sexuality in organisations. This literature shifts the focus of much of the work on sexual harassment, which showed how men in organisations use sex to manage gender relations, to looking at how it is sex which manages, constructs and reproduces gender relations in organisations.

What is meant by sexuality in the context of organisations? In contrast to the common-sense or biological view of sexuality which we discussed in the introduction to this chapter, most research and writing on sexuality in the workplace adopts a social constructionist approach. This suggests that 'our sexual feelings and activities, the ways we think about sexuality, and our sexual identities are not biologically determined but are the product of social and historical forces' (Richardson 1993:78), shaped by the culture in which we live. Specifically, it is the ways in which both the wider social culture and the culture and structure of the organisation construct the sexuality and the sexual identities of the men and women working within those organisations which form the focus of interest. Obviously this is a wide agenda, and different writers have focused on different aspects of these processes. Of key interest is the way organisational cultures are predominantly heterosexual and heterosexualising. In the next part of this section, we consider the various processes by which this happens.

Communication

In many organisations, sexuality structures the ways people communicate with each other. For many women workers, their structural location at the subordinate end of the hierarchy might mean that the politeness required to be shown to their superiors becomes infused with sexual expectations and connotations. For nurses, secretaries, personal assistants, catering and receptionist staff, 'politeness as implicit sexuality is part of the job' (Hearn and Parkin 1987:134), as the following examples demonstrate:

> The atmosphere was one of compulsory jocularity: solicitors and secretaries gaily exchanged insults and sexual banter with each other all day, and there was a great deal of friendly fondling and patting of bottoms...The women were clear that their role was to service men and were willing to put up with what was constant sexual innuendo. The overall feel of the place was not dissimilar to a brothel (Pringle 1989:93–4)

> Playing the doctor–nurse game – you have to play the hierarchy all the time and the sexual component is pretty central: doctors expect you to flirt with them and find them attractive. (Game and Pringle 1983:108)

Certain jobs have a clear 'sexual labour' content, whereby it is part of the job to service clients or customers in a sexualised way. Typically, it is women who fill these jobs: jobs such as airline hostesses, barmaids, waitresses and shop assistants (Hochschild 1983, Williams 1988, Adkins 1995). Although some of the communication with customers may be received as distinctly harassing, the most common forms are the daily routine of 'chatting up': 'treating a person as if they were an object which the observer has a right to' (Adkins 1995: 129).

> The men customers 'were always eyeing us up', and often 'saying things about our appearance', commenting on 'the way we looked in our uniforms...how they liked the way we looked in them'...[they] would often try to chat up the women workers: they were always trying to get us to meet them in the bar after work. (ibid.)

The fact is that for some, and probably many, women, their daily communication with men is frequently of a sexualised nature. This may be with men as colleagues, superiors, or customers, yet commonly these men hold power over women's employment position. This means that sexuality is something that women have to bring into the public realm: it is not something they can choose to leave at home. Importantly, it is a specific form of sexuality: a jolly, cheerful sort of heterosexuality which hints at constant availability, and which both men and women have to collude with, masking the power plays with the facade of 'having fun'.

Sexualised forms of communication are not solely restricted to groups of mixed sexes. Collinson (1988) notes how, within the all-male environment of a lorry-making factory, masculine sexual prowess was a pervasive topic of conversation. Often conducted through joking and bravado, the consistent aim was to reinforce the image of men as sexually insatiable, yet independent and powerful: ready to 'have it' with any one, at any time. By contrast, women were portrayed as 'passive, dependent, and only interested in catching a man' (Collinson 1988:191). Photos of female nudes adorned the walls, an objectification of women which was reinforced by the continual banter of the men. Hearn (1985) found that the physical proximity of men on the shop floor, or in institutions such as armies and prisons, may lead to contact of a much more physical kind. He terms this 'horseplay': the grabbing of genitals, play-fighting and hugging, yet all conducted in a macho, heterosexual male culture. Such sexual displays thus enable men to perform their masculinity, as well as to construct hierarchies between men and women, positioning women as subordinate to men and, at the same time, anxious for their sexual attentions. There is also some evidence that such overt and aggressive displays of macho masculinity are used to construct hierarchies between men, for instance marking out the men who might choose not to take part as 'wimps' or even 'poofters' or distinguishing the 'real men' on the shopfloor from the emasculated men in suits 'upstairs' (that is, the managers) (Roper 1988).

This is certainly not a function of class. Lewis's (1989) findings of how outstanding success on the trading floor of major banks is sexualised as (outrageous) masculinity reinforce these conclusions:

> If he could make millions of dollars come out of those phones, he became that most revered of all species: a Big Swinging Dick...Nothing in the jungle got in the way of a Big Swinging Dick...That was the prize we coveted...everyone wanted to be a Big Swinging Dick, even the women. Big Swinging Dickettes. (Lewis 1989:42–3)

Careers and mentorship

As we have already discussed, the importance of mentoring relationships in career development has been well documented, and has been noted as a factor especially critical to the career success of women (McKeen and Burke 1989, Colwill 1984, Hennig and Jardim 1979, Morrison *et al.* 1992, Noe 1988). However, the development of successful mentor relationships is not easy for women. Men are typically in more senior positions within the organisational structure, and therefore more likely to be in mentoring positions, yet physical proximity between individual women and men is frequently sexualised within organisational cultures. The assumption is that where men and women are together there must be sex. Fear of such gossip sexualising a work relationship may diminish the possibilities for a successful mentor relationship developing for women. Concerns about the 'public image 'of the relationship can cause men and women to avoid one-to-one contact behind closed doors or at the margins of the day.

Sexualities and self-presentation

The sexualisation of women means that women are often very self-conscious about the way they present themselves at work. The way they appear physically may be made to be of crucial importance for women, as inferences about sexuality are usually made on the basis of appearance. Style of clothes, including length of skirt and type of blouse, hair colour and style, amount of make-up and jewellery: all these artefacts carry sexual connotations, which women have to balance carefully. Women learn to manage their sexuality and gender and redefine their 'femaleness' as a necessary component of organisational membership (Sheppard 1989). They do this by very deliberate strategies of gender and sexual management. These include thinking carefully about dress, language and relationships with peers and superiors. Without this type of constant vigilance, women risk not being taken seriously, not being heard, and not receiving necessary information – in other words, of not being able to participate fully in the organisational system (Sheppard 1989). To maintain credibility, they have to de-emphasise their femininity and/or their sexuality, yet if they are perceived as 'too masculine' in appearance, they risk being labelled in ways which are seen as punitive: 'lesbian' or 'castrating bitch' (Sheppard 1989). For black women this problem may be particularly acute: for example, the black teachers in Al-Khalifa's (1989) study report the preoccupation of white men with their dress and appearance, which reflects an underlying view of the dominance of sexuality in their construction of black women.

However, for women in many jobs, the self-management of their appearance is beyond their individual control. Barmaids, catering assistants, receptionists and nurses are just a few occupations for which the wearing of a uniform is a necessary requirement. In some cases, this 'uniform' is overtly sexualised: for example, in Adkins' (1995) study of a theme park, women working in the bars had to wear their dresses 'off the shoulder', a requirement aggressively enforced by the bar manager who would often pull their dresses down into this position. These women thus had to offer their sexuality as part of the skills they brought to the job, a requirement that was not similarly made of the men. In fact, to put the case more strongly, sexuality or more specifically 'sexiness' to men was one of the most specific criteria for which women were employed: their physical appearance or attractiveness was the deciding factor as to whether and where they were placed. Even where women's uniforms are not overtly sexualised, they may be implicitly so: nurses' uniforms' are the butt of many a *Carry-On* style fantasy in popular cultural images of male sexuality. For researchers such as Sheppard (1989) and Adkins (1995), therefore, working women are seen to be in a no-win situation as regards their physical appearance: sexual connotations about dress and other physical features all work to undermine their authority. However, others have challenged this structural perspective, and have argued that some women in some positions may be able to use their appearance in a more empowered way. Either by dressing in 'power suits' or by deliberately sexualising their appearance, they gain attention which they can use to their own advantage (Pringle 1989; Hegelson 1990). For example, in the last chapter, we saw how some women managers deliberately play on their clothes and appearance to construct a certain type of image (Rowe 1999).

Relationships at work

Hearn and Parkin (1987) argue that hierarchical organisational structures also spill over into the structure of interpersonal relations
between people in organisations, including the sexual. They claim
that relations usually operate 'in one dominant direction – of men
over women' (Hearn and Parkin 1987:82) (in 74 per cent of the romantic relationships that occur at work, the male is in a higher position
than the female (Quinn and Lees 1984)), and this means that hierarchical divisions and thus interpersonal relations and sexuality are similarly gendered, with power and sex becoming interrelated. This both
reflects and is reflected by the perception of heterosexuality in the
wider social culture, wherein

> Erotic excitement, according to patriarchal ideology, depends on the tension
> created by setting men against women in a power struggle, setting them at
> cross purposes with conflicting interests that create the possibilities of vul-
> nerability and domination. (Hunter 1993:163)

From a structural perspective, it is this cultural more which sets the
scene within which sexual relations within organisations are tolerated.
As such, a male-boss – female-secretary relationship which develops
into the sexual, is deemed to be more acceptable than if the situation
was reversed, so that a female superior was having a sexual relationship with a male member of the rank and file. Generally, however,
within organisations sexual liaisons between members are looked upon
with disfavour. Where sexual relationships become more established
and perhaps threaten the ways of working in the organisation, reaction
from those in the upper levels of the hierarchy can be intense, with
threats, dismissals, reorganisations and so on (Hearn and Parkin
1987). In other words, one of the main sources of fear about sexual
relations within organisations is that they may cut across the supposedly rational–legal hierachy – in effect, this means that (hetero)sexu-
ality may undermine the gendered divisions of labour, enabling certain
women to benefit and gain what may be seen as unacceptable amounts
of power and influence.

An interesting contradiction thus exists about women's sexuality in
the popular discourses which abound in most organisations: on the one
hand, women are often perceived in no other terms than sexual ones
(MacKinnon 1979), yet on the other hand, if they are seen as actually
engaging in and enjoying sexual behaviour, they are scorned, resented

and even punished for it. Whereas men's active sexuality tends to be associated with the properties of valued labour and hierarchy, women's sexuality is negatively interpreted as a threat to all things Weberian (as we discussed in Chapter 2).

This is interestingly reflected in the ways in which women who do gain power and ascend to a managerial position are constructed. They may become desexualised by men workers within the organisation, confirming the idea that female sexuality and power must not be mixed. In other words, such women are defined by the absence of their sexuality: where sexuality fails as a means of controlling women or maintaining them in a subordinate position, it is abandoned. Gould argues that a woman in a high-status, high-income position 'loses in attractiveness . . . she poses a threat to a man's sense of masculinity . . . men are unsexed by failure' (Gould 1974:97–8). On the other hand, an alternative response by men is to reharness sexuality to women in high-status positions, as a more or less deliberate way of undermining them. Thus, women in power may be eroticised as exotic, out of the ordinary, and viewed as a challenge. Margaret Thatcher, for instance, was known to be the subject of male sexual fantasy for some of her colleagues and even the then French president Francois Mitterand spoke of her in physical terms.

So far, we have discussed how structural power combines with sexuality within organisations to maintain the existing gendered hierarchies. Through the discussion of the ways women are sexualised, the picture of power relations within organisations has been a ubiquitously male-dominated one, with women being sexualised by men as a way of marginalising them and minimising their power. However, this approach tends to assume that *all* women are subjected to the same sexualising processes, which they have little power to resist. Working from a poststructuralist perspective, Pringle (1989) seeks to widen our understanding of gender relations at work by focusing on the divisions within these processes, as well as challenging our understanding or the position of women within them (see also the 'Sexuality, Power and Pleasure' section in this chapter). She argues that relations within organisations are maintained and reinforced by several prevailing discourses, which not only emphasise the different sexualities of different members of the organisation, but also define the type and form of those sexualities. A number of such discourses exist: for women, which discourse is applied may be decided by her age, colour or seniority. All define her sexually in relation to the men within the organisation, not with her life in 'the private sphere'. Pringle (1989) looks particularly at secretaries working in contemporary organisations, and identifies three key discourses which she sees coexist to construct our understanding of them. The first discourse is that of 'the office wife', who takes her identity primarily from her boss, and is perceived primarily as an extension of him: loyal, trustworthy and devoted. She is expected to 'love, honour and obey', to look and sound 'like a lady': in short, to care for him, to act as both wife and mother. The second discourse is that of 'the sexy secretary'. Here it is the physical attractiveness and/or youth and sexual availability, if not proclivity, of the secretary which is emphasised. She is a 'dolly bird' or 'blond bombshell': not very intelligent, but big-bosomed, and above all, young. Pringle (1989) maintains that this discourse is so pervasive that *all* women workers, whatever their age, are put down as adolescent girls and assessed in terms of their physical attractiveness. The 'dolly' lacks the respect allocated to the office wife: she is valued only as a sex object. The third discourse is that of the 'career woman'. This discourse emphasises skill and experience and resists sexual and familial definitions and plays down the special relationship with the boss in favour of the notion of the management team. However, because the presence of sexuality is usually so dominant, so its absence merely recalls that presence.

Discussion

In this section, we have shown how an extremely important debate on organisational sexuality has emerged since the 1980s, which 'sees sexuality as penetrating the workplace at a depth such that the entire working environment is predicated on gender difference' (Brewis and Kerfoot 1994:15). Much of this debate has been framed within the structural perspective, which argues that the tendency to see women and men as distinct and different, and as such better suited to different types of work, is not only exacerbated by the pervasive (hetero)sexualisation of women but is actually constructed through this process. In other words, the sexual divisions which exist within an organisation – both horizontally, in terms of the division of labour, and vertically, in terms of divisions of authority – are produced, supported and maintained through these entrenching processes of sexualisation. Hearn and Parkin (1987) call this process 'the organisational structuring of sexuality'.

Pringle (1989) also reveals the ways in which gender relationships within organisational hierarchies are infused with sexuality, but from a poststructuralist approach. In particular, she draws our attention to the discursive association of women with sexual roles which pervade the wider social culture generally. While Pringle's (1989) notion of discourses, can, in one sense, be seen to be a way in which structural power is constructed and reinforced, Pringle (1989) also see that discourses open up possible spaces for contestation and resistance. It may be that in their interpretation of these discourses, individual women are able to modify or even rewrite them, according to the particularities of their own situation. In this conceptualisation, power is understood as being altogether more fluid, and exercised through many different versions of relationships. Through their modification of discourses, women may thereby mobilise power to construct themselves within organisations, rather than be constructed by them. We return to this discussion more fully in the section after the next one.

Lesbianism, homosexuality and organisations

Our discussion of the various ways in which gender relations in organisations are sexualised has revealed the extent to which they are 'profoundly heterosexualised' (Cockburn 1991). Indeed, Rich's notion of 'compulsory heterosexuality' (1984) can be seen to be of relevance here: for, as we have seen, the sexual normality of daily life in organisations is, as Pringle puts it, 'relentlessly' heterosexual (Pringle 1989), involving the domination of men's heterosexuality over women's heterosexuality and the subordination of all other forms of sexuality. From a structural perspective, heterosexuality at work may thus be usefully seen to be an organisational practice (Dunne 1992) by which inequalities of power between men and women within the organisation are reproduced and maintained. However, from a poststructuralist perspective, heterosexuality might also be seen to be a pervasive discourse or ideology within most organisations: the common-sense, 'taken-for-granted' pattern of ' "normal" adult living' (Dunne 1992:86), within which understandings and assumptions about organisational members are framed. Thus not only is it gendered power which is continuously mobilised but a specific version of this hegemonic heterosexual power. In the next section, we explore the ways that this not only underpins the assumptions behind formal organisational policies, but also, and perhaps more influentially, operates through daily informal interactions with colleagues at all levels.

The power of hegemonic heterosexuality

The power of hegemonic heterosexuality means that many non-heterosexuals have specific problems within the organisations in which they work, surrounding the issue of their sexual identity. They have to choose whether to come out, and manage this out identity, which, for many non-heterosexuals, allocates them to a social group defined precisely and only by its sexuality (Wilton 1992). Alternatively, they have to manage an identity in which their sexuality is hidden, in order 'to comply with the dominant discourse of hegemonic hetero-sexuality in order to safely negotiate what for them is often an intolerant and hostile world' (Clarke 1996:1). This means that, for gay men and lesbian women, their sexuality may be a source of disempowerment within their organisational lives. The choice appears to lie between either negative outcomes as a consequence of disclosure (that is, having one's sexuality identified and possibly used – against you – to identify the whole person), or negative outcomes as a consequence of concealment (that is, of having one's sexuality misunderstood) (Prince 1993:168).

Indeed, homosexuals are remarkably hidden in most organisations, with few making the decision to come out. For some organisation members, this decision is forced upon them: for instance, section 28 of the Local Government Act 1988 states that a local authority must not intentionally promote homosexuality or promote the teaching of the acceptability of homosexuality in any maintained school (this section is under review at the time of going to press). The consequence of this legislation and attitude has been to force many local government workers and teachers to conceal and protect their sexual identities in the augmentation of a climate which reaffirms what constitutes normal and acceptable sexual identity.

Kitzinger (1990) points out that coming out means different things to different people. For some, it means simply allowing others to know about their gayness or lesbianism. However, this is rarely a one-off event: there are always new colleagues and contexts, meaning this is something that has to be constantly redone:

> We are forced to make daily decisions about whether or not to say, whether or not to interrupt the assumptions being made about our presumed hetero-sexuality, weighing up the risks and possible repercussions of each and every situation. (p. 167)

This might mean that someone may be not entirely out or in, but constantly in an intermediate situation: out with some people and in with others, typically superiors in the organisational hierarchy. Hall (1989) found that for certain women who had decided to disclose their lesbianism to a friend at work, this had been the result of both premeditation and impulsiveness: 'I'd thought about it for a long time, but I didn't know when or if I was going to tell her... then one night we had a few drinks and it just came out' (Hall 1989:132)

The daily reality of being out may be a continual grinding strain, however, as the same limited set of reactions are met:

> the men who see me as a challenge ('all you need is the right man'), or as the embodiment of their sordid pornographic fantasies ('I've always wanted to go to bed with a lesbian'); the married women with small children who fall desperately in love with the mirage of freedom they imagine me to represent, the heterosexual women who are wary, cautious and distant as though lesbianism might be infectious, and the 'liberated' ones who are ostentatiously friendly to prove they know it isn't. (Kitzinger 1990:168)

Of course, sometimes the reaction to lesbians and gay men is not of this 'dripping-tap' (Kitzinger 1990) kind, but more openly hostile or even violent. Valentine notes that a national survey of attitudes to lesbians and gay men in the USA revealed that 25 per cent of respondents to the poll would strongly object to working around people who are gay. A further 27 per cent said they would prefer not to do so (Herek 1992, quoted in Valentine 1993a). The situation is probably much the same in Britain, as revealed by research from the Lesbian Employment Rights Group, who found that 151 out of 171 gay women questioned in London in 1984 had experienced some form of anti-lesbianism in the workplace (Hall 1989).

Because of these pressures, many gay and lesbian people decide not to disclose their sexual identity at work, choosing instead to pass themselves off as heterosexual. The consequence of this is that many lesbians and gay men have to manage and negotiate multiple sexual identities over space and time. They may maintain a heterosexual identity within the organisation, or they may try to make their sexuality somehow neutral and invisible, and then have a lesbian or gay identity in the 'private' spaces of home or gay bars (Valentine 1993b). Thus at work, in order to fit in and function with a minimum of attention to their personal selves, lesbian women may conform to a traditional 'feminine' identity, by wearing make-up and skirts and feigning sexual interest in men (Valentine 1993b, Clarke 1996, Hall 1989). Some augment this fictional heterosexual identity by making up a male partner's name, or by changing the pronoun 'she' to 'he'. However, as a result of adopting a gender-sexual identity which is devoid of meaning for them, some lesbians feel out of place at work (Valentine 1993b).

These strategies of sexual identity management within organisations reveal the tensions and contradictions which exist for lesbian women at work. But such juggling and secrecy is not without costs, in terms of the nature of friendships which may be established and the feeling that they are leading double lives (Clarke 1996). As one respondent explained: 'I'm a totally different person at work in terms of relationships with people than I am from a normal day in my life' (Clarke 1996:13). Valentine (1993b) points out that the number of identities may be even more multiple: at home, one may be a lesbian, in the neighbourhood, one of two women sharing a house for financial reasons, at the bank, a single, asexual career woman, and at work heterosexual. Whereas most of the women found this 'identity dilemma' (Valentine 1993b) difficult, some quite enjoyed it, finding as they got older it became much easier to slip in and out of their different selves. Further, sexual identity is frequently negotiated in a non-linear narrative: one might be in the closet in one job and out in another, depending on the culture of the different organisations.

What this discussion reveals is the complex and labyrinthine nature of the lesbian existence for people working within organisations. Cockburn (1991) suggests that difficulties may be even more fraught for gay men, for there is often a 'more frenzied' prejudice against homosexuality than lesbianism. This may be because homosexuality undermines a male solidarity and authority based on a cooperative domination of women's bodies. However, men are not in a position to marginalise homosexuality by ignoring it. As we have already demonstrated, the daily business of organisations depends on men generating a closeness in order to share and control information (Cockburn 1991). Homo-*sociality* – socialising between men – is the dominant cultural form in male-dominated organisations, whereby power is shared and distributed from one generation of men to another. Roper(1988) notes the close association of homosocial behaviour with homosexual, with the former relying on a nicely calculated amount of touching and intimacy which borders on the homoerotic. He argues that the managerial discourse itself is 'underlaid with male sexual definitions' and that promotion is dependent on the arousal of male desires. However, in contradistinction to this underlying culture, homosexuality is almost ubiquitously pilloried in organisations, with few openly supporting any initiative towards equality for homosexuals.

Differences do exist between the type of organisation: for example, Cockburn (1991) found a more tolerant climate in her study of the service sector than the retail. Whereas in the latter, any homosexual who might have inhabited the power structure was obliged to remain tightly closeted, with the distinct possibility of heterosexual men closing ranks against all gays, in the service sector, where some gay men had made it to the upper ranks of the hierarchy, the strategy was of an affirmation of a select group of middle-class, white males. The terms of this acceptance were strict, however: gays must play the fraternal game, and maintain the male hierarchical culture.

Thus although male homosexuality runs the risk of being aggressively opposed (but mostly by other men, not by women, who Cockburn (1991) found on the whole to be less intolerant), some homosexual men are able to be out and, at the same time up in the hierarchy of some organisations. Gay men are thus able to play a game that is closed to lesbian women. Whereas for lesbian women their safe option is to pass themselves off as a (usually powerless) heterosexual, stereotypically 'feminine' woman, gay men, by emphasising their similarity with the so-called 'white male brotherhood', may be able to negotiate the heterosexualised nature of organisations to their individual benefit.

Discussion

Our discussion of the marginalisation of homosexuality in many ways echoes those of sexual harassment and the pervasiveness of heterosexuality. From a structural perspective, we can see the coercive nature of the relationship that sexuality has with the dominant power sites within most organisations: sexuality becomes a fundamental mechanism by which the position of minorities (typically heterosexual women, gay men and lesbian women, black men and women) is maintained. Power and desire become inextricably linked: the desire of the dominant heterosexual man defines the way members of groups others are perceived within the organisation. By emphasising their sexuality, the other aspects of their identities, such as competence to do a particular job, are obsfuscated, reinforcing the justice of the heterosexual male monopolising positions of power and authority within organisations.

The extent to which our discussion has revealed the consistency of marginalising behaviour by dominant heterosexual men would suggest however that the job of maintaining the meanings attached to individuals is a fairly continual one: indeed, it can be seen as a form of work itself. Meanings have to be continually produced and reproduced, a daily if not hourly chore which, as we have seen, pervades the whole range of interactions between dominant men and others. The structural perspective reveals how their task is obviously aided by the context of the organisational and social structures in which they operate: structures which, if not fixed, do have a certain longevity (Pringle 1989).

However, as we saw earlier in the chapter, from a poststructuralist perspective discourses such as those of sexuality are understood as having 'fluidity of meaning', while power is understood as being dispersed between individuals, sometimes regardless of their formal structural position. This means that there are always possibilities for contestation, transformation and change within any (discursive) situation. Thus, while structural disadvantages shape the work experiences of many women, these do not necessarily make them 'hapless victims'. There *are* strategies of power and resistance open to them (Pringle 1989), which mean that there is no direct correspondence between structure and power. For example, people can resist the dominant discourses through which their sexual identities are constructed within organisations, and modify them in construction with other aspects of their identities. Valentine's (1993b) discussion of multiple identities echoes this line of thinking. While, from a structural perspective, separating sexual identity from other identities might be viewed as the enforced silencing of one's 'true self', this can also be seen, from a poststructuralist perspective, as a strategy of resistance which is sometimes pleasurable. The performance of one identity at work, and others at leisure, may be a means of resisting constraining definitions and consequent marginalisation by those with more structural power. As Pringle argues, through strategies such as these, 'Tables can be turned, roles reversed, outcomes changed' (Pringle 1989:28).

Sexuality, power and pleasure

According to Pringle's (1989) work on the boss–secretary relationship, one of the ways contestation and resistance to gender and structural power happens is through the possibilities which emerge through the discursive context in which gendered relationships exist. Modern western societies have accumulated a vast network of discourses on sex and pleasure. This range of discourses also infuse bureaucratic organisations; indeed, for many, the organisation is a central site for playing out a variety of sexual identities with a range of different people. As Pringle explains: 'It is undoubtedly true that for both men and women sexual fantasies and interactions are a way of killing time, of giving a sense of adventure, of livening up an otherwise boring day' (Pringle 1989:90). Thus, rather than seeing women as caught in an iron cage of oppressive and oppressing sexual relations, Pringle invites us to centralise the subject position of women, that is, to see them as 'sexual subjects' (Foucault 1980) in sexual discourses, engaging in relations with others because they derive pleasure from them. Furthermore, the ways discourses cut across and contradict each other, and the fact that they have to be reproduced by specific men and women, mean that there is room for change, play and experiment within each individual situation.

Such room for manoeuvre suggests that the interplay of power, pleasure and desire is highly complex. Pringle wishes to challenge a picture of power which automatically equates coercion with structural position: boss over secretary, man over woman. Instead, she argues that power operates more subtly than this: 'a person may "voluntarily" do what another wants, without any sense of coercion, or she may take pleasure in her situation' (p. 52). She singles out three sexual discourses which she sees structure gendered relationships within bureaucratic organisations: first, 'the master–slave' discourse, in which the boss is typically subject and the secretary the object; second, 'the mother/ nanny–son' discourse, in which the secretary is the subject and the boss may be positioned as 'naughty boy'. Third, 'the team' discourse, which evokes equality and modernity. Within these discourses, variations occur as the subjects and objects involved interact with each other and themselves. Masculine and feminine identities are never fully or permanently constituted and are always in some sense in a state of flux. Since meanings have to be reproduced in specific situations, there is room for negotiation and change: there is space for games to be played and roles to be reversed. What unites the discourses is the interaction of pleasure with power, and, in particular, how this is based on the close relationship between sado-masochistic relations and pleasure. For it is Pringle's case that, for both men and women, the pattern of unconscious emotions, fantasies and desires which underlie what are understood as normal, everyday interactions, draw heavily on the erotic elements of sado-masochism (Pringle 1989).

With this argument she is turning the relationship between sexuality and organisation on its head. That is, instead of seeing sexuality as a tool used by patriarchy or capitalism to structure and maintain gendered relations, she sees power inhering in sexuality, and as such more available to all. Thus whatever the basis of the structural relationship between people, sexuality has the power to challenge: it does not simply 'wither' away in egalitarian relationships, or coerce in inegalitarian ones. The unconscious acting out of fantasy means that bosses may subject themselves to "punishment" or secretaries may enjoy being submissive: in other words, sexuality may be the 'wild card' (Pringle 1989) in gendered relations by which women may both empower themselves by disrupting male rationality, and gain pleasure from their situation.

Pringle (1989) recognises the complex nature of this line of argument. She does not wish to deny the clear evidence that men have and abuse power, but wishes to question the extent to which women are victims, or whether they too can exercise sexual power. 'It is by no means certain that women are yanked screaming into "compulsory heterosexuality". Most actively seek it out and find pleasure in it.' (p. 95). Further, she notes that through men's willingness to enter into sexual games with women at different levels of the organisation, there lie opportunities for subversion. 'In their office humour and sometimes in public expression, secretaries use parody of themselves and their bosses to powerful effect. Much pleasure is derived from imitating, exaggerating and ridiculing the existing stereotypes' (Pringle 1989:103). Although recognising that these interventions are 'necessarily localised, sporadic and spontaneous' amounting to 'little more than letting off steam', they have a powerful place in challenging the masculinity of modern organisations.

The recognition of women's agency and pleasure in their own sexuality is turned into a normative recommendation by Cockburn (1991) in her agenda for the women's movement in organisations. She wishes to strengthen women's position and confidence by reintroducing into organisations women's bodies, their sexuality and their emotions on their own terms. She takes a slightly more sanguine view of the sexual power of women. As things stand at the moment, although women want to be free to be their fully sexual selves, at work as elsewhere, they find that, because of the power relations of heterosexuality, they are unable to do this without risk. Cockburn (1991) thus wishes to challenge this prescription of female sexual behaviour by arguing that what needs to change is not the sexiness or sexualised behaviour of women, but their vulnerability. It is not that the erotic should be suppressed or even banned from organisational life, but that women (as well as men) should be enabled to engage in it on equal terms.

This is a line of argument shared by both Burrell (1992) and Giddens (1992). Urging that the open and public celebration of sex is a framework for re-energising relationships between individuals (Brewis and

Grey 1994), they argue that organisations will benefit from a process of 're-eroticisation', in which sexuality and eroticism are specifically encouraged. At present, power relations in society and organisations are oppressive to women, and women have been disadvantaged by the modern regime by the lack of recognition of a female sexuality. Re-eroticisation, however, has an emancipatory and democratic ability, as everyone is seeking pleasure at the same time in the same place. This is not through merely sexual or genital activity and pleasure: 'it does not simply mean more orgasms' (Burrell 1992:78). It is rather 'the totality of pleasure-directed life instincts whose energy is derived from libido' (Bologh 1990:213, quoted in Burrell, ibid.). Closer to sensuality than sex, expanding 'not only the possible range of erotic acts, but also the intensity and length of erotic play' (Brewis and Grey 1994:72), this freedom of behaviour enables us to become 'fully human' (Irigaray 1991). Through re-eroticisation, therefore, women and men become empowered to challenge organisational hierarchies, and as a result, a growing number of alternative organisational forms may emerge, such as cooperatives, communes, ecological collectives, self-help groups and feminist groups.

Discussion

While on the face of it, the celebration of women's sexuality in organisations does seem to offer an emancipatory appeal to women, certain feminist writers have expressed some concern about the direction that these arguments are taking. Firstly, Adkins (1995) argues that Pringle (1989) and Cockburn (1991), in their plea to forward women's sexual pleasure in organisations, are assuming that there are *different sorts* of heterosexuality: the coercive and the non-coercive. Whereas coercive interactions make women powerless victims, non-coercive relations may afford women power, pleasure and excitement. In other words, these two types of heterosexuality are separated out, as if there were no connection between them. Radical feminists challenge this conception however by describing the whole of heterosexuality as a continuum, in which male dominance pervades to a lesser or greater extent (Kelly 1987). To separate sexuality from the hierarchical relations of the economic structure is to deny the reality of the relationship of gender, power and the labour market.

Further, Brewis and Grey (1994) have expressed deep concern with the implications of the arguments to 're-eroticise' organisations. Of particular import is the assumption that the erotic exists independently of those exercises of power which construct it. The two key arguments of re-eroticisation theory are that any erotic practice which emerges is worthwhile and, second, that the erotic practices which do emerge will reflect currently existing but repressed practices. By eliminating repression and taboo, the erotic emancipates all those who engage with it. However, the consequences of these assumptions may be quite dangerous for women, as sexual desires may be constructed in ways which are undesirable: for example, sado-masochism has a distinctly gendered inheritance which has involved the infliction of violence on women against their will. Sexuality and the erotic carry traces of essentialism which re-eroticisation theory has certainly not dispelled. This may make it very difficult for women to really define the terms of their own pleasure. It may be therefore, that that 'emancipation does not consist in the validation of such practices... but rather in recognising and challenging the social relations within which they are constructed' (p. 79).

Summary and conclusions

In this chapter, we have discussed the ways sexuality inflects organisational life and gender relations. We have demonstrated that whatever the form in which sexual behaviour is made explicit – whether this be sexual harassment, a dominant and domineering culture of heterosexuality, the marginalisation of lesbians and gay men or (the playful) acting out of prevailing sexual discourses – sexualised relations between the genders are seen to pivot on inequality: sexuality combines with power to act to differentiate and discriminate. In this final section, we pull out and explore more fully the range of theoretical explanations that have been offered to account for this. These theoretical approaches all take the concept of power to be central, but differ as to the way this is perceived: as regards its source, enactment and possibilities for resistance.

Structural approaches to sexuality and organisation

Through the discussions in this chapter, we have shown how structural approaches to sexuality and organisation establish themselves as a deliberate contrast to the 'common-sense' view of sexuality which tends to dominate popular thinking. Structural accounts claim that it is important to understand that sexuality is socially, not biologically, constructed, and that our sexual identities, feelings and activities are not innate but are the product of socialising processes. Further, structural approaches take as axiomatic that sexual harassment and predatory heterosexuality are the result of social factors and are patterned by social structures of domination and oppression. However, we have also seen in this chapter that there are variations in the ways structure is used to account for sexuality, power and organisation. Broadly, three positions have emerged.

First, social and sexual behaviour at work is seen to be the outcome and consequence of capitalism. For example, Hearn and Parkin (1987) argue that sexual harassment by men of women is particularly high in those industries which are characterised by alienating work conditions, such as lack of control of the product and act of production. Indeed, harassment could be interpreted as an attempt to create some human contact in reaction to alienation or as an attempt to exert some power in the face of structural powerlessness. Displays of pornography by men in the workplace also derive from men's boredom with their work, and are an attempt by men to escape this monotony.

However, this explanation of women's sexual oppression and objectification within organisations has been criticised for naturalising and essentialising heterosexual relations (Adkins 1992). By reducing sexuality to a by-product of capitalist processes, whereby sexual harassment is produced due to alienation, and men's sexuality is valorised over women's owing to their superior position in the labour market, a male-dominated heterosexuality is simply assumed. As Adkins asks, 'Why should capitalist hierarchies call into being a sexuality in which women are sexually exploited by men?' (Adkins 1995:47). Adkins argues that this model completely obscures the ways men control women through sexuality: it takes men's ability and desire to sexually harass women to be simply a characteristic of men's sexuality, and also takes a limited account of the ways patriarchal agents actively produce and maintain gendered divisions of labour within organisations.

A second explanation looks more specifically at organisational structures and hierarchies, rather than the prevailing economic system. Both authority and power are articulated through organisational hierarchies, and these hierarchical structures in turn construct hierarchical interpersonal relations between people – including sexual relations (Adkins 1992). Because men dominate the upper echelons of organisational structures, qualities associated with masculinity become prioritised and more highly valued: both through work and through other contexts, public as well as private, such as sexuality. Qualities such as control, activity, physical power and emotional distance thus come to define a whole range of behaviours, from management to sex. Sexuality is used as a way of reinforcing the status and position of the dominant people in the hierarchy. This may be done through sexual harassment: individuals may use their power and position to extort sexual gratification from their subordinates (Tangri *et al.* 1982). Although typically men harass women, in principle it is possible for women to sexually harass men: it is only less likely because women tend to be employed in occupations subordinate to men. However the economic vulnerability of this structural position means that women often lack the security necessary to resist sexual harassment, and may therefore play out the subordinate sexual role.

In this conceptualisation, organisations are placed in a central onto-logical position, from which other behaviours are 'read off'. However, the relationship between masculinity, femininity and sexuality is a secondary factor which is seen to come from organisational structures rather than lead into them. This approach has been criticised therefore for failing to identify adequately the gendered nature of both organisational and social sexual behaviour. That it is men that harass, and women that are harassed, may be not only to do with power but also to do with gender.

Thus a third approach, the radical feminist alternative, is to take a fundamentally gendered approach to explaining sexuality in organisations. That is, the wider reality of men's dominance over women must be recognised in any discussion of sexuality within organisations. Thus sexuality is viewed as one of the ways men control women in organisations, and reinforce their superior position not only within organisational hierarchies (Adkins 1992, 1995, Farley 1978, MacKinnon 1979, Stanko 1988) but also generally, as men. Thus, importantly, sexual relations at work, and in particular sexual harassment, are seen to be the metaphor for gender relations and sexuality in the wider society (Stanko 1986). 'Issues of maleness, femaleness, sexual power, economic power and social control coalesce within often mundane, seemingly ordinary work situations' (Stanko 1988:91).

In the radical approach to organisational sexuality, the predominant focus is on sexual harassment. This is yet another location where women are subjected to abuse by men, simply because they are women (Stanko 1988). In this way, sexuality and sexual work relations are seen to be central to both the gendered organisation of work and the forms of control and exploitation to which women workers are subject (Adkins

1995). In other words, rather than viewing sexuality as something which comes out of organisations or is 'read off' from them, it is seen to be one of the key ways men in organisations exploit women in the labour market and shore up their economic advantages. That is, sexuality, by being one of the criteria on which women are appointed (for instance as secretaries, receptionists and bar staff) *contributes to* organisational and labour market structures, rather than resulting from them.

In this approach, men and women are thus regarded as being fundamentally different. It is not the possession of structural power which leads people to exploit each other sexually; rather, it is a gender thing: something that men do by virtue of being men. As noted in other chapters, this approach has been criticised for being essentialist and universalistic. Not only are men seen to be ubiquitously heterosexual, but heteosexuality itself is seen to be ubiquitously male-dominated. Men are viewed as being constantly on the aggressive, harassing women whenever the circumstances permit them to do so. This is a view of heterosexuality which has been challenged by some heterosexual women wishing to accommodate their feminism with their heterosexuality (see, for example, the diverse collection of voices in Wilkinson and Kitzinger 1993). These readings point to the ways in which some heterosexual relationships can be seen to be based on equal terms, and terms which are pleasurable for women. Further, the view that women are victims in these large, unwieldy structures of male power has also been challenged. Although men quite clearly occupy superior positions in both social and organisational structures, writers who take a more poststructuralist approach to understanding power articulate ways women may resist and confront this male dominance (Pringle 1989).

Poststructuralist approaches

These focus on the ways sexuality, and its relationship with men, women, masculinity and femininity, are discursively produced within organisations. It stresses how the cultural and symbolic construction of men and women at work, and the ways in which specific occupations are represented and understood within organisations, frame identities, working conditions and power relations. For instance, if secretaries tend to be constructed and understood according to a limited paradigm of performances, such as 'mother/wife', 'sexy' or 'career woman', and, similarly, bosses to be either the 'master/husband', 'naughty boy' or 'superior colleague', then the women and men in these positions will also understand themselves as subjects along the continuum of these representations. Further, relationships will be played out according to these performances (Pringle 1989). Discourses thus have a relationship with structure, for representations and stereotypes structure relationships and define behaviour between managers and staff, men and women. However, the fact that power is seen to be mobilised through an abstract form, language, and not a material form, structure, means that there is potential for contestation and change.

For Pringle (1989), sexuality is central to these discourses, a primary means by which power is made more fluid. While her work focuses particularly on secretaries, she does see that these discourses have more general relevance to all women working within bureaucratic organisations. The stereotypical roles described above all have a sexual and/or familial connotation, and Pringle's case is that women at work are constructed in almost exclusively sexual terms. This means that sexuality is one of the key ways women are represented and understood within organisations, which, while making it difficult for them to divorce themselves from this aspect of their identities, does not make it impossible. As noted above, discourses do allow for variation and play, so that certain women may be able to construct more powerful identities for themselves within the specifics of their situation.

Although the discursive model breaks away from the ways gender and power are usually understood in feminist accounts of organisation, it has been criticised as sharing some of the same assumptions of these other models of explanation. For instance, Adkins (1995) claims that the issue of the relationship between the sexualised workplace identities accounted for in this model and the processes of formation of men's economic and other advantages in the labour market remain unclear. That is, for Adkins (1995), the ways in which symbolic and discursive processes actually gender the organisation of work are not made explicit. Thus although, for example, Pringle provides a lot of evidence of the ways male bosses appropriate women secretaries' labour, which include a tremendous amount of unpaid tasks such as entertaining, shopping and even laundry, she does not sufficiently explain how the symbolic positioning of bosses provide the conditions through which these various forms of work can be extorted from secretaries. Second, this model, by being relativist, has been criticised for not adequately tackling the ways in which men are more able to abuse their power and exploit women through their sexuality. Although women can be seen to gain some power through their sexuality, this is certainly not a means which is available to all women, either through choice (for lesbian women) or by default from the ways in which 'attractivenes' and sexiness are culturally bound to youth, physical ability and, to a certain extent, whiteness, in western society.

In this chapter we have demonstrated the multiple ways in which sexuality intersects with organisational life. We have shown that sexuality is a major tool through which the relationship between gender and power is constructed and reconstructed – chiefly, through reasserting the dominance of men and masculinity. By sexualising women and/ or subjugating them sexually, the hegemony of men's location in the upper sections of organisational hierarchies remains largely unquestioned, and the type of work carried out by organisational members becomes even more gendered. However, this is not to say that all women take this state of affairs lying down! The power of women's talk, humour and gossip, as well as their ability to play out different identities, may enable them to offer some resistance to this sexualised inscription.

Should organisations strive to rid themselves of sexuality, therefore? While this has been a plank of some feminist arguments about suitable responses to the prevalence of sexual harassment at work, it is difficult to see how such a 'disinfecting' might be achieved. Even if agreement could be reached about the boundaries of what was 'sexual' – and this is hard to conceptualise – we can be certain that many would oppose such a change and transgressions would be virtually impossible to police. An alternative scenario for change might be that organisations 'open up' and accept, even embrace, the sexual as part of organisational life (Pringle 1989, Cockburn 1991). Making visible the fact that organisations have long been implicitly dominated by male sexuality, may serve to problematise and undermine it, and enable a greater range of sexualities to flourish. If sexuality was made more explicit in organisational life, both women and men might be enabled to be more open about their sexuality without fear of punishment through marginalisation, discrimination, patronisation or even attack. Lesbian women, gay men and bisexual men and women would be able to come 'out' without fear of the consequences, while both women and men might be able to express a broader range of sexual identities, feelings and activities. However, the complex relationship of sexuality with the more private areas of life, makes this a difficult issue for organisational policy and practice, and a difficult arena for achieving any consensus, both within gender debates and outside them.

6

Challenging Gendered Organisation

Introduction

This book has elaborated the complex ways in which gender is enacted, sustained and generated across the structures and practices of organisational life. We have seen a mass of apparently contradictory evidence. On the one hand there are many instances where women are subjected to forms of dominance and control which seem to sustain male authority and privilege. On the other hand, we have seen repeated evidence of women acting as agents, rather than subjects, of power. In this chapter, we concentrate on the latter. We document the range of ways women have attempted to resist male power and masculine privilege inside work organisations. Such resistance is precisely about women exerting power. Some men too have been involved in challenging existing configurations of gender in work organisations. This represents a challenge to the hegemonic construction of organisational masculinity, demonstrating nicely that constructions and practices of gender within organisational life do not conform neatly to a binary division between women, on the one hand, and men, on the other.

However, in focusing on these challenges we show that their outcomes have been mixed. Simply making a challenge is not, of course, enough to bring about change. The unfolding stories of such challenges suggest a diverse range of conclusions about the nature of gendered power inside work organisations. While there are significant 'successes' – where challenges have achieved change – there are also stories which substantiate a more structural view of gendered power within organisations – where women's (or men's) challenges are met with resistance and effectively diffused altogether, apparently maintaining the original status quo. These mixed outcomes highlight the multiple forms of power operating inside contemporary work organisations. We can see the coexistence of masculine dominance with feminine resistance, of structural power relations with agentic exercises of power, and of organisational stability with organisational change. We return to these points later.

This chapter begins by categorising several forms of challenge to gendered organisation. We suggest four principal categories: individual resistances, collective actions, legislative challenges and voluntary initiatives undertaken by particular organisations. Examples of each type of challenge are given and, in each case, we present evidence on the extent and impact of these. Evaluating these challenges to organisational form and practice sharpens the political and theoretical question: what are we aiming for? What would a 'finished' gender-equal organisation look like? In practice, several different 'models' of change underlie the challenges described in the next section, and these are outlined in the section after that. As we show, each model depends not only on distinct understandings of 'gender' and 'organisation' but, critically, on a quite different interpretation of 'power'. In our conclusion we will suggest that it would be a mistake to see one of these models as accurate above the others. To do so would be to deny the multiple exercises of power inside work organisations and the ways in which these interact on a daily basis, as well as over longer periods of time.

Challenges

Individual Challenges

The literature which addresses challenges to gendered organisation does not, generally, take into account instances of resistance made by individual women (or men) during the routines of their daily working life. It is, rather, the more formal and collective forms of resistance which are the focus of attention (see pp. 184–203 below). However, if we look at empirical studies of gender and organisation (for example Hochschild 1983; Pringle 1989) we find that this research is littered with examples of everyday, individual resistances. In each case, we see evidence of individuals exerting agentic power, offering resistance to more pervasive and widespread forms of gender dominance in work organisations. We have divided these individual resistances into four subsections.

First, individuals may seek to limit the extent of organisational control over their life. We know that expectations of staff may extend way beyond contracted working hours and/or the confines of the organisation and that organisational norms and expectations about social life and domestic circumstances operate through gendered dynamics (see Chapters 3 and 4). Both women and men may resist these expectations by defending the home–work boundary against encroachment from organisational demands – for instance, by sticking firmly to office hours, refusing to be contacted at home or limiting overtime (Pringle 1989, Halford *et al.* 1997). Insistence on the compartmentalisation of home and work draws on strictly bureaucratic interpretations of organisational life, within which the public and the private are supposed to have clear boundaries. However artificial this may be, if separation is idealised as the norm then insisting on it in practice may be an effective strategy.

Workers may also restrict public knowledge of their lives outside work to prevent being subjected to discriminatory judgements. This represents an attempt to close down one mechanism of organisational power: absenting oneself from evaluation in the context of dominant organisational norms. This is commonly used by lesbian women (Hall 1988, Valentine 1993) and by gay men, and may be used by women getting married or becoming pregnant as well as those with families (Leonard and Malina 1994). Heterosexual men, leading conventional social and domestic lives, have nothing to conceal since these patterns are widely endorsed as evidence of stability and suitability (Collinson *et al.* 1990). Compartmentalisation may also close down avenues of extra-exploitation. Pringle (1989) found bosses demanding extra 'favours' (overtime, shopping, even washing) from their secretaries *as friends*, and using friendship to manipulate staff ('I know your husband, he won't mind you coming in on a Saturday for a few hours'). More directly, employees also challenge 'personal' requirements in the workplace. Air stewardesses' resistance to expectations about their appearance (weight, hairstyle, and so on) was so widespread that Hochschild concluded '[f]or a decade now, flight attendants have quietly lodged a counterclaim to control their own bodily appearance' (1983:126). Although male stewards objected to a beard ban, most resistance was practised by women, subjected to far more stringent controls. The ultimate sanction is for individuals to refuse to participate in the organisation at all, that is, to leave work permanently

(Marshall 1995)! Collinson *et al.* (1990) claim that this was common among women in the insurance industry. Certainly there is evidence that women are leaving managerial jobs far faster than men (McDowell and Court 1994), prompting widespread suggestions that this indicates gender-specific dissatisfaction with large corporations.

Second, individuals may resist by deliberately failing to fulfil objectionable job requirements. This is a subtle calculation. Resistance must be noted but not constitute grounds for dismissal. It is a question of gauging how much power one can exert within the broader confines of organisational power relations, without being subject to the ultimate expression of organisational power – that is, being sacked. This was widely practiced by secretaries in Pringle's study. She cites the following as a classic example:

Q: Did you refuse to make him cups of tea?

A: No, I didn't. But he didn't like the way I made it! I used to load up the sugar or take out the sugar accordingly when I was really mad with him ... I used to rebel a little bit ... because he was so rude (1988:165–6)

Hochschild (1983) gives us another example, where stewardesses resist employers' demands that they project a genuinely friendly and happy persona to passengers. While they must maintain some show of warmth this may be deliberately so superficial that the resistance beneath is intentionally exposed. Hochschild terms this 'going into robot' and summarises it thus: 'I'll pretend, but I won't try to hide the fact that I'm pretending' (1983:129). Since the airlines place great commercial value on stewardesses' personalities, this constitutes resistance which Hochschild refers to as the 'war of smiles' (p. 127). Even minute facial adjustments by the stewardesses can dim the company's message. Both Pringle and Hochschild suggest that this form of resistance may be more effective than outright challenges, since the degree of subtlety makes it difficult to counteract.

Third, individuals may manipulate personal identities as a form of resistance. This is not a case of making oneself unavailable for evaluation by organisational norms (as described above) but a deliberate representation of oneself exploiting the images and identities privileged within organisational culture. This involves playing the organisational game, on its own terms, but within this seeking to find new sources of personal power. For example, some women may portray exaggerated supposedly masculine traits (competitiveness or aggression) in an effort to convince employers that they are as capable as (stereotypical) men. Alternatively, some women may deliberately deploy aspects of gender or sexual difference as a means of gaining status and control. One response that air stewardesses made to their powerlessness was to deliberately exploit stereotypical feminine identities – the sexually desirable mate and the supportive mother – to try and win regard from others and to gain their compliance (Hochschild 1983; see also McDowell and Court 1994 on merchant banking). There is evidence that black staff, and black women in particular, may have to make particular, efforts in this regard. Davis and Watson (1982), for example, suggest that '[i]n order to fit in, one has to assume a new identity, negotiate a truce between the old one and the required self' (p.10). (See Chapter 3 on organisational cultures for more examples.) On a more positive note, Hill-Collins (1990) suggests that stereotypical roles such as mother and/or community leader may be consciously deployed by black women in order to make alliances with each other across organisations.

Hill-Collins also suggests that a key form of individual resistance involves making a conscious distinction between a 'work' identity and a 'real' identity. For black women in particular, Hill-Collins emphasises the importance of refusing externally imposed identities and maintaining a sense of self which transcends these:

> While they pretend to be mules and mammies and thus appear to conform to institutional rules, they resist by creating their own self definitions and self valuations in the safe spaces they create among one another. (1990:142)

Similarly, Hochschild's stewardesses viewed the distinction between a 'real' self and an 'acting' self as 'a way to avoid stress, a wise realisation, a saving grace' (Hochschild 1983:183).

The fourth and final type of individual resistance involves deliberate exposure of organisational inequalities. Gender inequalities inside modern bureaucratic organisations do not only, or even commonly, rest on overt forms of discrimination and oppression. While organisational forms and practices certainly contribute to gender differences and inequalities, at the same time many of these norms and expectations are widely accepted as gender-neutral, fair and reasonable (see Chapter 2). In this context, organisational power is understood rather as 'authority' – distributed according to technical and rational criteria – counterposed to 'power' which is unruly and unfair, distributed through prejudice and coercion. Exposing the power relations inside the rational shell of 'authority' can also serve as an effective lever for change. Naming the dynamics of oppression can constitute a powerful form of resistance. Hochschild gives the example of a stewardess challenged by a male passenger for not smiling. She replied: 'I'll tell you what. You smile first, then I'll smile'. The businessman complied and then was told 'Good. Now freeze, and hold that for fifteen hours.' Then she walked away'. (1983: 127). Hochschild concludes:

> In one stroke, the heroine not only asserted a personal right to her facial expressions but also reversed the roles in the company script by placing the mask on a member of the audience. She challenged the company's right to imply... that passengers have a right to her smile. (1983:127–8)

Each of these individual resistances has limits. Limiting the scope of organisational control by restricting hours may well be interpreted as lack of commitment (Young and Spencer 1990, McDowell and Court 1994). This may be particularly severe for men who, unlike women, are often supposed to place work above all else. Furthermore, concealing domestic and/or social relationships may be insufficient in organisations where opportunities are restricted to those who can openly demonstrate the approved home and/or social life. The ultimate sanction of resignation may only reinforce prejudices about women's lack of resilience and unreliability (Collinson *et al.* 1990). Employers may fight other challenges more directly, with disciplinary action, legal action or dismissal. National Airlines in the USA fired a stewardess because she was deemed 'too fat' at four pounds overweight (Woolf 1990). The manipulation of identity may also have limits. Women who try to project masculine traits may not be viewed positively. As well as being criticised for being unfeminine, they may find that whereas aggression or competitive behaviour in a man is interpreted as a good thing, in women it is seen as a liability. Furthermore, many women simply do not want to abandon femininity in favour of some stereotypical notion of masculinity (Pringle 1989). However, using exaggerated feminine identities may also be problematic. Hochschild (1983) argues that the stereotypical roles through which air stewardesses attempt to secure (some) control for themselves are *already* appropriated by the airlines as ideal stewardess characteristics, thus emptied of any subversive potential. Finally, doubts have been expressed about the psychological consequences of fragmenting the self, for this means relinquishing a 'healthy sense of wholeness' (Hochschild 1983: 184), damaging to the individual concerned. Of course, this assessment depends on a particular, normative view of 'identity' as whole and coherent. Alternative understandings of identity suggest that identity is, in any case, always fragmented composed of conflicting elements. This latter interpretation would suggest less cause for worry about the air stewardess's strategy.

These resistances demonstrate some of the ways power is embedded in routine, daily organisational practices, and how women (and some men) appropriate this power for their own ends. Clearly, women are not simply passive victims of organisational power relations: creative and determined individual resistances take place every day. This high-lights the diffuse nature of organisational power. Because of the indi-vidualised, and unsystematic, documentation of these resistances it is impossible to know their extent and difficult to assess their effective-ness. We may never know if individual resistances resulted in perman-ent change. Even if one individual's challenge does result in change, it may never be recognised or documented as such. Furthermore, as we have seen, instances of individual resistance may well meet resistance themselves, taking place, as they do, within a broader context of masculine power and privilege. The key points, however, are that organisational power relations are not set in stone, or inevitable, and many (if not all) individuals may – at times – mobilise power within work organisations in order to express their own interests.

Collective challenges

Individual resistances to gendered aspects of organisational life may, on occasion, inspire others to engage in collective challenges. Pringle (1989) cites a list of possible triggers: A boss may prevent a secretary ringing home after school to see if her child is alright . . . Dress rules are enforced . . . A particularly nasty piece of harassment is exposed. Some-one is sacked unfairly' (p. 266). In such instances, lightning strikes, go-slows or other organised protests can be highly effective (see also Hochschild 1983, p. 126) but their impact is usually confined to the trigger issue and dissipates quickly. However, collective resistance also involves longer-term campaigns about specific aspects of organisa-tional life, for instance around equal pay. (In the UK, see for example Beale 1982 and Boston 1987 for details of the celebrated equal pay campaign waged by women sewing machinists at Ford's in the UK during the late 1960s.)

Workplace trade unions may also offer women opportunities for collective challenge to gendered organisation. Trade unions have substantial resources, including money and full-time officials, and have access to employers via formal negotiating mechanisms. In this way, trade unions have a recognised place within the formal organisational hierarchy. They have a right to exert power: institutional power is formally accorded to the unions. Unions are understood – defined even – in terms of challenging established organisational practices, especially managerial preferences, and have large memberships which might be mobilised in support of their claims. All these resources constitute considerable *potential* to challenge gendered organisations.

However, feminist research on women and trade unions reveals mixed views. On the one hand, there are those who claim that 'a woman's place is in her union' (Beale 1982, Barrett 1980, Rowbotham 1989). This position stems both from a belief in the utility of union resources to women's campaigns for change and from fundamental concerns with the need to address class-based inequalities as well as gender inequalities. The origin and rationale of trade unions as representatives of the working class makes them obvious vehicles for such change. On the other hand, it has been argued that trade unions' potential has been appropriated by *male* working-class interests, that trade unions have been a vehicle for organised male power, that they have shown little interest in representing women workers, and are themselves implicated in the construction of gender inequalities (Walby 1986, Rowbotham 1989). In what follows, we briefly summarise these competing accounts of the relationship between trade union power and gendered power relations in work organisations. We concentrate on examples from British history, although many of the same general points are made in feminist debates in the US (Cobble 1990, Gabin 1989) and elsewhere (see, for example, Cockburn 1996 on European trade unions.)

In the past many trade unions excluded women from membership. They argued that women entering the labour market would increase the supply of labour and therefore reduce wages; that women might steal men's jobs because they were cheaper than men; that women should either be excluded from the workforce, or paid less than men, because they were not family breadwinners; and finally, simply that women's proper place was in the home (Walby 1986, Grint 1991). Many trade unions actively supported the Factory Acts (1844–1901) which 'protected' women by barring them from certain jobs (Walby 1986) and supported the 'family wage' principle (whereby male workers were paid enough to support their wives and families independently).

Although male unions began admitting women from the late nineteenth century onwards (Walby 1986), by 1874 an independent Women's Trade Union League had already been established. In 1901 there were 90 associated women's societies and by 1918 the National Federation of Women Workers had 80 000 members (Coote and Pattullo 1990). When the male unions offered mergers most women's unions accepted, but this did not mark the end of women's marginalisation within unionism. First, women lost their leadership positions and control of resources (Walby 1986). Second, most unions remained committed to maintaining 'men's jobs' and 'women's jobs', again arguing that allowing women into men's jobs would undermine wages. The mobilisation of women during the First and Second World Wars only took place on the basis of a strict agreement between unions and governments that it would be temporary (Grint 1991, Walby 1986). Third, the merged unions did nothing to encourage women's activism, which continued to lag behind men's (MORI 1985). Because of domestic commitments many could not spare the time and there were widespread complaints about meeting times and places (often evenings in a pub) as well as the pervasive sexism and 'macho' culture of union life (Cockburn 1987, Ledwith *et al.* 1990). Fourth, the unions continued to address the same old issues (pay, overtime rates, and so on) paying scant attention to issues of particular interest to women (occupational segregation, *equal* pay, maternity rights, part-time work, and so on) (Boston 1987). Although the TUC had been committed to equal pay since 1888, little substantive action had been taken and by 1966 it was still describing the prospect as a 'distant' one (Beale 1982).

Since the 1970s this pattern has begun to change. Rapid expansion of women's labour market participation in the context of severe decline in the traditional base of union membership (skilled male manual work) has meant that unions had to encourage the unionisation of 'non-traditional' workers including semi-and unskilled women workers in the service sector and part-time workers (90 per cent of whom are women) in order to 'stem the haemorrhaging of members' (Grint 1991:230). Women unionists were also increasingly demanding access to, and changes in, union practice and policy (Boston 1987), while, more generally, the political climate made it less acceptable to claim that women should be at home, or were worth less than men (Walby 1986).

Over the past two decades unions have taken action in two main ways. First, explicit efforts have been made to 'empower' women members. This has included efforts at grass-roots level to give women the power to articulate their views as well as efforts to give women greater access to officially sanctioned union power by enabling more of them to move into hierarchical positions of power within the union. Varying greatly between different unions (Boston 1987), this has involved: training women members, for example in meeting skills; changing the times of meetings; altering the style and culture of meetings; reserving seats for women, for example on national executive bodies; and even proportional representation of women and men in official posts (Coote and Pattullo 1990, Cockburn 1991, Cunnison and Stageman 1993). These efforts to challenge the gendering of trade union organisation have improved levels of unionisation amongst women. By the end of 1997, women accounted for 39 per cent of the membership of major British trade unions, following a steady rise in female membership in the context of a continuous, and steeper, fall in the numbers of male union members (EOR, 83, 1999). The number of women in official posts has also risen, although rarely to levels which reflect the proportion of women members.

Second, emerging from these (limited) successes in improving women's representation and activism some new policy priorities have been established challenging aspects of gendered organisation and – again to varying degrees – these have been pursued through employer–union negotiations. Here the unions are involved in challenging forms of male power embedded in organisational practice. Tackling women's low pay has been a particular priority. As well as actively supporting claims for equal pay some unions have negotiated job re-evaluation or harmonisation schemes with employers. Job reevaluation involves recognising that some jobs may be low-graded simply because they are done by women, rather than because they involve less skill, experience or responsibility. Reevaluation schemes construct new, (supposedly) gender-neutral criteria for evaluating job grading and commonly result in the upgrading of women's jobs. (However, see Acker's (1992) critique of job evaluation schemes in Chapter 2.) Harmonisation means bringing manual workers terms and conditions in line with the typically far better terms and conditions enjoyed by white-collar workers (longer holidays, shorter working week, flexitime, and so on), benefiting both male and female workers. Other new priorities have included the negotiation of improvements to employment terms and conditions such as maternity pay, paternity leave, and time off for sick dependants – all efforts to renegotiate organisational expectations about the accommodation between home life and work life for both sexes. Unions have also adopted policies to try and improve part-time workers conditions and have tackled the use of sexist language and images, while many have made policy statements about sexual harassment in the workplace (Boston 1987).

However, despite active support from some male unionists (see Rowbotham 1989, Cockburn 1991 for examples), it appears that many of the new policies have met with only limited success. Although special seats may be reserved for women in the union hierarchy, there are still remarkably few women trade union leaders or even women delegates to the Trades Union Congress (a collective national organisation for trade unions) Prejudicial attitudes to women remain entrenched in many local branches, and as Grint (1991) concludes, 'if men think [regardless of the evidence] that women make poor union members they will do little to recruit or retain them' (p. 231). Here we see the power vested in sexist images of women and in masculinised conceptions of the 'good' union member. If a 'good' union member is, essentially, masculine, it is hardly surprising that women may be seen as not good enough. Less subtly, it seems that cliques of powerful men inside unions have resisted efforts to challenge *their* power and women who do break into positions of power are often treated appallingly both by lay members and their peers. For instance, Heery and Kelly (1989) found that 85 per cent of women trade union officers had experienced sexual harassment from lay members and/or from male union officials. Such treatment serves to effectively disempower the female trade union leader, even if she stays in post, as (for instance) her contribution is marginalised or even ignored. As far as addressing 'women's issues' is concerned, while national policy statements may be progressive and far-reaching, at a local level some male unionists have opposed or even boycotted equality initiatives (Stone 1988), resenting what they see as 'political correctness' or simply 'going too far' (Cockburn 1991). Here we see how national policy statements of intent may be divested of any power, if rank-and-file refuse to implement them, leaving nothing but empty rhetoric.

In sum, the British evidence suggests that hostility to women's trade union activism is endemic. Encouraging women to take up more powerful positions in union hierarchies and changing policy priorities within unions both displace the power of particular men and challenge the power embedded in particular endorsements of masculinity. It is perhaps then not surprising that there has been resistance to change. However, it would be a mistake to conclude that nothing has changed, that women have been entirely unsuccessful in challenging the male dominance of trade unions. Female membership of British trade unions continues to rise, new policies are in place and many are implemented, there is at least a formal level of support for equality and the political discourse of trade unions has been transformed over recent decades. While these developments do not guarantee a total transformation of the unions or of organisational practice, they do illustrate the effective power of women's challenges and the real changes which can take place.

Legislative challenges

The third form of challenge to gendered organisation has involved appeal to the law to uphold equality between women and men at work. This strategy has not met with unequivocal support from feminist theorists or campaigners, who have long been stuck with an ambivalent view of the law, and of the state more generally. On the one hand, feminists have been highly critical of the role which state institutions (the government, the law, education, the police, and so forth) have played in the construction and maintenance of gender differences and inequalities. On the other hand, many feminist demands are directed towards the state, for example provision of childcare, contraception, or action on domestic violence. Either way, the state is understood to occupy a position of power, either as an oppressor of women or as a (potential) liberator. The tension between these two positions has been played out in responses to 'equality' legislation.

Since the 1960s equality legislation has been introduced by most western governments, making it illegal to discriminate against women in employment or pay In the US the Equal Pay Act 1963 was swiftly followed by requirements that all companies working for the federal (central) government should implement 'affirmative action' programmes. This goes beyond requiring simply that employers do not discriminate, placing the onus on companies to make more proactive interventions towards equality. This may include, for instance, practicing positive discrimination: if there are several equally well-qualified candidates then US companies may, quite legitimately, choose to appoint a black or ethnic minority candidate over a white candidate.

Equality legislation was introduced almost a decade later in Britain, and still does not make such general provision for positive discrimination (see below). In the 1970s the Labour government introduced two major pieces of legislation aimed at women workers: the Equal Pay Act

1970 and the Sex Discrimination Act 1975. The Equal Pay Act (EPA) makes it unlawful to discriminate between men and women with regard to pay and other contractual terms and conditions (for example, holiday pay, sick leave or redundancy). To be covered by this legislation women had to be engaged in identical, or broadly similar work, to men or prove, through a job evaluation study, that their work was of equivalent value to that done by men. There was no obligation for an employer to carry out such an evaluation study. Under the EPA the onus was on individuals to take action and there were no provisions for 'class actions', as there are in the US, whereby groups of women across employers could take collective action (Coyle and Skinner 1988).

The Sex Discrimination Act (SDA) applies to training, education, the provision of services and the disposal and management of premises (renting or selling housing or other property) as well as to employment. The act makes it unlawful to practice either direct discrimination or indirect discrimination against either sex or against people on the grounds of marital status. Direct discrimination refers to instances where a woman (or man) is treated differently simply by virtue of sex. Indirect discrimination refers to instances where no explicit mention is made of sex, yet where factors are brought into play which affect men and women differently. For instance, were a job advertisement for a clerical assistant to state that all applicants should all be six feet tall, this would constitute indirect discrimination because more men than women would be able to meet the requirement and there is no justifiable reason for specifying this criterion (Straw 1989). The SDA allows sex-specific recruitment to only if sex can be established as a 'genuine occupational qualification' for that job. This is the only instance of discrimination still allowed by law; any other 'positive' discrimination for either sex remains illegal in Britain. Examples include female social workers to work with women who have been beaten by their husbands or where the job holder has to be a man because of pre-existing legislation preventing women from certain work (for example, health and safety, overtime, night shift legislation). The latter example is important because it illustrates the premise that, at the time it was introduced, the SDA did not take primacy over pre-dated legislation. Rather, the earlier legislation was taken as binding. (This was changed in 1989 – see Figure 6.2 below). The Sex Discrimination Act 1975 also established the Equal Opportunities Commission (EOC). As well as producing research publications and campaigning for change, the EOC has the specific power to issue notices against employers (and others) found to be discriminating against women (or men) requiring them to desist and to take legal proceedings employers fail to respond. The EOC also acts to advise members of the public and can take legal action on their behalf.

It is widely believed that this legislative 'equality package' marked a milestone in the history of efforts to challenge workplace gender inequalities. Symbolically, the government had legitimated women's claims for equal treatment. This alone can be interpreted as a significant exercise of power, redefining dominant and socially acceptable meanings and identifying the state as a guarantor of women's equality. *Practically*, for the first time, there was a legal right to challenge inequality, offering women the power of legal compulsion if employers were found discriminating. However, there is a widespread consensus that the challenges apparently offered by the original legislation have, in practice, been severely limited, and this has prompted some to take a more cynical view of state action on equality.

Although estimates on the impact of the EPA vary, an optimistic calculation claims that women's earnings increased by 15 per cent relative to men's earnings as a direct consequence of the act (Zabalza and Tzannatos 1985). Others calculations are far lower (Gregory 1982, Atkins 1986, Marsh 1988). Whatever the precise figure, by 1997 – twenty-one years after the implementation of the EPA – the average hourly wage for full-time women workers was still only 80 per cent of the average wage for men whilst the hourly rates for part-time women workers were lower still (see Figure 6.1). Weekly earnings were lower, at 72.7 per cent of male earnings.

There are two broad explanations for this continued inequality. First, many employers took evasive action in the period between the passing of the act (1970) and its implementation (1975). Snell *et al.* (1981) found that over half the organisations they researched had taken deliberate action to reduce their obligations, for example by making sure that women and men were thoroughly segregated, or had different job titles or different job content, so that they could no longer be compared with one another. This would have been illegal after 1975. As it was, Snell *et al.* found few cases of outright non-compliance after the act came into force, although Glucklich (1984) claims that employer non-compliance persisted in 'borderline' cases which were less likely to go to, or win at, tribunal. Second (and as the employers above had recognised), the EPA failed to consider the fact that women and men *do not* typically do identical, or even broadly similar, work but are segregated into sex-stereotyped occupations. 'Women's jobs' have always been particularly badly paid, and there is evidence that this is less to do with the skill, experience or

Figure 6.1 Women's earnings as a percentage of men's

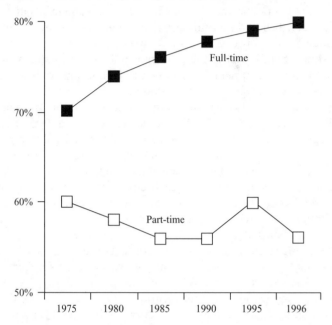

Source: Equal Opportunities Review (1997a). Reprinted with permission.

responsibility involved in those jobs and more to do with the fact that it is women in the posts. Yet, in practice, the EPA tackled only cases where women and men were being paid different rates for the same job and did not allow comparisons to be made across job categories or sectors of the economy. Even here, the onus was on individuals to pursue their claim through a costly, lengthy and rarely successful industrial tribunal process. Between 1976 and 1983, only 10 per cent of equal pay claims were upheld; for as many as 40 per cent of these, the increase in pay was less than £8 per week and claimants reported victimisation and harassment in their workplaces (Leonard 1987), despite the fact that the EPA and SDA were supposed to prevent this. These success rates have improved but, the vast majority of cases still do not result in a successful outcome.

Furthermore, the EPA did nothing to challenge the fact that few women reach senior positions in their organisations. (See Chapter 4 above.) 'Women's jobs' are often not linked into promotion hierarchies *et al.*, and even where women are in jobs on career ladders they are far less likely to be promoted than men (Halford *et al.* 1997). This is linked partly to childcare breaks, which give women less time in the labour market to build careers but also – as we have discussed throughout this book – to the gendered values and assumptions which underlie much organisational practice.

The SDA might have been expected to intervene here, but in practice it has also had a limited impact. Snell *et al.* (1981) found that the main action taken by employers involved superficial changes to wording of job advertisements (no longer specifying sexist preferences, except where the post was exempted from the act). Beyond this, employers did little to change organisational practice, claiming that they were already 'equal opportunities employers' (ibid.). Nonetheless, Snell *et al.* found examples of overt discrimination. Over half of the managers interviewed in over a quarter of the organisations studied admitted that they would continue to discriminate in the future. Despite this, not one of these cases had been pursued under the provisions of the SDA. Examples of illegal sex discrimination after the act are plentiful and successful tribunal cases remain unusual. In 1992–3 the average compensation for successful claims of sex discrimination was £1416 (EOR 1994a). Furthermore, even if the employer loses at tribunal, this may not be enough to enforce a change in practice (Chambers and Orton 1990).

In short, the initial effect of the acts was limited, largely because of the way they were (or were not) implemented and because the acts themselves failed to get to the root of organisational gender inequalities, were vague in their terms (Rubenstein 1999, and earlier editions documents over 300 court cases which have been necessary in order to clarify implementation), did not ensure effective grievance procedures and failed to recompense adequately. In 1980 the Equal Opportunities Commission announced that there would be no further progress unless the acts were amended (Glucklich 1984). Since then, some of the limitations of the EPA and the SDA have been addressed through legislative amendments and changes in guidelines (see Table 6.1).

Perhaps the most significant of these is the 1984 amendment to the EPA, which ends the requirement for women and men to be in broadly similar work in order for an equal pay claim to be made. Claims are no longer restricted to equal pay for equal work, but can be made on the basis of equal pay for work of equal value. An early case involved a female warehouse worker who claimed that the job was of equivalent value to that carried out by male warehouse checkers. This case could not have been made under the 1975 legislation, but in the light of EU law was upheld by the English law lords in 1988 (Grint 1991). By the end of 1995, 8,500 equal value applications had been made to industrial

Table 6.1   Key UK legislative interventions (including European Union legislation)

1957	Treaty of Rome: EC agreement binding member states to ensure that women and men receive equal pay for equal work.
1970	Equal Pay Act (UK): Makes it illegal to discriminate between women and men in terms of pay or contractual conditions where they are employed to do the same work (implemented 1975).
1973	Britain joins the EEC.
1975	Sex Discrimination Act (UK): Makes it illegal to practice direct or indirect discrimination between women (includes sexual harassment). Also established the Equal Opportunities Commission.
1976	Employment Protection Act (UK): introduces the statutory right to paid maternity leave.
1977	Extension of equality legislation to part-time workers.
1984	Equal Pay Act (Amendment) (introduced in the UK following EC intervention): allows comparisons to be made between jobs which may be considered of equal value although not broadly similar. If the comparison is judged valid the Equal Pay Act applies.
1986	Equal Pay Act (Amendment) (introduced in the UK following EC intervention): extends the Act to include collective agreements, small businesses and employment in private households.
1987	End to compulsory sex-specific retirement ages.
1989	Employment Act: repeals pre-existing 'protective' legislation applying to women's employment (with the exception of protection linked to pregnancy).
1993	Government budget: pensionable retirement age equalised at 65. Ceiling of £11 000 on sex discrimination compensation removed.
1994	Extension of employment rights to part-time workers in line with EC law. EC Pregnant Workers Directive: extension of UK maternity provisions in line with EC law.
1995	Reduction to minimum hours requirements for cases of unfair dismissal
1997	Protection from Harassment Act: makes harassment a criminal as well as civil offence. Intended to deal with stalkers, can also be used for sexual and racial harassment at work.
	Labour government signs European social chapter.
1999	Introduction of a national minimum wage.
	Employment Relations Act.

tribunals, involving approximately 640 employers. Of these, the tribunals had referred 180 cases (involving 1800 applicants) to independent experts. However, by 1996 only 27 cases had been upheld. The vast majority (108) had been withdrawn or settled 'privately'. Nonetheless, it is estimated that since the amendment employers have now paid out around £4.75m. in settlement of equal value cases. This figure looks set to rise following the success of the Enderby case (settled in 1997), in which a claim was made for equal value between speech therapists (predominantly female) and occupational psychologists and pharmacists (predominantly male). The Enderby case took 11 years to settle, and up to 1500 further claims are still outstanding. It is estimated that the eventual settlement in this case could cost as much as £30m. (EOR 1997b). In a similar vein, 1993 saw the abolition of the £11 000 ceiling on sex discrimination compensation, dramatically increasing the potential sanctions on employers who break the law. A woman army major was recently awarded almost £300 000 in a series of cases against the Ministry of Defence which totalled £60m. Other major changes up to 1996 included the extension of employment rights to part-time workers and the extension of maternity provision – these latter two changes both made to keep Britain in line with EU law.

The election of a Labour government in 1997 brought with it a number of further significant changes. We are yet to see the full implementation and/or impact of these changes, but the following seem particularly significant. First, the new government reversed the Conservatives opt-out of the Maastrict treaty, and signed Britain up to the European Union's social chapter. Amongst other things, this committed the government to the establishment of parental and family leave for employees. Second, a national minimum wage was introduced in 1999 and it is thought that this will affect as many as one in ten of all women workers (EOR 1998d). Third, the government's Employment Relations Act (1999) extends statutory maternity leave from 14 to 18 weeks and equalises the rights of part-time and full-time workers. The Act has also introduced the right to up to 3 months (unpaid) leave for both mothers and fathers to care for children in the first seven years of life. At present, this right only applies to those children born after the introduction of the Act.

Overall, it seems that the law has been most effective in imposing clear-cut and finite changes to terms and conditions but far less effective in encouraging employers to reconsider normative assumptions about career paths, promotion qualities or the expectations they have of their workers. There has been no compulsion for employers to do anything other than stick to the letter of the law and – until recently, at least – very few employers chose to go beyond this. We suggested at the beginning of this section that the power of the state to effect change lay both in the scope to instil new meanings and in the authority to enforce rules. While equalities legislation has placed women, work and organisation on the mainstream political agenda, new interpretations of why and how gender difference persists at work have been superficial, within restricted boundaries and ultimately limited. This is reflected in the rules which, even when they are enforced effectively, offer limited potential for change. Both, in turn, are linked to the dominance of liberal conceptions of gender and the state–where equality between citizens is thought to be secured through the banning or outlawing of discrimination, and without challenging more fundamental social structures or the discourses surrounding 'gender', 'organisation' and 'equality'. Certainly, state institutions have more potential power to achieve change than is expressed in these legislative developments. The fact that this hasn't been utilised could be interpreted as an expression of masculine dominance inside the state, and linked to the claim that, in a patriarchal society, the state will inevitably serve the long-term interests of men (for a review see Halford 1992). But this may be over-conspiratorial, rely too heavily on a functionalist view of the state (as a tool in the hands of men) and serve to deny those changes which have taken place.

Organisational challenges

The legislative interventions described above enshrine some basic rights for women workers, but organisations were only required to ensure that they did not break these laws and, as we have seen, this has had limited effect in challenging the gender inequalities embedded within work organisations. However, in Britain it was always hoped that legislation would prompt extended voluntary initiatives (Dickens 1989). Although such actions were rare at first, by the late 1970s a few British local authorities had begun to take some action. Initially, these were highly politicised interventions, originating with feminists organised within urban, left-wing Labour Parties, who successfully pressurised for the establishment of women's committees and equal opportunities committees (Halford 1989a). These committees commonly addressed a broad range of issues including those of interest to the local community (for example funding women's groups, campaigning on sex shops, establishing women's health programmes) as well as those of interest to women working for local authority organisations. Some extended the meaning of this beyond the local authority itself to include all organisations contracted by the authority, for example to supply goods or services. In these cases, the authorities insisted that any firm they contracted should comply with certain equal opportunities employment requirements. Since local authority contracts could be very lucrative indeed, many firms were keen to join in. This practice is known as contract compliance and, as we saw above is commonly accepted practice in the US (where it comes under affirmative action provision). In Britain, the practice was made illegal in 1988.) Most of these initiatives employed feminist women as bureaucrats, or 'femocrats', to devise and coordinate policy across the organisation. Throughout the 1980s the number of these initiatives expanded rapidly, beyond the pro-feminist urban left, and by 1988 as many as 69 per cent of all local authorities had made some policy commitment to equality for women workers, although many of these involved no specialist staff or budget (Halford 1989b). The early 1980s also saw the beginnings of organisational intervention in a few other British organisations (the BBC, the Inner London Education Authority, Littlewoods, Barclays Bank, London Weekend Television, Thames TV, Austin Rover (Straw 1989, Stamp and Robarts 1986)) but it was in the second half of the decade that such organisational interventions really began to take off. In 1989, a survey by the British Institute of Management revealed that as many as 30 per cent of employers had equal opportunities policies (Dickens 1989). In 1991, the British government-backed organisation Business in the Community launched the programme Opportunity 2000 to provide an organisational umbrella for employers wishing to pursue proactive equality interventions. Broad goals – principally relating to improving the *numbers* of women across organisational hierarchies – were encouraged by Opportunity 2000 and affiliated employers established their own commitments within these guidelines. The aim was to establish a bandwagon effect, whereby peer pressure would spread commitment across organisations. At its launch 61 employers affiliated (including giants like Sainsburys, the National Health Service, Grand Metropolitan and Kingfisher) and by 1998 there were 325 members, representing approximately a quarter of the national workforce. The original impetus for Opportunity 2000, as well as many individual organisational interventions, was commonly cited as fears about the falling numbers of school-leavers entering the labour market (the so-called 'demographic time bomb'), and the consequent need to make better use of women workers, although other significant factors included women workers' own campaigns for change, concern about organisational image and actual, or threatened, investigations by the EOC. High street banks had been particularly affected by EOC actions and all of the major British high street banks have joined Opportunity 2000, as well as taking earlier independent action (Scouller 1991).

The degree of organisational intervention has varied as have assessments of the extent of change. In what follows we will describe the

Table 6.2   Forms of organisational intervention

1. Improving women's access to jobs and enhancing women's careers
    -   reviewing and monitoring recruitment and selection procedures
    -   reviewing appraisal and promotion procedures
    -   women-only training
    -   job re-evaluation
    -   new career grades

2. 'Family-friendly' policies
    -   improved maternity leave
    -   paternity leave
    -   career break schemes
    -   childcare provision or support
    -   time off for sick dependents

3. Challenging sexism
    -   equal opportunities training
    -   awareness training
    -   sexual harassment grievance and complaints procedures

4. New forms of organisation
    -   alternative ways of working
    -   challenging/establishing informal networks

types of intervention which have been most common and then consider the issue of impact and effectiveness.

Organisational interventions fall into four categories (summarised in Table 6.2).

First, and most popularly, there have been interventions which aim to improve women's access to jobs and particularly to improve women's chances of building hierarchical careers. Such policies are partly premised on notions of 'fairness' and giving women and 'equal chance' to occupy positions of organisational power, both seen as ends goals in themselves. But there is also a hope that more women in structurally powerful positions will, as a consequence, transform organisational life. Kanter (1977) for instance, strongly advocates a 'critical mass' argument, claiming that once enough women are in managerial positions then the mechanisms which maintain masculine dominance (see Chapter 2) will cease to operate. In other words once women 'have' power, sex will cease to be a significant feature inside work organisations.

In order to achieve this, common policies include *new recruitment and selection procedures* designed to ensure that women know about jobs; that they feel encouraged to apply; that there are clear job descriptions and person specifications; that sexist questions (about menstrual cycles, pregnancy plans or childcare arrangements, for example) are not asked;

that all candidates are asked the same questions; and that all interviewers have undertaken sexism awareness training. Personnel departments may also monitor applications and appointments to see if there are systematic sexist biases in outcomes. *Training* has been another policy to enhance women's career opportunities, including women-only assertiveness training, support for vocational part-time study to improving chances of promotion or enable women to move into traditionally male occupations (especially skilled manual work). Finally, *job re-evaluation schemes* have been used to upgrade women's work, sometimes resulting in new promotion opportunities. Linked to this, some employers have also introduced new posts or new grades enabling workers previously segregated into an area of work with a short career ladder to link into other, longer career ladders. One way of measuring the success of these policies involves setting targets for increasing the numbers of women in non-traditional and senior positions and monitoring the gender composition of organisational workforces. Targets have been highly controversial, since many believe they entail appointing or promoting women even if they are *less* suited than men to particular posts. There is little research evidence of this. To the contrary, it seems to continue to be the case that women have to be *more* suitable than men in order to be appointed. Some organisations have been effective in reaching their targets although it should be pointed out that these targets, are sometimes set rather low.

The second category of interventions involve enhanced organisational support for workers' responsibilities outside the workplace, particularly around childcare, and are sometimes referred to as 'family friendly policies' (Rees 1992). Here, staff are no longer conceptualised in the abstract, as a set of skills or capacities (see Acker 1992), but acknowledged to be rooted in complex familial relations. On the basis of this, expectations of staff may be modified and there is a re-evaluation of the place of the organisation in accommodating the private with the public. These policies became more widespread towards the end of the 1980s but, perhaps because they are expensive for employers, they are less common than those initiatives described in the category above. In the UK, all women who have worked for an employer for six months or more by the end of the fifteenth week before their before their baby is due are legally entitled to *maternity leave* (with some pay), but extending this provision is a common policy (in 1993, 62 per cent of Opportunity 2000 employers had made some improvement). Some employers now allow women up to one year's maternity leave (mainly unpaid) with the right to return to the same

job after this time. Several days' *paternity leave* have also been introduced by some organisations, and this will shortly be made a legal right
in line with European Union legislation. *Career break schemes* extend
the amount of time workers may take off work for childcare, sometimes up to five years, but there are rarely guarantees that workers can
return to the same job which they held previously. In 1989, 10 per cent
of firms had established a career break scheme, principally for management staff (Rees 1992). Some organisations have also become involved
in the provision of childcare, whether directly (by setting up nurseries)
or indirectly (by providing childcare vouchers). Most direct provision
(up to 80 per cent) and indirect provision is by local authorities (Rees
1992, Income Data Services 1989) but surveys carried out in the late
1980s revealed that 2 per cent of employers provided childcare (Income
Data Services 1989) and 11 per cent of women managers had workplace crèche facilities (Aitkenhead and Liff 1991). The difference
between these two figures may suggest that there may have been
changes between 1989 and 1991; or that women managers are disproportionately concentrated in organisations where there is childcare
provision; or that women managers get better access to nursery provision, perhaps it is only they who can afford it; or simply that there were
differences in the sample of organisations taken by the two pieces of
research. *Job-sharing* may also benefit workers with domestic responsibilities. It is, of course, well known that many women work part-time
as a means of coping with other responsibilities, but also that part-time
work is mainly available in low-skill, low-paid jobs with few career
prospects. By splitting full-time jobs into a job-share between two or
more people, new types of work become available for those who wish
to work fewer hours. Local authorities and other parts of the public
sector have again been most active but overall, in 1989, only 7 per cent
of employers had job-share schemes (Income Data Services 1989).
Finally, a few employers allow *time off to care for sick dependants*.
However, for most the only option is to save annual holiday leave
for such emergencies. Of course, some of these 'family friendly' policies
apply to men as well as women and as such could be interpreted as an
effort to enable a renegotiation in the gendered division of labour.
However, take-up by men has been very limited, even in Scandinavian
countries where there is a legal right to parental leave.

   The third category of organisational intervention involves challenging sexism inside the organisation. This is about changing sexist
attitudes towards both female and male workers. *Equal-opportunities
training* is provided by some employers in a bid to challenge precon-

ceived assumptions about women, or men. In some organisations
this is voluntary, in others it is compulsory for all those involved
in interviewing job candidates and taking promotion decisions,
while in others still it is compulsory for all staff. The issue of sexual
harassment will frequently be one subject in this training. That is,
encouraging awareness of what constitutes harassment and how
to tackle it. Although sexual harassment is covered by the Sex
Discrimination Act, cases have proved difficult to pursue under
this legislation (Stockdale 1991), and a few organisations have
established special grievance and complaints procedures. (See also
Chapter 5.)

The fourth and final category of organisational challenges promises
more fundamental disruption to the gendering of organisation and to
gendered power relations within organisations. 'Changing the culture
of the organisation' entails questioning fundamental aspects of 'organisation', such as ways of working and how hierarchies are constructed,
and may include investigation of the ways gender is embedded in
everyday practice and in the cultural assumptions and expectations
beneath this. Here, 'culture' is understood as something which an
organisation 'has' (rather than 'is') and as something which can be
manipulated to desired ends. (See Chapter 3 on organisational cultures.) In some local authority initiatives officers pioneered collective
working, which some claim is more suited to women's ways of being
and more compatible with feminist politics (Ferguson 1984, Brown
1992). (See Chapter 2 for further discussion.) Other examples might
include: examination of the informal bars to women's success, for
example male networking, (lack of) role models and mentors (Rees
1992); re-evaluating expectations of systematic overtime (Kanter
1989); or reconsidering established norms for managerial posts, such
as geographical mobility (Collinson *et al* 1990). Such changes have
been more widespread than one might immediately imagine, although
not so much because of pressure to improve women's opportunities as
because of new models of organisation and management (which
emphasise, for example, the need for flexibility, innovation, flatter
structures and protecting workers from burnout) which have been
sweeping management textbooks and training programmes (see, for
example, Peters and Waterman 1982, Kanter 1983). Some have suggested that women will do especially well within these new paradigms
(Skinner 1988, Maddock 1993), although there also appear to be
grounds for caution (Jewson and Mason 1994, Halford and Savage
1995).

Clearly, then, there are some examples of imaginative new policies. Here, organisational challenges are not just a case of respecting the power of the law. Rather, there is an effort to go beyond these basic requirements, to recognise the pervasiveness of male privilege inside organisations, and to promote new meanings around gender, work and organisation. Independent voluntary initiatives slowed during the 1990s as local governments struggled to deal with reductions in funding and changes in the rules governing their practice, as the driving force of the left wing in Labour local government continued its demise and as economic recession and unemployment made the demographic time bomb seem less threatening. Furthermore, even where organisations continue to make policy commitments in the areas described above, we cannot be certain that those policies actually become practice. Although we may know what organisations *say* they do, it is far harder to know what actually happens in interview rooms, or whether sexist and/or racist assumptions continue as a concealed dimension of decision-making. There is certainly good evidence that many staff simply ignore the requirements placed on them by equal opportunities policies. This may be partly because compliance entails extra work or doing things in an unaccustomed way. It may also be that staff object morally or politically to equal opportunities policies. For instance, in a 1990s documentary on the introduction of women on board Royal Navy ships one officer claimed this to be a sign that Britain as a nation was a 'morally corrupt'. Less dramatically, but perhaps more significantly, research reveals that organisational equality policies may bestow a tokenistic status on women, and blacks, who are seen to benefit from them. A 'discounting process' seems to operate whereby women and blacks (and perhaps especially black women) in senior positions are seen to be no more than tokens of liberal commitment by the organisation, rather than good at their jobs (Heilman *et al.* 1992, Liff and Dale 1994, also Cockburn 1991). Linked to this, equal opportunities interventions may be seen to challenge the 'maleness' of organisational power, challenging assumptions about the right of men to manage and, as such, provoke counter-resistance designed to reinstate male privilege.

Nonetheless, once more, despite all these reservations, we should not deny the changes which have taken place. Of course, nothing is guaranteed and change may itself be met with resistance. However, there is also some evidence of success. For instance, in the UK, it is reported that Opportunity 2000 organisations now have significantly higher numbers of women in senior positions than is the national average

Table 6.3 Women in management roles – Opportunity 2000 organisations (1996)

	Opportunity 2000	*National Survey*
Corporate managers/administrators	33.0	29.6
Directors	11.2	3.3
Senior managers	17.5	6.5
Middle managers	30.6	12.2
Junior managers	41.2	14.4

Source: Adapted from Hammond (1997).

(see Figure 6.4) and that as many as 66 per cent of these organisations offer maternity leave and/or pay arrangements over and above the statutory minimum (Hammond 1997).

Summary

This section has shown just how widespread and varied challenges to gendered organisation have been. From individual resistances, to collective union activities, to new legislation and independent organisational initiatives, the gendering of organisation is clearly a dynamic and a contested matter. All the challenges represent efforts to deploy power in order to disrupt or even transform gendered processes embedded within organisational life. However, as we have seen, these challenges are constituted within existing frameworks of power and the outcomes can never be predictable. While there may be some significant changes, we have no examples of total transformation, of a 'finished' equal-gender organisation. So can the gendering of organisation ever be fully challenged, and what would this take? The answer to this depends on how we conceptualise our end goal. What would the ideal organisation look like? In the next section we review the range of answers which have been offered and consider the implications for understanding gender, power and organisation.

Approaches to equality and organisational change

The diversity of the challenges described above demonstrates that there is no single, coherent or cohesive form of resistance to organisational gender inequalities. Not only may challenges take place on an individual, collective, legislative or organisational basis, but embedded within these categories are several understandings of equality and how organisations might achieve equality. In this section we widen our focus from detailed consideration of particular challenges to examine these different analytical approaches more directly. Researchers involved in deconstructing the different models embedded within challenges to gendered organisation have commonly identified two broad approaches which are usually labelled the liberal approach and the radical approach (Jewson and Mason 1986, Forbes 1991, Meehan and Sevenhuijsen 1991, Aitkenhead and Liff 1991).

In an influential article Jewson and Mason (1986) lay out an ideal-type model which distinguishes 'liberal' conceptions of equal opportunity from 'radical' conceptions. (See Table 6.4).

The liberal approach to equal opportunities merges liberal understandings of gender, of organisation and of the way power relations operate inside organisations. While individual skills and abilities are understood to be *independent* of sex the problem is that some prejudiced individuals behave *as if* sex was an important factor. In order to combat this, the liberal perspective places emphasis on the establishment of formal procedures designed to ensure that all individuals are treated on grounds of their own merit, rather than unfounded assumptions about the qualities or responsibilities of one sex or the other. The main problem is thus conceptualised as the exercise of individual sexist prejudices which may prevent women, or indeed men, from entering an organisation, or being promoted. A prime example of interventions emerging from this perspective are the new recruitment and selection procedures described in the previous section) above. Here the main mechanism of change is formalisation with an underlying belief that the right rules and procedures can determine equal treatment (see also the discussion of Kanter in Chapter 2). Thus, the liberal approach aims to remove unfair barriers to free competition (Jewson and Mason 1994) between essentially like individuals in a fundamentally gender-neutral environment. Once satisfactory procedures are in place it is assumed that the outcomes of those procedures are fair (Aitkenhead and Liff 1991). Even if-sex biased patterns of recruitment and selection persist, this can no longer be explained by discrimination but is understood as the aggregate consequence of differences between particular individuals' with regard to skill, experience or abilities.

It is this liberal conceptualisation which most commonly underlies the challenges to gendered organisation which we have described in the

Table 6.4 Models of equal opportunity

	Conceptualisations of equal opportunity	
Elements of equal opportunity	*Liberal*	*Radical*
Principles	fair procedures	fair outcomes
Implementation	bureaucratisation	politicisation
Perceptions	justice seen to be done	consciousness raising

Source: Adapted from Jewson and Mason (1986).

previous section, particularly British legislative interventions. The model draws on socially acceptable analogies such as 'the level playing field' and encompasses a strong sense that men too should benefit from new policies. The model leaves Weberian notions of the bureaucratic organisation intact, albeit with some improvements which make it even *more* effectively rational. Here, the unsanctioned exercise of power to sustain sexist practices is seen as counter-productive to organisational efficiency and is challenged by the imposition of rules upheld by the rational-legal authority of bureaucracy.

The liberal model of equal opportunities has been criticised on several grounds. First, it is argued that the conceptualisation of discrimination is essentially individual – in terms of both discriminators and those discriminated against – trivialises, ignoring structural inequalities of power between social groups. Second, it has been pointed out that formal procedures themselves may continue to be biased, asking for qualifications or experience which are not really required or fixing the job specification to match an individual already in line for the job. Liberals may of course respond that this is just a failure of the procedures and can be dealt with by the introduction of new procedures. However, this reliance on formal procedures is judged by some to be naive. It is argued, that even where formal procedures are adhered to, judgements may still be made on sexist grounds (Jewson and Mason 1986, Cockburn 1991, Halford 1991, section 7.2iv)). Third, the liberal conceptualisation of power inside organisations may be seen as rather superficial. Here power is treated as if it only resides in organisational rules and procedures or, at least, it is assumed that unsanctioned episodes of power can be effectively dealt with by bureaucratic rules and procedures. The aim then is to ensure that there are adequate rules and procedures to deal with any such eventuality and that the rules and procedures themselves are disinfected of gender (and other) biases, rendering them nothing but the manifestation of technical, rational, bureaucratic authority. However, evidence suggests that even if prejudicial decisions are *not* made during formal interviews there may be other, more diffuse and pervasive ways in which organisational practices are based on gendered assumptions, values and attitudes. It is clearly not possible to bureaucratise everything which goes on inside organisations and individuals will always be able to exert some independent power. Fourth and last, there are more fundamental critiques still, which claim that 'equality' within the liberal perspective is itself a gendered concept – that is, that women are being allowed to compete with men on male terms, that 'equality' presupposes a norm 'which in practice tends to be defined as what is characteristic of the most powerful groups in society' (Meehan and Sevenhuijsen 1991: 3–4). This critique has parallels in feminist writing about other core political concepts such as 'citizenship' and 'justice', see for example Pateman 1988 and Phillips 1991.) If all that is happening is that some women are being offered the chance to mimic masculine patterns of work and career, the chances are that they will still be less successful than men (who fit established organisational norms more readily) and the fundamental structures of inequality remain in place (Forbes 1991).

In contrast to the liberal model outlined above, radical models place less faith in traditional bureaucratic procedures arguing instead that in order to achieve equality more fundamental transformations in organisational practice and models of organisation must take place. In this formulation, gendered power is more diffuse and more embedded across structures, cultures and individual identities than the liberal perspective acknowledges. Within this we can discern two related but distinct perspectives. First, the radical model outlined by Jewson and Mason (1986) focuses on outcomes rather than procedures and insists that if outcomes are unequal then this must mean that discrimination still persists:

> In this view since it is manifestly the case on a priori grounds that women and black people are the equals of men and whites the actual distribution of occupational rewards should be made to reflect this fact. (Jewson and Mason 1986: 315)

In this perspective fairness is identified with equality of *outcome*, and discrimination is identified as a collective or systematic feature of organisational life, rather than the prejudices of a few isolated individuals. Bureaucratic procedures are not assumed to bear legal-rational authority unless proven otherwise, and unequal outcomes are taken to mean that masculine (and white) power is still in place. Transforming inequalities within this perspective means laying aside established organisational norms and procedures and making political decisions with equality of outcome in mind (Jewson and Mason 1994). Although bureaucratic procedures may be used within this approach, as above, they are not thought to be sufficient. Instead, it is necessary to ensure that all organisational members, especially managers, recognise systematic discrimination throughout the organisation and ideally, practice positive discrimination in favour of the disadvantaged social groups. Positive discrimination is illegal in Britain (although it has been used in the United States), but some actions by British local authorities during the 1980s used loopholes in the law and their funding arrangements to promote policies based on radical principles (ibid.). Thus, despite recognition of deeply embedded gender inequalities, and gendered power, this perspective understands masculine power inside organisations to be contestable, if we are willing to focus on outcomes, and maintains a belief that bureaucratic organisations can be made 'fair'. Achieving this may take some radical interventions, which in and of themselves may not seem properly bureaucratic (for example, positive discrimination allows the rejection of standard technical criteria for appointments in pursuit of political goals) but the outcome, again, will be a more effectively functioning bureaucracy.

While the explanations and prescriptions for dealing with gender inequality differ markedly between the liberal and radical models described so far, they both entail a common underlying belief that women and men are 'equal' and that this equality rests on the underlying 'sameness' of women and men. The second radical model shares many of the critiques of liberal approaches we have outlined above, but is distinguished by a core belief in the essential differences between women and men. Here established organisational life is understood as a mirror of masculinity. Hierarchies, rationality, technocratic procedures, as well as organisational cultures are essentially masculine. Because bureaucratic organisations mirror masculinity they are seen, inevitably, to mobilise male power. Organisations may be presented as if they were gender-neutral but, since bureaucracy is essentially masculine to aim to treat women the same as men will continue to disadvantage women. Instead women's difference must be taken into account, if fair outcomes are to be achieved. Change means recognising fundamental gender differences and enabling women to do things in their own, feminine, ways. Policies might include special training for women, endorsement of women's special organisational skills, and encouragement of alternative ways of working to suit women. Ultimately, change might even mean relinquishing bureaucracy to men and establishing independent feminine forms of organisation.

The specific literature on gender and organisations offers fewer critiques of either radical model than those made of the liberal model. However, borrowing from feminist theory more widely, both models can be criticised for universalising women and men and making essentialist claims about them (that is, assuming that all women on the one hand and all men on the other share common identities and oppressions and will benefit from universal equality policies). Particular criticisms have been made by black women, who argue that policies drawn up to recognise women's difference are in fact based on the interests of a small group of white, middle-class women. For instance, career break schemes and management training programmes will be of little use to the disproportionately large numbers of black women concentrated in manual and junior posts unconnected to the mainstream organisational hierarchy. Similarly, sexual harassment policies may fail to recognise the specific forms of harassment experienced by black women. More generally, equal opportunities policies are criticised for compartmentalising 'sex' and 'race' – working for women or black people, but failing to consider the specific circumstances and needs of black women. Indeed, none of the perspectives outlined here, and almost none of the challenges described in the previous section, have taken account of the intersection of gender and race.

The debate over these issues has recently been central to much feminist research and writing and is widely referred to as the 'equality versus difference debate'. On the one hand are those who argue that sexual difference ought to be irrelevant, that women should be treated the same as men (liberal feminists). On the other are those who claim that women have special needs and interests and should be treated as a distinct category (radical feminists). Scott (1988) claims that this polarisation of 'equality' and 'difference' faces feminists with an 'intellectual trap' (p. 43) and an impossible political choice. It seems that if women want to claim equality we have to ignore the ways in which gender shapes women's lives differently from men's. However, if we want to recognise those differences we must forfeit claims to equality. Taking a feminist post-structuralist perspective (see Chapter 1), Scott claims that in order to move beyond this impasse we need to unpick the meanings attached to 'equality' and 'difference' and reveal how they are constructed to be mutually exclusive. It is only through challenging language and meaning that we can find a way forward. Scott challenges the common-sense meanings attached to both. First, she shows that 'equality' does not have to mean that women and men are understood to be universally identical. In fact, 'equality' in the political theory of rights has been used to mean

> ignoring differences between individuals for a particular purpose or in a particular context... [presuming] a social agreement to consider obviously different people as equivalent (not identical) for a stated purpose. In this usage, the opposite of equality is inequality or inequivalence... equality might well be defined as deliberate indifference to specified differences. (1998:44)

Second, Scott shows that 'difference' does not have to be used in a categorical way to claim generalised differences between all women on the one hand and all men on the other. Instead, we can specify the particular aspects of difference between women and men which are being highlighted and the particular social and/or spatial and/or historical context in which they are being made. Furthermore, we should examine how claims of categorical sex differences work to repress differences *within* gender groups.

In this analysis, Scott is not only trying to reconcile 'equality' with 'difference'. She is also illustrating her poststructuralist conviction that language and discourse are infused with power: that patriarchy (a term she uses) resides in meanings and common-sense understandings and that this serves to constrain feminist intellectual and political possibilities. Thus, it is *patriarchal power relations* which construct 'equality' and 'difference' as binary opposites, and feminists must refuse to make a choice between equality and difference defined in these terms. Instead we can argue for both difference *and* equality although, as Scott points out, claims will be inevitably contingent and specific. For example:

> There are moments when it makes sense for mothers to demand consideration for their social role, and contexts within which motherhood is irrelevant to women's behaviour, but to maintain that womanhood is motherhood is to obscure the differences that make choice possible. (1998:47)

Scott's theoretical claims are certainly compelling, although we must question – as she herself does – the ease with which political claims and policy interventions might mobilise these insights. While Scott is surely correct to claim that, rather than being timeless absolutes, equality and difference have been constructed through social relations, the power embedded within the oppositional construction lies precisely in the way it is accepted *as if it were* timeless and absolute. Making claims which break out of this established paradigm is extremely difficult, as Scott's own revealing analysis of a particular US court case shows. In this case, the Equal Employment Opportunities Commission (EEOC) claimed that the company Sears were discriminating against women and should be forced to treat women no differently from men when making appointments to commission-based sales jobs. The EEOC brought in an expert witness to argue their case. Sears however high-lighted that the expert witness had argued elsewhere that gender did indeed make a difference when looking at women's history of employ-ment. This, Sears claimed, meant that the witness was making contra-dictory claims and was therefore unreliable and not credible. In a legal context which privileged consistency and 'the truth', this apparent contradiction could not be contained, and the EEOC lost the case.

Yet, Scott believes, we have no choice but to break out from the constraints of either–or sameness–difference. She suggests:

> Perhaps as we learn to think this way solutions will become more readily apparent. Perhaps [there is] theoretical and historical work we do can pre-pare the ground. Certainly we can take heart from the history of feminism, which is full of illustrations of refusals of simple dichotomies and attempts to demonstrate that equality requires the recognition and inclusion of differ-ences. (1988:48)

Concluding discussion

This chapter has analysed the range of challenges which are made to gendered organisation and the different models of change on which they draw. Throughout we have implied that *men* as well as women may act to challenge established gender relations inside work organ-isations. In fact, we have found very few documented examples of resistance by men. Nonetheless these do exist. Cheng (1997), for ex-ample, describes how Asian American men reject hegemonic, white, macho masculinity, presenting instead a quieter, gentler and less assuming 'Confucian' masculinity. Elsewhere there is evidence that some men are refusing to subsume their domestic commitments to the demands of work in the way that would have been routinely accepted in the past (Halford *et al.* 1997). Focusing on resistance reveals the range of ways in which power is embedded in the everyday life of work organisations. By exploring the issues which generate resistance we are offered a 'window' onto the often invisible dynamics of masculine power in privilege inside organisations. Documenting resistance also demonstrates the multiple power relations which coexist inside work organisations, as different forms of resistance – personal, collective, legal and bureaucratic – challenge established practices and beliefs enshrining masculinity and male dominance. The focus on resistance in this chapter shows that women are not simply subjected to 'masculine' power, and that men's exercises of power are not necessarily coherent. Rather, some women (and some men, although it seems rather fewer) attempt to exercise power in order resist dominant masculine paradigms of organisational life. *Gendered power inside organisations is not monolithic or one-directional: gendered organisation is contested.*

We have also seen that challenges made to gendered organisation are greeted with resistance themselves. Overall, then, how do we interpret the challenges which have been made? Has masculine power inside work organisations been eroded? Or have the challenges been effectively dismissed through the operation of those very same dynamics of masculine power? Is masculine dominance inside work organisations inevitable? Or do the challenges here indicate that it is possible to move beyond this? Is one form of challenge 'better' than the others? Or do they all meet with the same inevitable dead end? The answers depend, of course, on how you look at it! On the one hand, we could argue that reforms to gendered organisation are no more than a tokenistic buy-off for feminist challenges – of any sort. In this structuralist account, any apparent 'victories' are in fact a subtle calculation, in which women are *allowed to think* that they have effectively wielded some power and changed organisations when, in fact, the changes are insignificant within the broader structure of patriarchal dominance. Within this perspective, individual challenges would be deemed the most ineffective: how can individuals challenge such monolithic structural oppression? At the same time, collective resistances would at least hold potential to galvanise women as a social group and perhaps lead to more fundamental challenges to patriarchy. Whether any of the challenges described above could be seen as such is doubtful. Even legislation, underlain as it is by liberal notions of equality between citizens, may be interpreted as a state response to quell feminist demands with a token of action, and thus to be in the long-term interests of patriarchy. This kind of functionalist structuralism assumes that men simply have power and that – in the absence of profound structural change – any apparent exercise of power by women is a kind of controlled safety-valve: women are effectively powerless. It attributes supreme knowledge and intent to patriarchy and, conversely, assumes that feminists (or women and/or men making challenges to patriarchy) can have only partial vision and be 'bought off' with little difficulty.

Alternatively, the challenges described above might be seen as significant in the erosion of established masculine power inside organisations. We could argue that small changes may set precedents for the future, or may have as yet unknowable knock-on consequences. Maybe it is, in fact, very difficult to conclude that a challenge is utterly ineffective. It is hard to know exactly how engaging in resistance may affect a particular individual in the short or long term, just as it is hard to know the ultimate effect of such resistance on others within an organisation. In this sense, we might say that individual challenges may be just as important as broader collective or legislative challenges. This is to move away from an 'episodic' view of power (see Chapter 1), which suggests that power has been exerted only where one individual is clearly seen to make another do something which she or he would otherwise not have done. Rather, it is to suggest that power takes less clear-cut and simply definable forms. More generally, it might be argued that the masculinity of organisation is not infinitely stable or predetermined, but that it requires constant shoring up – constant re-creation – and that it is only ever contingent and is therefore vulnerable to challenge at any time. Of course, this is not to deny that resistances to gendered organisation are constituted within existing frameworks of power. However, following Foucault's work on power it would suggest a rather different interpretation of our evidence on challenges to gendered organisation (Foucault 1981, 1986, 1988). Rather than trying to identify who *has* power, Foucault argues that we should look at how power *works*. In doing so, he claims that power does not belong to individuals, to one class, or to one sex but that power circulates: power enters all social relations and everyone is engaged in the exercise of power. This is clearly to refute the more structuralist argument above that men always have power and women, even if they seem to be exerting power, are always powerless. Conversely, Foucault argues that the circulatory nature of power means that 'as soon as there is a power relation there is a possibility of resistance. We can never be ensnared by power. We can always modify its grip' (1988: 122–3). Resistance should not be dismissed simply because it takes place within the broad parameters of established inequalities. As Pringle (1989) argues, following Foucault, individuals are never simply victims within power relationships, but rather that they are free subjects faced with choices and alternatives and hence that the possibility for resistance is ever present.

Both positions hold their appeal. Even if we were to accept the latter position in principle, organisational expressions of masculine power and privilege seem remarkably resilient to change. As we enter the twenty-first century, organisations are still significantly characterised by gender inequalities. Despite a century or more of pushing for change, men still dominate organisations in every sense – in terms of hierarchy, status, rewards and opportunities – while particular constructions of masculinity continue to be perceived as the norm to which all should (and can) aspire. But, even as we emphasise these points, we are unable to endorse a vision of all-knowing, all-seeing patriarchy building masculine organisations in its own image and able to fend off any challenges by feminists who will, by and large, be satisfied with what tokenistic change they are given. The level of functionalism, of total control and intent is difficult to give credence to.

In short, can we bring together the insights from competing accounts in order to construct a new approach to gender, power and organisation. In the remaining chapter we attempt to do this, building on the analysis presented in our book so far, drawing on contemporary feminist and organisational theory to highlight the key themes which must be resolved, and suggesting a way forward.

7

Gender, Power and Organisation

Introduction

In the preceding chapters of this book we have revealed the range of ways gender is enacted, sustained and generated across the structures, practices and discourses of organisational life. We have striven to show how the relations between gender and organisation are extremely diverse, complex and multi-dimensional, and may be viewed from different perspectives. Although we have reported many instances of persistent gender discrimination, and shown how it is, primarily, women who are made the minority in both power and material reward, we have also offered evidence to show that the traditional relations between women and men in organisations are being thoroughly challenged. In the contemporary organisational landscape, there is a coexistence of familiar structural patterns of gender with significant change in gender relations. Today it is the case that many women are located in jobs, roles or work relationships that are far from subordinate, rather than a noteworthy few. Many women are resisting the traditional gendered stereotypes by which their occupational choices, performance, achievement and relations may have previously been constrained. Similarly, many men are also challenging the definitions of workplace masculinities that have dominated organisations, prescribing which jobs they should do, and how they should be performed. Not only are more men entering jobs which have been traditionally viewed as 'women's work', but they are also reframing the models of how equally traditional 'men's work' is done, as well as their relations with women in organisations.

This book also aims to offer some understanding of this complex picture. Many existing accounts offer clear, but *partial*, explanations of particular aspects of the relations between gender and organisation. Our recognition of the multiplicity of organisational life, the coexistence of familiar patterns of gender structure with relations which contradict these, means that we have held a range of perspectives in tension. Rather than impose one view of gender or organisational life, our analysis is multi-perspectival, pulling together a mix of evidence and explanations, all of which have resonance in a contemporary analysis of gendered organisational life.

By definition, as we argued in Chapter 1, this means that the picture that has resulted is not only complex but also contradictory. However, we have also argued from the beginning that a focus on power is key to understanding how all this can be so. It is through the concept of power that we can come to understand how these many competing situations and phenomena are able to jostle alongside each other in the same organisational arena. It is our aim to forward the concept of power, to make it integral to gender and organisation.

While existing accounts certainly present the relationship between gender and organisation as essentially one of power, the concept is often implied and embedded within the analysis and only rarely pulled out for rigorous examination. In Chapter 1 we demonstrated how the term is used by different writers to refer to quite different understandings of processes, actions and relations. Our aim, in subsequent chapters, has been to pull out and reveal these different understandings of power, and to demonstrate how existing explanations of gender and organisation have hinged on a particular, singular interpretation of the concept. However, we have also made it clear in this book that we hold that *all* the understandings of power may be useful to our understanding of the relationship between gender and organisation. A multi-dimensional understanding of power allows us to transcend the barriers between the conventional perspectives on gender and organisation, and enables us to admit to the complex and contradictory picture in its entirety, released from the pressure to deny or prioritise particular aspects. Further, and perhaps more importantly, it enables *explanation* of the diverse relations between gender and organisation which have been documented throughout this book.

Power, gender and organisation

Through our examination of the different organisational processes and practices in the preceding chapters of this book, we have shown how power is exercised in multiple ways to gender organisations. We started, in Chapter 2, with our look at organisational structures. We saw that western organisations are typically designed as a series of tiers or levels: if drawn diagrammatically, the picture which results is much the same as that produced in geology, to indicate how the earth's crust is constructed. In organisations, people are slotted into occupations that are located at different levels, each level gaining progressively more power as it nears the top. Thus at the bottom level, employees are understood to have very little power, while at the top a select group of named individuals have considerably more. We saw in particular that gender has a significant relationship with organisational structures, such that women tend to be more likely than men to be located at the bottom levels of organisational structures. Different arguments exist to explain the relationship between gender and organisational structures, and we explained that these hinge on different understandings of power. Indeed, as we argued in Chapter 2, 'the particular interpretation of power in each case *defines* the relationships which are understood to exist between organisational structures and gender in organisational life' (p. 38). In other words, how power is understood shapes how organisational structures are conceptualised, and the connections that may be made between gendered patterns of difference and discrimination.

Chapter 2 reviews four different arguments, which have dominated the literature on gender and organisational structures. The first is rooted in the work of Max Weber. Weber maintained that a wholly neutral equality, and therefore ultimate efficiency, is ensured by the democratic configuration of power that results through the construct of bureaucracy. Bureaucracies are ruled by organisational structures which permit only one sort of power as legitimate: that of rational-legal authority. Those who have power have earned it through the strict application of objective procedures. This equitable and democratic process means that all individuals are judged by their merits and abilities rather than by any personal attributions such as gender or race. In other words, this argument maintains that there is no such thing as gender discrimination, and that there is no noticeable relationship between gender and organisational structures. The dominance of the rational-legal form of power means that processes and procedures are entirely objective and gender-neutral.

In the second argument examined, power is understood more widely. Kanter (1977) sees that it is not just a neutral authority that exists in organisations, but an authority which, owing to the contingency of historical events, has become associated with men. However, it is not their *gender* that determines their possession of power, but their managerial status. This means that power is still understood as organisational, rather than personal, and is, as such, essentially benign and malleable. Organisational structures are thus understood as *not necessarily* gendered: they are so at present owing to almost accidental historical circumstances, rather than any conscious gender design. Once organisational structures are redesigned as egalitarian for both women and men, power will become redistributed between the sexes according to criteria that are gender-neutral.

The third argument discussed sees organisational structures as much less independent of gender. Structures are seen as merely the tools of men: it is men who hold power, not structures. In other words, men are the primary agents of power, and they are so *because they are men*. They use organisational structures to mobilise their power over women. A structural relationship therefore exists between male power and organisational hierarchies, rules and procedures: all are used as means by which women can be kept at the bottom of organisational structures, with little power or material reward.

The fourth argument we examined was Ferguson's (1984) case against bureaucracy. For Ferguson, bureaucratic organisational structures are male – or, rather, they are *masculinity*. Thus not only do they work to support male power but their every aspect is merely a performance of masculinity, of the male way of doing things. Power is thus understood here to be far more than the exercise of rules or procedures to maintain gender hierarchies; it is understood as so thoroughly embedded in the design of bureaucratic organisations that it is a 'knowledge', in the sense of an unquestioned way of thinking and doing. Bureaucratic structures are thus a performance of a knowledge, a belief system or a discourse, which is also male power. However, it is possible for women to resist bureaucracies and therefore male power. Their special position as women enables them to envision alternative ways of organising, perhaps entirely separately from men. The alternative organisations which would result would lead to the dissipation of male power.

These four arguments articulate quite different conceptions of power. The first two draw on essentially liberal understandings of power, wherein power is seen to be centralised, and exerted in the form of democratic laws or procedures to produce (if not now, in the very near future) fair organisational structures. The third argument rests on a structuralist understanding of power, and sees that power (as male dominance) operates through organisational structures, such that they simply and inevitably articulate and sustain the position of men. In the fourth argument, poststructuralist understandings of power are mobilised to present power as a disciplinary regime or knowledge, which dominates not only women but all those subjected to it. At first sight, these broad arguments about gender and organisational structures present themselves as mutually exclusive – each one offering a clear political and social strategy through which gender discrimination in organisations may be challenged. However, by focusing on the concept of power embedded within these arguments, we can see that it is possible to see that all the arguments have bearing, all offer explanations which account for some aspect of organisational life. We have demonstrated how complex organisational life is, how different women and men may work alongside each other yet experience their organisations in very different ways. For some people, organisations offer a way of understanding themselves, their relationships with others, and the world generally; for others, they are a site of conflict, either to establish their own positions or to resist the positions of others; while for others still they offer a set of guidelines for relations and behaviour which are accepted in that part of life: they also may be all of these things, either simultaneously or at different moments in time.

This conclusion is supported, and embellished, through our discussion of gender and organisational cultures in Chapter 3. Here we saw that two arguments dominate the research in this area. The first takes a structural perspective to conceptualise culture as a tool by which men may dominate women and organisations. Men's experiences and attitudes determine the dominant belief systems that operate within organisations and consequently shape gender relations. The result is that women are subordinated not only at the (more material) structural level but also at the ideological level – through language, ideas, images and behaviour. From this perspective, therefore, organisational culture *is* male power.

The second argument takes a more eclectic approach, combining insights drawn from social interactionism and poststructuralism. Organisations are seen as unstable and ever changing, as they respond to a combination of political and economic forces. This means that there is no single stable cultural regime, but that many competing ideas and beliefs circulate within them. They cannot therefore be seen as clearly gendered in any one way: different gender cultures, with different patterns of gender relations, coexist in different groups, between different people and in different situations. Power is thus conceptualised as a more of a process than a possession – it does not adhere to a single group, but may be held by both men and women, at different times and in different places. Thus whereas the first explanation of organisational culture rests on a structural conceptualisation of power, seeing culture as an almost mechanical construction and expression of male power, the second takes a poststructuralist approach, seeing culture as fluid and unstable, dominated by different groups of people at different times, but with the possibility of resistance being ever present. Power is thus understood to circulate between all organisational members, rather than being the restricted possession of a few.

In the final summary of Chapter 3, we recognised that the liberal understanding of power, as more individual and observable, can also be seen to have relevance to explaining the relationship between organisational culture and gender. Clearly, individual men wield power over individual women on a daily, observable basis, either through direct action or non-action. However, far from being mutually exclusive, we saw from the examples of organisational cultures that we discussed throughout Chapter 3 that it may be useful to hold all of these conceptualisations of power as relevant when searching for a better understanding of gender and organisation. We saw how strong traditional ideas about gender relations may coexist alongside other, contradicting patterns of gender. The point we made was that gender and gender relations have to be performed, by the day, by the minute, with every person of contact – a continual, never ending process. Within a structural perspective, this process must be understood as more or less seamless, performed by all men, against all women. Certainly we saw that within some organisations, or within some parts of organisations, this is achieved successfully. However, within other organisations, or other sections of the same organisation, the patterns of gender relations that exist may seem to be better explained by focusing on men and women as individuals rather than as cohesive (political) groups. Importantly, the poststructuralist view allows us to recognise and account for circumstances where structural or liberal interpretations seem to be contradicted by instances of slippage and resistance, found to occur at all levels, and between all individuals, within organisations.

Through our study of gender and management in Chapter 4, we saw that the key questions about women and management which dominate both research organisational theory are also questions of power. The first question, which asks, ostensibly, 'Why are there so few women managers?', is also seeking to establish why, how and by whom is power is being exercised to prevent women from succeeding to the upper levels of organisational structures. The evidence produced to answer this question falls primarily within either a liberal or a structural view of power, or sometimes merges the two together (see, for example, Schwartz 1989). From a liberal perspective, power is mobilised in episodic ways to marginalise women: male managers operate from stereotypical attitudes and beliefs about women, and they draw on these when making decisions about appointments and promotions. Evidence of the *systematic* exclusion of women from jobs, social activities and training also supports an interpretation that rests on a structural conceptualisation of power, with men working in unison to safeguard their superiority within organisations.

The research evidence that exists to answer the first question is powerful and convincing. However, the fact remains that women managers *are* increasing in numbers, and this has led to a second question, which focuses primarily on the differences that may exist between women and men managers. Various arguments are produced to answer this question, all of which rest not only on different conceptualisations of power, but also on different conceptualisations of the relationship they see existing between women, men and power. The first argument, which works from a liberal understanding of power, contends that women are different sorts of managers than men: they offer different qualities, all of which are beneficial to organisational and as such should be appreciated. Power is thus conceptualised as organisational, something which should thus be shared, to enable both men and women managers to flourish and 'do their own thing' within organisations.

The second argument is more structural, and radical. While agreeing that women and men managers manage differently, this position maintains that women are *better* managers than men and, as such, should be enabled to revolutionise contemporary managerial practice. This may be achieved by recognising women's qualities and appointing many more women managers, and/or retraining men, so that they learn to incorporate feminine qualities into their managerial style. Failing this, women should organise separately from men, and establish their own organisations where their highly individual style may flourish. Power is thus viewed here as a personal possession: at present held by men, but now being challenged. Further, however, this argument maintains that, once power is in their possession, women then use it differently – that is, more democratically than the authoritarian model typically adopted by men.

A third argument draws on poststructuralist understandings of power to answer the question in a wholly different way. To see men and women managers as so different, as so black and white, is, it is maintained, reductive and simplistic. As many differences exist between men as managers as there do between women as managers, such that gender may be less of a point of difference than other factors. People are highly individual, and their circumstances and experiences are interpreted in highly different ways. There is no one feminine style, nor is there one dominant masculine style. Thus power is viewed neither as an organisational possession, nor as belonging primarily to a social group, but as something that constantly shifts according to individual and local circumstances, people and situations.

Clearly, management is as much about power as about reward. Chapter 4 demonstrates that it is a highly contested level of most organisations, and that gender is clearly significant in that it is one of the qualities by which people may be excluded and/or made to feel unwelcome. In some organisations, gender is one of the most significant barriers to gaining entry to the top. However, as we enter the twenty-first century, the gender patterning of management tiers within organisations is constantly shifting and changing shape. The changing social and political climate has challenged the right of men to wield structural power, such that men's ubiquity in management positions is diminishing in most occupational sectors. However, spaces still exist for groups of men, or individual men, to exert power and sometimes these exertions are successful, while at other times they are resisted. It is a complex picture, and one to which all the various conceptualisations of power contribute to achieve a better understanding.

In Chapter 5 we showed that one of the ways power is exercised in organisational structures, cultures and management is through sexuality. Once again, various arguments exist to explain the relationship between organisation and sexuality, and these also draw on the various conceptualisations of power. First, structuralists maintain that there is an integral relationship between sexuality and social structure. Those who hold power in organisations (namely, men) are able to use it to manipulate others – and the sexual is a method of oppression used by the powerful against the powerless. This oppression may take a variety of forms – from sexual harassment to the more covert use of innuendo, 'humour', rules about dress, appearance and job performance, and so on. There are two versions of this argument. The first focuses on sexuality as a means by which the powerful in organisations can maintain their position; these are usually men, but not necessarily so: women in power may also use their power to sexually oppress. In other words, sexual oppression is a function of structure, not gender. A second, more radical version of this view forwards the concept of gender as well as that of power, claiming that sexuality is the key way men oppress women. Sexuality is a mobilisation of male power. One of the ways this is achieved is through the construction of an organisational culture which not only assumes but values heterosexuality, and this works to marginalise gay men and lesbians, as well as straight women, through their sexuality.

A second argument draws on poststructuralist conceptualisation of power to argue that a top-down, male-dominated understanding of sexuality and gender relations does not reflect the complexity and contradictions that exist in many (sexual) relations. Once again, there are variations to this argument. Some look at language to point out that it is difficult to establish agreement as to what constitutes an abuse of power through sex . Without denying that some experiences may be unequivocally harassing, others are more grey: what is harassment to one person may be a site of pleasure to another. Others look at the way sexual relations are defined within cultural discourse, and these may offer a means by which those in structurally less powerful positions may acquire power with a superior. A secretary may play the role of the 'master' to her 'slave' boss a relationship which may give pleasure to both of them, but on a small, local basis may confuse their structural relations. In this way, we may see how both the structural and the poststructuralist perspectives on power work to offer important explanatory frameworks for sexuality and organisation.

Finally, in Chapter 6, we looked at challenges made by women to the masculinity and male privilege of gendered organisations. The outcome of such challenges is that contemporary organisations appear to be a mixed complexity of male and female success and failure. As we stated in Chapter 6, 'we can see the coexistence of masculine dominance with feminine resistance; of structural power relations with agentic exercises of power; and of organisational stability with organisational change' (p. 179). Four methods of challenge were discussed. First, we focused on challenges made by individuals to organisational life. We demonstrated how power is embedded in the routine and daily practices, but also how women may adapt these practices to appropriate power, and use it for their own ends. Flight attendants may resist attempts to modify their appearance, nurses may handle patients according to personal rather than hospital guidelines, secretaries may refuse to do photocopying or make tea – there are as many examples as there are individuals. Women are not the passive recipients of male structural power, although, at the same time these resistances undeniably do take place in the broader context of male privilege and power.

Second, we focused on collective challenges by groups of women to male power. We look particularly at women's experiences in British trade unions, and show how men have been successful in maintaining their structural advantages and largely resisting any support for women and women's issues. At the same time, while there has been a general decline of many trade unions, in some women have found the support they have needed to challenge instances of sexism and sexual harassment. This leads us to our third form of challenge – those through the legislature. On one level, equality laws can be interpreted as a significant exercise of women's power, a mark of success in redefining the dominant and socially accepted meanings of gender, and ensuring these are backed up by the state. There is also, however, plenty of depressing evidence that demonstrates how men are successfully able to resist broad and bald legal standards through a variety of covert means.

Finally we looked at organisational challenges: challenges made by groups of women getting together within organisations. Through the construction of locally based equal opportunities groups and working parties, women have been able to challenge and change such issues as promotion, recruitment and selection procedures, childcare issues, sexism and organisational culture.

Clearly, then, these diverse examples of challenge demonstrate that gendered power inside organisations is not monolithic or one-directional, but is something that is often contested. However, in the final analysis, how successful are these challenges in substantially undermining male power? In Chapter 6 we offered two possibilities in answer to this question – which one is chosen depends on the model of power which is felt to operate. From a structural perspective, the kinds of challenges we have discussed can be seen to be merely something that might be happening in the shop-window, as it were; in effect, no real or effective power is given away: challenges are always effectively dealt with by an all-seeing, all-knowing patriarchy. Alternatively, the whole issue is seen to be more ephemeral. Challenges may indeed lead to erosion of male power, but perhaps not in a directly observable, linear fashion. It is difficult to know to what extent male power is being undermined, but as it requires constant shoring up if it is to be maintained, any hiccup may be problematic. Power here is seen as less clear-cut: what is of interest is not so much who has it, but how it works.

In summary, the wealth of evidence of the ways organisations are gendered that we have covered in this book thus also demonstrates clearly how integral the concept of power is to any interpretation of events. We have seen how a range of actors exercises power, and that power has various manifestations and effects. We have seen that power cannot be reduced to its individualised-episodic, social-structural or discursive–agentic poststructural instances – although, clearly, examples of all three can be identified. Power is not only mobilised by individuals, or social structures, or discourses. Power cannot be conceptualised as any one type of action; or as having one effect; or as only repressive; or only productive; or as only top-down or only bottom-up: it is all of these things.

Theoretical connections

This formulation of the ways relationships between gender and organisation are constituted across multiple power relations has some significant and potentially productive points of connection with the diverse works of Giddens, Foucault and Clegg. In what follows, we elaborate on these points of connection and draw on the insights each of these writers offers on how power may be understood as a multiple concept.

Giddens's theory of structuration (Giddens 1984) was devised as a general explanatory model for the constitution of society at the broadest level, rather than concentrating on power *per se*. He does however make important comments on the question of power in particular and, furthermore, the formulation of power relations that we outlined above has some striking resonance with his more general position. In his critiques of both interpretative and structural sociologies, Giddens is concerned to redefine what is understood by both social 'structure' and human 'agency' and to see the relationship between structure and agency as one of *duality*. By 'structure' Giddens is referring to the structural properties of social systems, specifically to *signification* (codes of meaning, symbolic orders and modes of discourse), to *domination* (through the authorisation and allocation of resources through political and economic institutions) and to *legitimation* (normative regulation principally through legal institutions). However, distinguishing himself from the conventional structuralist treatment of these structures, Giddens does not suggest that they hold a position of primacy over human agency. To the contrary, within structuration theory, human agency is not determined by social structures. Nor, according to Giddens, do structures serve merely to *constrain* human action or human acts. By 'agency' Giddens is referring to action by human subjects understood as both knowledgeable and capable. These actions *may* be constrained by social structures, but these same structures also offer the possibility for enabling certain human action. Structures do not just *stop* people from doing things, but also provide the opportunities and possibilities for people to take action. In turn, this human agency may come to modify or even reconstitute those structures. In this way, Giddens argues that his model of structuration transcends both the deterministic views of structure (within structural sociology) and the voluntaristic views of agency (within interpretative sociology). Instead, structure and agency are locked together as a duality: each is shaped by and shapes the other. Structure is activity-dependent; and agents draw upon the structural properties of society in making their actions (Clark 1990). Agents may transform structures but, equally, agency is not totally 'free' or random, but rooted and routinised within the context of social structure. To use Giddens's own phraseology 'the personal transient encounters of daily life' are essentially bound up with the 'long term sedimentation of social institutions' (Cloke *et al*. 1991:105).

Whilst Giddens's primary concern is not with power *per se*, power inheres across his model of structuration, being embedded in both structure and agency. Giddens suggests that power is vested in structural resources, specifically authority and property, which 'enable and constrain social interactions through the exercise of control over people and over the material world' (Cloke *et al*. 1991:101). Everyday life is structured by the distribution of these authority and property resources and, in turn, everyday life reproduces particular distributions of these resources. Here then, the duality of structure and agency is clear, although – as far as power is concerned – the emphasis appears to lie heavily towards the structural side. However, Giddens's understanding of structures as enabling, rather than simply constraining, and his commitment to the duality of structure and agency, mean that power is also mobilised through the everyday actions of human subjects. Far from being 'programmed' by social structures, human agents are exercising power in their everyday social interventions, making choices and achieving skilled accomplishments which may lead to broader patterns of social change.

This understanding of the duality of power bears some surprising similarities to Foucault's work. Across the range of his work, Foucault too identified power as operating in rather different ways, although he was less concerned – initially, in any case – to specify the connections between these different manifestations of power. In his earlier work, Foucault was concerned with the way the exercise of power had transformed during the transition in the west from feudal to capitalist societies (Foucault 1977). While the former were characterised by direct, physical and often brutal forms of discipline and punishment which were practised by individuals with sovereign powers (kings, aristocracy and their agents), Foucault saw that emergent capitalist societies had come instead to be dominated by 'disciplinary power'. According to Foucault, disciplinary power is exercised through the constant monitoring, assessment and judgement of individuals and, in this way, 'individuals are controlled through the power of the norm and this power is effective because it is relatively invisible' (McNay 1994:94–5). Thus, disciplinary power ensures a widespread and efficient form of social control, without the need for one-to-one physical domination as was the case in feudal times. Of course, Foucault's archetype of disciplinary power was the prison, where prisoners were totally monitored and controlled, but his analysis is extended to modern society more generally, with particular emphasis placed on the role of social workers, doctors, teachers and so on, who are seen to serve as the arbiters of normality. Here then, Foucault's understanding of power is clear: power is repressive and excluding, a one-directional and monolithic force. There is no sense in which power is seen as exercised by individual subjects. Indeed, in his early work, Foucault was driven by a rejection of the enlightenment construction of a free, rational, interior self, which led him to deny the human subject altogether (McNay 1994). Seen at its most extreme, then, disciplinary power is understood to operate directly on the body, rendering it inert and docile, leaving no room for mediation by a thinking, willing or responsible subject (ibid.).

However, as Foucault became more and more concerned to explore the permeation of power beyond prisons, and across modern society, he also came to modify his understanding of power and his understanding of the nature of the subject. As best expressed in his work on the history of sexuality (1981) Foucault came to see power as 'regulative' rather than simply 'repressive' (Wood 1985) and to understand power as subjectivising – operating at the level of individual consciousness – rather than objectivising – bypassing the subject and acting directly on the body (McNay 1994). Critically, in this admission of the subject, power came to be exerted through people rather than over them (Smart 1988). In this formulation, then, human subjects come to be involved in interpreting and responding to regulative power and, critically, may not necessarily comply with the pressures for normalisation. Capturing this point very neatly, Foucault proclaims that 'where there is power there is resistance' (Foucault 1977:95). Here, then, power becomes far more complex than the simple domination of individuals; it also comes to constitute the possibility for their freedom, expressed as freedom to act and to – attempt to – influence others' actions (McNay 1994). The study of sexuality provides Foucault's particular example of this point. Whereas it had conventionally been argued that the nineteenth century obsession with naming and cataloguing sexual practices was repressive, for example in the way these stigmatised and marginalised homosexual activities, Foucault argues that the explosion of knowledge about sexuality and the development of a language of sexuality opened up new and positive spaces for naming alternative lifestyles, provoking debate and enabling dissent from so-called normality. As Foucault explains:

> [A]s soon as there's a relation of power there's a possibility of resistance. We're never trapped by power: it's always possible to modify its hold, in determined conditions and following a precise strategy. (Foucault in Gordan 1980:13)

In sum, Foucault's later work came to see that power was not a top-down force exerted *over* the population, but was also exerted *by* the population in diverse ways.

The different understandings of power within Foucault's early and later works do not sit comfortably together (Smart 1988, McNay 1994). Characteristically, Foucault himself was not especially concerned with this inconsistency (Foucault 1988), although he did express dissatisfaction with the term 'power', referring to 'this all-embracing and reifying term' (in Hindess 1996:100). In taking up this challenge, McNay (1994) suggests that we should in fact delineate three simultaneous forms of power within Foucault's work. First, Foucault allows the concept of sovereign power to remain. Indeed, he acknowledges that this is perhaps the most visible locus of power vested in individuals, specifically the king and state officials, who have the power to make laws controlling social actions. It is not that he wishes to deny this form of power, but rather that he sees this as relatively insignificant compared with other forms of power which permeate contemporary societies. Second, we should accept the ascendancy of disciplinary power in modern society, whereby normalising pressures act to organise, discipline and dominate the human body. Third, and perhaps most importantly, however, is the 'range of infinitesimal power relations that permeate the body, sexuality, the family, kinship, discourse, etc.' (McNay 1994:117). McNay refers to this third understanding of power as 'governmentality'. While this form of power works again to render the subject in a receiving position to a larger, normalising 'state' power, there is no direct or causal relationship. Rather, it works in an 'indirect and erratic fashion, through a multiplicity of mediatory power networks' (ibid.). It is this understanding which captures the everyday relations between individuals, where individuals mobilise power and act as conduits in the network of power relations which crisscross the social landscape. It is here that we see the reintroduction of individuals as subjects with (some) freedom and autonomy, and it is here that we (may) see individuals resisting, 'in a mundane and invisible fashion, the normalising pressures exerted over their lives' (McNay 1994:102). However, we must still not see power as *possessed by* subjects, but as an *exercise*. Power is the effect of one action on another action, although to explain it we need to understand 'the field of possible actions' in which the action occurs (Couzens Hoy 1986). Not only will the action inhibit other possible actions, but it may increase the probability of other actions. In other words, according to Foucault, 'power is not like two adversaries confronting each other; it is comparable to "government" in a broad sense, where to govern means "to structure the field of the eventual actions of others" (Couzens Hoy 1986:135).

Thus we can see that, taken across his work, Foucault is effectively critical of any singular notion of power, maintaining instead three distinct forms of power. What then of the relationship between these forms of power? McNay (1994) argues that while sovereign and disciplinary power can be seen as 'meta-powers', with some coherence and stability, the key to their existence and persistence is the decentralised, everyday circulation of power between individuals. Foucault himself ties together this macro-and the microphysics of power thus:

> [T]his meta power [specifically, here, state power] ... can only take hold and secure its footing where it is rooted in a whole series of multiple and indefinite power relations that supply the basis for the great negative forms of power. (Foucault in Gordon 1980:122)

Elaborating on the same point, he says

> [O]f course, we still have to show who those in charge are, we know that we
> have to turn, let us say, to deputies, ministers, principal private secretaries,
> etc., etc. [that is, the bearers of sovereign power]. But this is not the impor-
> tant issue, for we know perfectly well that even if we reach the point of
> designating exactly all those people, all those 'decision makers' we will still
> not really know why and how the decision was made, how it came to be
> accepted by everybody and how it is that it hurts a particular category of
> person. (Foucault 1988:103–4)

Clearly, then, Foucault wishes to maintain the significance of sovereign power *and* of disciplinary power *and* of the agentic exercises of
power across everyday life. For what is of interest is not *who* possesses
power, but *how* it is exercised, and this involves looking at every actor
involved, not only at the actions of the dominant class. Power is not
simply a possession or privilege of the dominant class, but rather it is a
strategy, 'and the dominated are as much a part of the network of
power relations and the particular social matrix as the dominating'
(Couzens Hoy1986:134).

Finally, our multi-dimensional analysis of the ways power constructs relations between gender and organisation shares some very
close concerns with Clegg's more generalised research on 'frameworks
of power' within organisations (Clegg 1989). Once again, Clegg's
starting-point is to dispute a unitary concept of power. Instead,
Clegg asserts, power must be understood, simultaneously, as more
than one concept: '[T]here is no such thing as a single all-embracing
concept of power *per se* but there are at least three family groupings
clustered around loci of dispositional, agency and facilitative concepts
of power' (p. xv). Put simply, the grouping around 'agency' refers *to
episodic power relations between agencies*, most obviously individuals
(although, according to Clegg, 'agency' may be interpreted to include
animals, machines or even germs). The exercise of power through
agency involves direct and causal action by an identifiable sovereign
actor: a supreme agency, to which other wills bend. This family group
is then centred on traditional liberal notions of episodic power, a
concept Clegg wishes to retain: clearly this exercise of power *does*
occur, and the concept does tell us something about power relations
between A and B. However, Clegg argues, this concept of episodic
power alone does not tell us anything about the 'relational field' within
which A and B are situated. It does not tell us anything about the pre-
existing privileges or handicaps which particular individuals may bear

(for example, gender, or class, ethnicity, position in the hierarchy, and so on), or the ways these factors may shape the exercise and outcome of episodic power relations.

Here we must extend our analysis of power to include the family groupings around dispositional and facilitative power. Dispositional power is a term developed from Wrong's (1979) research, and refers most strictly to the latent capacities of individuals or social groups, whether they are actually exercised or not. For example, the knowledge that a male manager *could* sack a female secretary if she were to complain about his language or physical contact may be enough to stop her from doing so. Here there has been no identifiable instance of episodic power but clearly power has been exerted nonetheless. More generally, these latent capacities are embedded in the 'rules of practice'. As we saw in Chapter 3, 'how things are done around here' has been interpreted by analysts interested in gender and organisation as the sedimentation, or fixing, of particular configurations of male power. However, it may not be recognised or experienced as such, by either women or men. The power operating in this grouping is then quite distinct from the direct, observable and causal episodic power relations discussed above.

Clegg's final family group is the cluster of power relations operating around 'facilitative power'. This is quite different again from episodic and dispositional power. As with dispositional power, the focus is not on individual agency, but broader configurations of power. But whereas dispositional power refers to power embedded in the processes of *social* integration, specifically in rules of meaning and membership, facilitative power refers to power embedded in processes of *system* integration. In this, Clegg is referring to the techniques of production and discipline which are used to perpetuate the social system (in this case the organisation) and, specifically, the ways these techniques are deployed with the effect of empowering some agencies (individuals) and disempowering others. This form of power is then far more specific, in relation to organisation at least, focusing on the way the system (organisation) pursues achieves its goals – principally, maintaining and developing itself effectively.

What then of the relations between these three groupings of power? Clegg suggests that, while there may be instances where the exercise of power is confined solely to one grouping, this is unusual and more commonly power should be understood as a process which may pass through two or even three of the groupings or 'circuits'. For instance, there might be cases where power can be exercised through agency alone, as in the traditional sovereign conception of agency. Indeed, Clegg says that this is a particularly effective, efficient and economic exercise of power:

> [P]ower which makes only one circuit, which has no need to struggle against relations of meaning and membership, nor to institute new disciplinary techniques of production or of force, is an economy of power. It is a power which can efficiently deploy given capacities where resistance ... will be overwhelmed. (1989:18)

More commonly, however, Clegg suggests that episodic power necessarily trades off 'some extant fixing of facilitative or dispositional power' (p. 215). That is to say, individual, episodic exercises of power only work because of the configurations of power embedded in the other circuits of power. Similar points are made about all three circuits of power: the exercise of power may be confined to one particular circuit, but it is more likely that the exercise of power in one circuit depends on the configuration of power across the other circuits.

Throughout, Clegg emphasises that power relations are far from permanently fixed. Episodic exercises of power, he says, will 'invariably be accompanied by resistance' (1989:215) as agencies compete with each other, attempting to pursue their own interests (as they see them). In the circuit of dispositional power, Clegg argues that there is a constant struggle over the rules of practice and meaning. Indeed, he says, the rules of practice are 'at the centre of any stabilisation or change in the circuitry [of power]' (ibid. 215). Nonetheless, techniques of discipline and production in the circuit of facilitative power also offer constant potential for resistance. In particular, Clegg suggests that the ongoing process of innovation in these techniques may 'as readily subvert as reproduce' (p. 216) domination.

Conclusions

There are, then, some obvious similarities between the arguments being made by Giddens, Foucault and Clegg. Most importantly, all three writers are suggesting that power relations have a certain degree of fixity, and all three combine this with an understanding of the instability of power relations. The question of agency is critical to all arguments, in that agents both *enact* and *resist* embedded formations of power. At this general level then, these arguments all serve to support our own conclusions and, in their detail, they offer considerable promise for the development of fuller understandings of the relations between gender, power and organisation.

Of course, Giddens, Foucault and Clegg do not all arrive at these general conclusions in the same way and, in the details of their arguments, there are many points of difference between them. Perhaps most obviously, their analytical models differ. Giddens offers us a duality (of structure and agency), while Foucault appears to be delineating three forms of power and Clegg suggests a clear framework showing three interconnected circuits of power. More theoretically, the three writers differ on the question of *interests*. That is to say, whether particular social and/or economic interests are embedded in the more fixed formations of power, which they recognise. While Giddens recognises class society and sees that capitalist interests are embedded across property and authority structures, Foucault actively denies the existence of any clear set of objective interests which would account for the broader formations of power, and this is a position also adopted by Clegg. Instead of attempting to identify what individuals or social groups' 'real' interests are, Clegg suggests we can only examine how individuals or groups come to *perceive* their interests in certain ways and, in turn, attempt to mobilise power accordingly.

This latter point underlines the fact that all three theorists acknowledge that power is exercised not only in ways that can be observed – in the form of direct actions, but also at the level of the unseen, in the form of ideas and perceptions which circulate, sometimes at the level of unconscious. In our discussions in this book of power and organisation in this book, we have shown many examples of both overt and covert practices of power. We have shown that these emanate not only from those with structural/organisational power, but also from those at the receipt of such power. However, in our suggestion that the overwhelming effect of these practices of power, when combined, is largely to support an assumption of male dominance in gender relations, we have followed Clegg and Foucault to argue that what is of importance is the way interests are perceived, and the ways power is consequently mobilised. Men perceive that it is in their interests to acquire and maintain organisational power. Accordingly, power relations in organisations do embed themselves into a 'larger', overarching system of gender relations, which becomes more or less fixed in sustaining persistent patterns of difference and inequality between women and men. This is what is perceived as 'normal', and as such is reflected both in the material (such as the distribution of money, official authority, divisions of labour) and in the discursive (for example, language, truth and meaning). In order to persist, however, these formations of power have to be constantly maintained, or enacted. They are not guaranteed, existing as abstract structures regardless of social action. Rather, they must be maintained by everyday actions at the 'smaller', local level. Here power relations are less embedded, determined and systematic. Individualised perceptions of gender relations demonstrate themselves through individual episodes of power as well as agentic engagements in networks of power.

In other words, exercises of power at the individual level *constitute* the organisational, yet there is always the possibility of change as individuals interpret their situation in different ways. Thus exercises of power at the individual level may erode or even transform embedded power relations at the organisational level. In this way, gender relations within an organisation may change: as more people at the local level resist or modify the gendered cultural assumptions of the organisational, then the larger system of power may start to change shape. Or it may not – since exercises of power at the individual and local level take place also within the context of embedded power relations at the larger, organisational level. Exercises of power do not take place within a vacuum of individual freedom but are shaped by (not determined by) the broader material and discursive formations of power. Just as everyday exercises of power at the individual level hold the potential to transform broader formations of power, they may also be routine and mundane, enacting and sustaining persistent and systematic gender divisions and inequalities.

In this way, we can see how liberal, structural and poststructuralist analyses of power all converge to contribute to our understanding of organisational processes. In common with Giddens, Foucault and Clegg, we have acknowledged a larger system of power that structures action and defines choices at the smaller and local level. We have seen how this larger system is bound up with ideas about gender difference which mean that in many cases individual episodes of power combine to reflect dominant cultural understandings of gender, and thus sustain men's interests. However, we have also discussed how these cultural understandings are far from uniform: they are being constantly challenged and redefined as other cultural discourses offer diverse ideas about gender. Our performances in our work organisations are bound up with our individual identities, and, as such, changing gender identities in other aspects of life may offer models of resistance and change.

It is clear that the relationships between gender, power and organisation are constantly moving and changing: yet to what extent the picture of gender and power achieves substantial and systematic change will remain one of the key research questions for organisations as we enter the new millennium.

References

Acker, J. (1990) 'Hierarchies, Jobs, Bodies: A Theory of Gendered Organisations', *Gender and Society*, **4**(2), 139–58.

Acker, J. (1992) 'Gendering Organisational Theory', in Mills, A. and Tancred, P. (eds), *Gendering Organisational Analysis*. London, Sage.

Acker, J. and Van Houten, D. (1974) 'Differential Recruitment and Control: The Sex Structuring of Organisations', *Administrative Science Quarterly*, **19**(2), 152–63.

Adams, J., Kottke, J. and Padgitt, J. (1983) 'Sexual Harassment of University Students', *Journal of College Personnel*, **24**, 484–90.

Adkins, L. (1992) 'Sexual Work and the Employment of Women in the Service Industries', in Savage, M. and Witz, A. (eds), *Gender and Bureaucracy*, Oxford: Blackwell Sociological Review.

Adkins, L. (1995) *Gendered Work: Sexuality, Family and the Labour Market*, Buckingham: Open University Press.

Aggarwal, A. (1987) *Sexual Harassment in the Workplace*, Toronto and Vancouver: Butterworths.

Aitkenhead, M. and Liff, S. (1991) 'The Effectiveness of Equal Opportunities Policies', in Firth-Cozens, J. and West, M. (eds), *Women at Work: Psychological and Organisational Perspectives*, Buckingham: Open University Press.

Alban-Metcalfe, B. (1984) 'Current career Concerns of Female and Male Managers and Professionals: An Analysis of Free Response Comments to a National Survey', *Equal Opportunities International*, **3**(1), 11–18.

Alban-Metcalfe, B. (1985) 'The Effects of Socialisation on Women's Management Careers', *Management Bibliographies and Reviews*, **11**, 3.

Alban-Metcalfe, B. and Nicholson, N. (1984) *The Career Develoment of British Managers*, London: British Institute of Management Foundation.

Alban-Metcalfe, B. and West, M. (1991) 'Women Managers', in Firth-Cozens, J. and West, M. (eds), *Women at Work: Psychological and Organizational Perspectives*, Buckingham: Open University Press.

Alexandre, H. (1990) *Les Femmes cadres*, Paris: APEC.

Alimo-Metcalfe, B. (1987) 'Male and Female Managers: An Analysis of Biographical and Self-concept Data, *Work and Stress*, **1**(3), 207–19.

Alimo-Metcalfe, B. (1993) 'Women in Management: Organizational Socialization and Assessment Practices that Prevent Career Advancement', *International Journal of Selection and Assessment*, **1**(2), April, pp. 68–83.

Alimo-Metcalfe, B. (1994a) 'Waiting for Fish to Grow Feet!', in Tanton M. (ed.), *Women in Management: A Developing Presence*, London: Routledge.

Alimo-Metcalfe, B. (1994b) 'Women in Business in the UK', in Davidson, M. and Cooper, C. (eds), *European Women in Business and Management*, London: Paul Chapman.

Al-Khalifa, E. (1988) 'Pin-money professionals? Women in teaching', in Coyle, A. and Skinner, J. (eds), *Women in Work: Positive Action for Change*, London: Macmillan.

Al-Khalifa, E. (1989) 'Management by Halves: Women Teachers and School Management', in De Lyon, H. and Migniuolo, F. W. (eds), *Women Teachers: Issues and Experiences*, Milton Keynes: Open University Press.

Allen, I. (1988) *Any Room at the Top?* London: Policy Studies Institute.

Alvesson, M. and Billing, Y. (1992) 'Gender and Organization: Towards a Differentiated Understanding', *Organization Studies*, **13/12**, 73–103.

Anderson, C. and Hunsaker, P. (1985) 'Why There's Romancing at the Office and Why It's Everybody's Problem', *Personnel*, **62**, 57–63.

Antal, A. and Krebsbach-Gnath, C. (1994) 'Women in Management in Germany', in Adler, N. and Izraeli, D. (eds), *Competitive Frontiers: Women Managers in a Global Economy*, Cambridge, MA: Blackwell.

Asplund, G. (1988) *Women Managers – Changing Organizational Cultures*, Chichester: John Wiley.

Atkins, S. (1986) 'The Sex Discrimination Act 1975: The End of a Decade', in *Feminist Review*, **24**, 57–70.

Baack, J., Carr-Ruffino, N. and Pelletier, M. (1993) 'Making It to the Top: Specific Leadership Skills: A Comparison of Male and Female Perceptions of Skills Needed by Women and Men Managers', *Women in Management Review*, **8**(2), 17–23.

Bachrach, P. and Baratz, M. (1963) 'Decisions and Nondecisions: An Analytical Framework', *American Political Science Review*, **57**, 641–51.

Barrett, M. (1980) *Women's Oppression Today: Problems in Marxist Feminist Analysis*, London: New Left Books.

Barrett, M. and Phillips A. (1992) *Destabilizing Theory: Contemporary Feminist Debates*, Cambridge: Polity Press.

Barron, J., Davis-Blake, A. and Bielby, W. (1986) 'The Structures of Opportunity: How Promotion Ladders Vary Within and Among Organisations', in *Administrative Science Quarterly*, June, **31**, 248–73.

Basil, D. (1972) *Women in Management*, New York: Dunellen.

Baudrillard, J. (1981) *For a Critique of the of the Political Economy of the Sign*, St Louis, MI: Telas.

Beale, J. (1982) *Getting It Together: Women as Trade Unionists*, London: Pluto.

Bell, E. (1990) 'The Bi-cultural Life Experience of Career-Oriented Black Women', in *Journal of Organisational Behaviour*, **11**, 459–77.

Bell, E. and Nkomo, S. (1992) 'Re-Visioning Women Managers' Lives', in Mills, A. J. and Tancred, P. (eds), *Gendering Organizational Analysis*, Newbury Park, CA: Sage.

Bell, E., Denton, T. and Nkomo, S. (1993) 'Women of Colour in Management: Towards an Inclusive Analysis', in Fagenson, E. (ed). *Women in Management: Trends, Issues and Challenges in Managerial Diversity*, London: Sage.

Bem, S. (1974) 'The Measurement of Psychological Androgyny', *Journal of Consulting and Clinical Psychology*, **42**, 155–62.

Bhattacharaya, G. (1994) 'Offence is the Best Defence? Pornography and Racial Violence', in Brant, C. and Too, Y. (eds), *Rethinking Sexual Harassment*, London: Pluto.

Billing, Y. (1994) 'Gender and Bureaucracies', in *Gender, Work and Organization*, **1**, 179–93.

Blum, L. and Smith, V. (1988) 'Women's Mobility in the Corporation: A Critique of the Politics of Optimism Signs', *Journal of Women in Culture and Society*, **13**(2), 528–45.

Bologh, R.(1990) *Love or Greatness*, London: Unwin Hyman.

Boston, S. (1987) *Women Workers and the Trade Unions*, London: Lawrence & Wishart.

Bourantas, D. and Papalexandris, N. (1991) 'Sex Differences in Leadership – Leadership Styles and Subordinate Satisfaction', *Journal of Managerial Psychology*, **5**(5), 7–10.

Bowman, G., Wortney, B. and Greyser, S. (1965) 'Are Women executives People?', *Harvard Business Review*, **43**, 14–28, 164–78.

Brandser, G. (1996) Women – the New Heroes of the Business World?', *Women in Management Review*, **11**(2), 3–17.

Brant, C. and Too, Y. (eds) (1994) *Rethinking Sexual Harassment*, London: Pluto.

Braverman, H. (1974) *Labour and Monopoly Capital: The Degradation of Work in the Twentieth Century*, New York: Monthly Review Press.

Brenner, J., Tomiewics, J. and Schein, V. (1989) 'The Relationship Between Sex Role Stereotypes and Requisite Management Characteristics Revised', *Academy of Management Journal*, **32**(3), 662–9.

Brewis, J. and Kerfoot, D. (1994) 'Selling our "Selves"? Sexual Harassment and the Intimate Violations of the Workplace', paper presented at the British Sociological Association Annual Conference, University of Central Lancashire, March.

Brewis, J. and Grey, C. (1994) Re-eroticizing the Organization: An Exegis and Critique *Gender, Work and Organization*, **1**(2) (April), 67–82.

Brown, H. (1992) *Women Organising*, London: Routledge.

Brownmiller, S. (1975) *Against Our Will: Men, Women and Rape*, Harmondsworth, Penguin.

Burden, H. (1997) 'Pat Chapman-Pincher', *Guardian*, G2, 27 May, p. 4.

Burrell, G. (1988) 'Modernism, Post Modernism and Organizational Analysis 2: The Contribution of Michel Foucault', *Organization Studies*, **9**(2), 221–35.

Burrell, G. (1992) 'The Organization of Pleasure' in Alvesson, M. and Willmott, H. (eds), *Critical Management Studies*, London, Sage.

Butler, J. (1990) *Gender Trouble: Feminism and the Subversion of Identity*, New York, Routledge.

Cairns, K. (1997) 'Femininity' and Women's Silence in Response to Sexual Harassment and Coercion', in Thomas, A. M. and Kitzinger, C. (eds) *Sexual Harassment: Contemporary Feminist Perspectives*, Buckingham: Open University Press.

Calas, M. (1992) 'An/Other Silent Voice? Representing "Hispanic Woman" in Organizational Texts', in Mills, A. and Tancred, P. (eds), *Gendering Organizational Analysis*, Newbury Park, CA: Sage.

Calas, M., Jacobson, S., Jacques, R. and Smircich, L. (1991) 'Is a Woman Centred Theory of Management Dangerous?', paper presented at the National Academy of Management: Women in Management Division, Miami, FL, August.

Calas, M. and Smircich, L. (1993) 'Dangerous Liaisons: The "Feminine in Management" Meets "Globalization"', *Business Horizons*, March-April, 71–81.

Canadian Human Rights Commission (1984) *Unwanted Sexual Attention and Sexual harassment: Results of a Survey of Canadians*, Ottawa: Research and Special Studies Branch/Ministry of Supplies and Services, March.

Carby, H. (1982) 'White Women Listen! Black Feminism and the Boundaries of Sisterhood', in CCCS Collective, *The Empire Strikes Back*, London: Routledge.

Carroll, C. (1982) 'Three's a Crowd: The Dilemma of Black Women in Education', in Hull, G., Scott, P. and Smith, B. (eds), *But Some of Us Are Brave*, New York: Feminist Press.

Case, S.S. (1994) 'Gender Differences in Communication and Behaviour in Organizations', in Davidson, M. and Burke, R. J. (eds) *Women in Management: Current Research Issues*, London: Paul Chapman.

Chambers, G. and Orton, C. (1990) *Promoting Sex Equality: The role of Industrial Tribunals*, London: Policy Studies Institute.

Cheng, C. (1997) ' "We Choose Not to Compete": The "Merit" Discourse in the Selection Process and Asian and Asian American Men and their Masculinity', in Cheng, C. (ed.), *Masculinities in Organisations*, London: Sage.

Chodorow, N. (1979) *The Reproduction of Mothering: Psychoanalysis and the Sociology of Gender*, London: University of California Press.

Cianni, M. and Romberger, B. (1995) 'Interactions with Senior Managers: Perceived Differences by Race/Ethnicity and Gender', in *Sex Roles*, **32**(5–6), 353–73.

Clark, J. (1990) 'Anthony Giddens, Sociology and Modern Social Theory', in Clark, J., Modgil, C. and Modgil S. (eds), *Anthony Giddens: Consensus and Controversy*, Basingstoke: Falmer Press.

Clarke, G. (1996) 'Conforming and Contesting with (a) Difference: How Lesbian Students and Teachers Manage Their Identities', *International Studies in Sociology of Education*, 6(2), 191–209.

Clegg, S. (1989) *Frameworks of Power*, London: Sage.

Clegg, S. (1990) *Modern Organisations*, London: Sage.

Cloke, P., Philo, C. and Sadler, D. (1991) *Approaching Human Geography*, London: Paul Chapman.

Coates, J. (1989) Gossip Revisited: Language in All-female Groups, in J. Coates and D. Cameron (eds), *Women in their Speech Communities*, London: Longman, pp. 94–121.

Coates, J. (1991) 'Women's Cooperative Talk: A New Kind of Conversational Duet?', in Uhlig, C. and Zimmerman, R. (eds), *Proceedings of the Anglistentag 1990 Marburg*, Tubingen: Max Niermeyer Verlag.

Coates, J. (1995) 'Language, Gender and Career', in Mills, S. (ed.), *Language and Gender: Interdisciplinary Perspectives*, London: Longman.

Cobble, D. (1990) 'Rethinking Troubled Relations Between Women and Unions: Craft Unionism and Female Activism', *Feminist Studies*, **16**, 519–48.

Cockburn, C. (1987) *Women, Trade Unions and Political Parties*, Fabian Research Series no. 349, London: Fabian Society.

Cockburn, C. (1991) *In the Way of Women*, London: Macmillan.

Cockburn, C. (1996) 'Strategies for Gender Democracy – Strengthening the Representation of Trade Union Women in the European Social Dialogue', *European Journal of Women's Studies*, 3(1), 7–26.

Collins, E. and Blodgett, T. (1981) 'Sexual Harassment – Some See It, Some Won't', *Harvard Business Review*, 59(2), 76–95.

Collinson, D. (1988) 'Engineering Humour': Masculinity, Joking and Conflict in Shop-Floor Relations *Organization Studies*, 9(2), 181–99.

Collinson, D. and Hearn, J. (1994) 'Naming Men as Men: Implications for Work, Organization and Management', *Gender, Work and Organization*, 1(1), 2–22.

Collinson, D., Knights, D. and Collinson, M. (1990) *Managing to Discriminate*, London: Routledge.

Colwill, N. (1982) *Women and Men in Organisations*, Palo Alto, CA: Mayfield.

Colwill, N. (1984) 'Mentors and Proteges, Women and Men', *Business Quarterly*, Summer, 19–21.

Colwill, N. and Vinnicombe, S. (1991) 'Women's Training Needs', in Firth-Cozens, J. and West, M. A. (eds), *Women at Work*, Buckingham: Open University Press.

Cooper, C. and Davidson, M. (eds) (1984) *Women in Management*, London: Heinemann.

Coote, A. and Patullo, P. (1990) *Power and Prejudice*, London: Weidenfeld & Nicolson.

Couzens Hoy, D. (1986) 'Power, Repression, Progress: Foucault, Lukes and the Frankfurt School', in Couzens Hoy, D. (ed.) *Foucault: A Critical Reader*, Oxford: Basil Blackwell.

Coward, R. (1999) 'Women are the New Men', *Guardian*, G2, Thursday 1 July pp. 4–5.

Coyle, A. and Skinner, J. (eds) (1988) *Women and Work: Positive Action for Change*, London, Macmillan.

Crompton, R. and Jones, G. (1984) *White Collar Proletariat: Deskilling and Gender in Clerical Work*, London: Macmillan.

Crompton, R. and Sanderson, K. (1990) *Gendered Jobs and Social Change*, London: Allen & Unwin.

Cunnison, S. (1989) 'Gender Joking in the Staffroom', in Acker, S. (ed.), *Teachers, Gender and Careers*, Lewes: Falmer Press.

Cunnison, S. and Stageman, J. (1995) *Feminising the Unions: Challenging the Culture of Masculinity*, Aldershot, Avebury.

Czarniawska-Joerges, B. (1992) *Exploring Complex Organizations: A Cultural Perspective* Newbury Park, CA: Sage.

Dahl, R. (1957) 'The Concept of Power', in *Behavioural Science*, 2, 201–5.

Dahl, R. (1961) *Who Governs? Democracy and Power in an American City*, New Haven, CT: Yale University Press.

Dahl, R. (1986) 'Power as the Control of Behaviour', in Lukes, S. (ed.), *Power*, Oxford: Blackwell.

Daly, M. (1984) *Pure Lust: Elemental Feminist Philosophy*, London: Women's Press.

Davidson, M. (1991) Women Managers in Britain – Issues for the 1990s', *Women in Management Review and Abstracts*, 6(1), 5–10.

Davidson, M. (1997) *The Black and Ethnic Minority Woman Manager*, London: Paul Chapman.

Davidson, M. and Burke, R. (1994) *Women in Management: Current Research Issues*, London: Paul Chapman.

Davidson, M. and Cooper, C. (1983) *Stress and the Woman Manager*, London: Martin Robertson.

Davidson, M. and Cooper, C. (1992) *Shattering the Glass Ceiling: The Woman Manager* London: Paul Chapman.

Davies, C. (1995) *Gender and the Professional Predicament in Nursing*, Buckingham: Open University Press.

Davies, C. (1996) The Sociology of the Professions and the Profession of Gender, *Sociology*, **30**(4), 661–78.

Davis, A. (1981) *Women, Race and Class*, London: Women's Press.

Davis, C. and Watson, C. (1982) *Black Life in Corporate America: Swimming in the Mainstream*, New York: Anchor Press/Doubleday.

Deal, T.E. and Kennedy, A (1982) *Corporate cultures: The Rites and Rituals of Corporate Life*, Reading, MA: Addison-Wesley.

DeMatteo, L. (1994) 'From Hierarchy to Unity Between Men and Women Managers: Towards an Androgynous Style of Management', *Women in Management Review*, **9**(7), 21–8.

Denton, T. (1990) 'Bonding and Supportive Relationships Among Black Professional Women: Rituals of Restoration', in *Journal of Organisational Behaviour*, **11**, 447–57.

Devanna, M. (1987) 'Women in Management: Progress and Promise', *Human Resource Management*, **26**(4), 469–81.

Dickens, L. (1989) 'Women: A rediscovered Resource?', in *Industrial Relations Journal*, **20**, 167–75.

Dinnerstein, D. (1977) The Mermaid and the Minotaur: Sexual Arrangements and the Human Malaise, New York: Harper & Row.

Dowling, C. (1988) *Perfect Women*, New York: Summit Books.

du Gay, P. (1996) *Consumption and Identity at Work*, London: Sage.

Driscoll, J. and Bova, R. (1980) The Sexual Side of Enterprise, *Management Review*, **69**, 51–62.

Dumas, R. (1980) 'Dilemmas of Black Females in Leadership Positions', in La Frances Rogers-Rose (ed.), *The Black Woman*, London, Sage.

Dunne, G. (1992) 'Difference at Work: Perceptions of Work from a Non-Heterosexual Perspective', in Hinds H., Phoenix, A. and Stacey, J. (eds), *Working Out: New Directions for Women's Studies*, Brighton: Falmer Press.

Eakins, N. and Eakins, G. (1976) 'Verbal Turntaking and Exchanges in Faculty Dialogue', in Dubois, M. and Crouch, I. (eds), *The Sociology of the Language of American Women* Papers in Southwest English IV, Trinity University, San Antonio, TX.

EOC (1996) *Briefings on Women and Men in Britain: Pay*, London: HMSO.

EOC (1997a) *Briefings on Women and Men in Britain: The Labour Market*, London: HMSO.

EOC (1997b) *Briefings on Women and Men in Britain: Management and the Professions*, London: HMSO.

EOC (1997c) *Briefings on Women and Men in Britain: Income and Personal Finance*, London: HMSO.

EOR (1994a) *Equal Opportunities Review*, vol. 54.

EOR (1994b) *Equal Opportunities Review*, vol. 55.

EOR (1995) *Equal Opportunities Review*, vol. 59.

EOR (1997a) *Equal Opportunities Review*, vol. 74.

EOR (1997b) *Equal Opportunities Review*, vol. 76.

EOR (1998a) *Equal Opportunities Review*, vol. 77.

EOR (1998) *Equal Opportunities Review*, vol. 78.

EOR (1998b) *Equal Opportunities Review*, vol. 79.

EOR (1998c) *Equal Opportunities Review*, vol. 81.

EOR (1998d) *Equal Opportunities Review*, vol. 82.

EOR (1999) *Equal Opportunities Review*, vol. 83.

Epstein, D. (1997) 'Keeping Them in their Place: Hetero/sexist harassment, Gender and the Enforcement of Heterosexuality', in Thomas, A. and Kitzinger, C. (eds) *Sexual Harassment: Contemporary Feminist Perspectives*, Buckingham: Open University Press.

Essed, P. (1991) *Understanding Everyday Racism*, London: Sage.

Evetts, J. (1994) 'Gender and Secondary Headship: Managerial Experiences', in Evetts, J. (ed.), *Women and Career: Themes and issues in Advanced Industrial Societies*, Harlow: Longman.

Exworthy, M. and Halford, S. (1999) *Professionals and the New Managerialism in the Public Sector*, Buckingham: Open University Press.

Fagenson, E. (1986) 'Women's Work Orientations: Something Old, Something New', *Group and Organization Studies*, **11**, 75–100.

Farley, L. (1978) *Sexual Shakedown: The Sexual Harassment of Women on the Job*, New York: Warner Books.

Feber, M., Huber, J. and Spitze, G. (1979) 'Preference for Men as Bosses and Professionals', *Social Forces*, **58**, 466–76.

Ferguson, K. (1984) *The Feminist Case Against Bureaucracy*, Philadelphia, PA: Temple University Press.

Fernandez, J. (1980) *Racism and Sexism in Corporate Life*, Lexington: MA, Lexington Books.

Fierman, J. (1990) 'Do Women Manage Differently?', *Fortune*, 17 December, pp. 115–18.

Fisher, S. (1991) 'A Discourse of the Social: Medical Talk/Power Talk/Oppositional Talk', *Discourse and Society*, **2**(2), 157–82.

Fitzgerald, L., Shullman, S., Bailey, N., Richards, M., Swecker, J., Gold, Y., Ormerod, M. and Weitzman, L. (1988) 'The Incidence and Dimensions of Sexual harassment in Academia and the Workplace', *Journal of Vocational Behaviour*, **32**, 152–75.

Forbes, I. (1991) 'Equal Opportunities: Radical, Liberal and Conservative Critiques', in Meehan, E. and Sevenhuijsen, S. (eds), *Equality, Politics and Gender*, London: Sage.

Foucault, M. (1977) *Discipline and Punish: The Birth of the Prison*, London, Allen Lane.

Foucault M (1980) 'The History of Sexuality: An Interview', trans. G. Bennington, *Oxford Literary Review*, **4**(2), 13.

Foucault, M. (1981) *The History of Sexuality*, vol. 1, Harmondsworth: Penguin.

Foucault, M. (1986) 'Disciplinary Power and Subjection', in Lukes, S. (ed.), *Power*, Oxford: Blackwell.

Foucault, M. (1988) 'On Power', an interview with Michel Foucault (1978), reprinted in Kritzman, L. (ed.), *Foucault: Politics, Philosophy and Culture*, London: Routledge.

Freeman, J. (1975) *The Politics of Women's Liberation* New York: David McKay.

Friedan, B. (1965) *The Feminine Mystique*, London: Gollancz.

Gabin, N. (1989) *Feminism in the Labor Movement: Women in the United Auto Workers 1935–75*, Ithaca, NY: Cornell University Press.

Game, A. and Pringle, R. (1983) *Gender at Work*, London: Pluto.

Garrett-Gooding, J. and Senter, R. (1989) 'Attitudes and Acts of Sexual Aggression on a University Campus', *Sociological Inquiry*, **57**, 348–71.

Gerson, K. (1985) *Hard Choices: How Women Decide about Work, Career and Motherhood*, Berkeley, University of California Press.

Ghazi, P. (1999) '*1980 Superwoman, 1990 Downshifter, 2000 Portfolio Parent*', *Guardian*, G2, Wednesday 26 May, pp. 8–9.

Gherardi, S. (1996) 'Gendered Organizational Cultures: Narratives of Women Travellers in a Male World', *Gender, Work and Organization*, **3**(4), 187–201.

Giddens, A. (1984) *The Constitution of Society*, Cambridge: Polity Press.

Giddens, A. (1992) *The Transformation of Intimacy*, Cambridge: Polity Press.

Gilligan, C. (1982) *In a Different Voice: Psychological Theory and Women's Development* Cambridge, MA: Harvard University Press.

Gilman, S. (1985) *Difference and Pathology*, Ithaca, NY: Cornell University Press.

Glucklich, P. (1984) 'The Effects of Statutory Employment Policies on Women in the UK Labour Market', in Schmid, G. and Weitzel, R. (eds), *Sex Discrimination and Equal Opportunity*, New York: St Martin's Press.

Gordon, C. (ed.) (1980) *Michel Faucault: Power/Knowledge: Selected Interviews and Other Writings 1972–1977*, Hemel Hempstead, Harvester Wheatsheaf.

Gould, R. (1974) 'Measuring Masculinity by the Size of a Paycheck', in Pleck, J. and Sawyer, J. (eds), *Men and Masculinity*, New York: Prentice-Hall.

Grant, J. (1988) 'Women as Managers: What They Can Offer to Organizations', *Organisational Dynamics*, **16**(3) (Winter), 56–63.

Grant, L. (1997) 'The Age of Optimism', *Guardian* G2, Tuesday 27 May, pp. 2–7.

Green, E. and Cassell, C. (1996) 'Women Managers, Gendered Cultural Processes and Organizational Change', *Gender, Work and Organization*, **3**(3) (July), 168–78.

Greenhaus, J., Parasuraman, S. and Wormley, W. (1990) 'Effects of Race on Organisational Experiences, Job Performance Evaluations and Career Outcomes', in *Academy of Management Review*, **33**(1), 64–86.

Gregory, J. (1982) 'Some Cases that Never Reached the Tribunal', in *Feminist Review*, **10**, 75–89.

Grint, K. (1991) *The Sociology of Work*, Oxford: Polity Press.

Guardian (1997a) '50 Most Powerful Women', 26 May, 2–9.

Guardian (1997b) '50 Most Powerful Women', 27 May, 2–7.

Gutek, B. (1985) *Sex and the Workplace: The Impact of Sexual Behaviour and Harassment on Women, Men and Organizations*, San Francisco, CA: Jossey-Bass.

Gutek, B. (1989) 'Sexuality in the Workplace: Key Issues in Social Research and Organizational Practice', in Hearn, J., Sheppard, D., Tancred-Sheriff, P. and Burrell, G., (eds), *The Sexuality of Organization*, London: Sage.

Gutek, B. And Dunwoody, V. (1987) 'Understanding Sex in the Workplace', in Stromberg, A. Larwood, L. and Gutek, B. (eds), *Women and Work: An Annual Review*, 2, Newbury Park, CA: Sage, pp. 249–69.

Hadjifotiou, N. (1983) *Women and Harassment at Work*, London: Pluto.

Halford, S. (1989a) 'Local Authority Women's Initiatives 1982–1988: The Extent, Origins and Efficacy of Positive Policies for Women in British Local Government', Urban and Regional Working Papers no. 69, University of Sussex.

Halford, S. (1989b) 'Spatial Divisions and Women's Initiatives in Local Government', in *Geoforum*, **20**(2), 161–74.

Halford, S. (1991) 'Local Politics, Feminism and the Local State: Women's Initiatives in British Local Government in the 1980s', Unpublished Ph.D. thesis, University of Sussex.

Halford, S. (1992) 'Feminist Change in a Patriarchal Organisation: The Experience of Women's Initiatives in Local Government and Implications for Feminist Perspectives on State Institutions', in Savage, M. and Witz, A. (eds), *Gender and Bureaucracy*, Oxford: Blackwell.

Halford, S. and Savage, M. (1995) 'Restructuring Organisations, Changing People: Gender and Restructuring in Banking and Local Government', in *Work, Employment and Society*, **9**(1), 97–122.

Halford, S., Savage, M. and Witz, A. (1997) *Gender, Careers and Organisations: Current Developments in Banking, Nursing and Local Government*, Basingstoke: Macmillan.

Halford, S, and Leonard, P. (1999) 'New Identities? Professionalism, Managerialism and the Construction of Self', in Exworthy, M. and Halford, S. *Professionals and the New Managerialism in the Public Sector*, Buckingham: Open University Press.

Hall, M. (1989) 'Private Experiences in the Public Domain', in Burrell, G. and Hearn, J. (eds), *The Sexuality of Organisation*, London: Sage.

Hall, S. (1997) 'The Work of Representation', in Hall, S. (ed.), *Representation: Cultural Representations and Signifying Practices*, London: Sage.

Hammond, V. (1997) 'Cultural Change and Equal Opportunities: Learning from Opportunity 2000', in *Equal Opportunities Review*, no. 75, 14–22.

Hänninen-Salmelin, E. and Petajaniemi, T. (1994) 'Women Managers: The Case of Finland', in Adler, N. J. and Izraeli, D. N. (eds), *Competitive Frontiers: Women Managers in a Global Economy*, Cambridge, MA: Blackwell.

Hansard Society Commission (1990) 'Women at the Top', London: Hansard Society.

Harding, S. (1988) *The Science Question in Feminism*, Ithaca, NY: Cornell University Press.

Harlan, A. and Weiss, C. (1980) *Moving Up: Women in Managerial Careers: Third Progress Report*, Wellesley, MA: Wellesley Center for Research on Women.

Harragan, B. (1977) *Games Mother Never Taught You*, New York: Warner Books.

Hearn, J. (1985) 'Men's Sexuality at Work', in Metcalfe, A. and Humphries, M. *The Sexuality of Men*, London: Pluto Press.

Hearn, J. and Parkin, W. (1987) *'Sex' at 'Work': The Power and Paradox of Organisation Sexuality*, Brighton, Wheatsheaf Books.

Heery,E. and Kelly, J. (1989) 'A cracking Job for a Woman: A Profile of Women Trade Union Officers', in *Industrial Relations Journal*, **20**, 192–202.

Hegelson, S. (1990) *The Female Advantage: Women's Ways of Leadership*, New York: Doubleday/Currency.

Heilman, M., Block, C. and Lucas, J. (1992) 'Presumed Incompetent? Stigmatisation and Affirmative Action', *Journal of Applied Psychology*, **77**(4), 536–44.

Henley, N. (1977) *Body Politics, Power, Sex and Nonverbal Communication*, Englewood Cliffs, NJ: Prentice-Hall.

Hennig, M. and Jardim, A. (1979) *The Managerial Woman*, London: Marian Boyars.

Herek, G. (1992) 'Physiological Heterosexism and Anti-gay Violence: the Social Psychology of Biogtry and Bashing', in G. Herek and K. Berrill (eds), *Hate Crimes: Confronting Violence Against Lesbians and Gay Men*, London, Sage.

Hill-Collins, P. (1990) *Black Feminist Thought*, London: Routledge.

Hindess, B. (1996) *Discourses of Power*, Oxford: Blackwell.

Hochschild, A. (1983) *The Managed Heart: Commercialization of Human Feeling*, Berkeley, CA: University of California Press.

Hochschild, A. (1989) *The Second Shift: Working Parents and the Revolution at Home*, London: Piatkus.

Hollway, W. (1984) 'Gender Difference and the Production of Subjectivity', in Henriques, J., Hollway, W., Urwin, C., Venn, C. and Walkerdine, V. (eds), *Changing the Subject: Psychology, Social Regulation and Subjectivity*, London: Methuen.

Horner, M. (1972) 'Toward an Understanding of Achievement Related Conflicts in Women', *Journal of Social Issues*, **28**, 157–76.

Hunt, R. (1994) 'Seventy Times Seven? Forgiveness and Sexual Violence in Christian Pastoral Care', in *Rethinking Sexual Harassment*, London: Pluto.

Hunter, A. (1993) 'Same Door, Different Closet: A Heterosexual Sissy's Coming Out Party', in Wilkinson, S. and Kitzinger, C. (eds) *Heterosexuality: A Feminism and Psychology Reader*, London: Sage.

Ianello, K. (1992) *Decisions without Hierarchy: Feminist Interventions in Organization Theory and Practice*, New York: Routledge.

Ibarra, H. (1993) 'Personal Networks of Women and Minorities in Management: A Conceptual Framework', in *Academy of Management Review*, **18**(1), 56–87.

IDS (1993) *No Offence*, London: Industrial Society.

IHSM Consultants (1995) *Creative Career Paths in the NHS*, London: IHSM.

Income Data Services (IDS) (1989) *Women in the Labour Market*, IDS Report 8, Labour Market Supplement, London.

Institute of Management and Renumeration Economics (IoMRE) (1996) *1996 National Management Salary Survey* London.

Irigaray, L. (1991) *The Irigaray Reader*, Whitford, M. (ed.), Oxford: Blackwell.

Jewson, N. and Mason, D. (1986) 'Theory and Practice of Equal Opportunities Policies', in *Sociological Review*, **34**(2), 307–34.

Jewson, N. and Mason, D. (1994) ' "Race", Employment and Equal Opportunities: Towards a Political Economy and an Agenda for the 1990s', in *Sociological Review*, **42**(2), 591–617.

Kahn, W. and Crosby, F. (1985) 'Discriminating Between Attitudes and Discriminatory Behaviour: Change and Stasis', Larwood, L., Stromberg, A. and Gutek, B. (eds), *Women and Work: An Annual Review 1*, Beverly Hills, CA: Sage.

Kanter, R. (1977a) *Men and Women of the Corporation*, New York, Basic Books.

Kanter, R. (1977b) *Work and Family in the United States: A Critical Review and Agenda for Research and Policy*, New York: Russell Sage Foundation.

Kanter, R. (1983) *The Change Masters: Corporate Entrepreneurs at Work*, London: Routledge.

Kanter, R. (1989) *When Giants Learn to Dance: Mastering the Challenges of Strategy*, London: Routledge.

Kanter, R. (1993) *Men and Women of Re Corporation*, 2nd edn, New York: Basic Books.

Kelly, E. (1987) 'The Continuum of Sexual Violence', in *Women, Violence and Social Control*, Basingstoke: Macmillan.

King, M. 'Human Capital and black women's occupational mobility'. *Industrial Relations*, vol.34, No.2, pp. 282–98.

Kitzinger, C. (1990) 'Beyond the Boundaries: Lesbians in Academe', in Lie, S. and O'Leary, V. (eds), *Storming the Tower: Women in the Academic World*, London: Kogan Page/Nichols/GP.

Kitzinger, C. (1994) 'Anti-Lesbian Harassment', in Brant, C. and Too, Y. L., *Rethinking Sexual Harassment*, London: Pluto.

Kitzinger, C. and Thomas, A. (1995) 'Sexual Harassment: A Discursive Approach', in Wilkinson, S. and Kitzinger, C. (eds), *Feminism and Discourse: Psychological Perspectives* London: Sage.

Korabik, K. (1990) 'Androgyny and Leadership Style', *Journal of Business Ethics*, *9*, (4 and 5) (April/May), 283–92.

Korabik, K. (1981) 'Androgyny and Leadership: An Integration', paper presented at the meeting of the Association for Women and Psychology, Boston, MA.

Korabik, K. and Ayman, R. (1987) 'Androgyny and Leadership: A Conceptual Synthesis', paper presented at the meeting of the American Psychological Association, New York.

Kritzman, L. (ed.) (1998) *Foucault: Politics, Philosophy and Culture*, London: Routledge.

Labour Force Survey (1995) London: HMSO.

Ledwith, S., Colgan, F., Joyce, P. and Hayes, M. (1990) 'The making of women trade union leaders', in *Industrial Relations Journal*, **21**, 112–25.

Legge, K. (1995) *Human Resource Management: Rhetorics and Realities*, Basingstoke: Macmillan.

Leggon, C. (1980) 'Black female professionals: dilemmas and contradictions of status', in La Frances Rogers-Rose (ed.), *The Black Woman*, Lara, Sage.

Leonard, A. (1987) *Pyrrtic victories*, London: HMSO.

Leonard, P. (1995) 'Gender/Organisation/Representation: A Critical and Poststructuralist Approach to Gender and Organisational Theory', Unpublished Ph.D. Thesis, University of Southampton.

Leonard, P. (1998a) 'Women Behaving Badly? Restructuring Gender and Identity in British Broadcasting Organizations', *Harvard International Journal of Press Politics*, **3**(1), pp. 9–25.

Leonard, P. (1998b) 'Gendering Change? Management, Masculinity and the Dynamics of Incorporation', *Gender and Education*, **10**(1) (March) 71–84.

Leonard, P. and Malina, D. (1994) 'Caught Between Two Worlds: Mothers as Academics', in Davies, S., Lubelska, C. and Quinn, J. (eds), *Changing the Subject: Women in Higher Education* London: Taylor & Francis.

Lewis, M. (1989) *Liar's Poker: Two Cities, True Greed*, London, Hodder & Stoughton.

Liff, S. and Cameron, I. (1997) 'Changing Equality Cultures to Move Beyond "Women's Problems"', *Gender, Work and Organization*, **4**(1), 35–46.

Liff, S. and Dale, K. (1994) 'Formal Opportunity, Informal Barriers: Black Women Managers within a Local Authority', in *Work, Employment and Society*, **8**(2), 177–98.

Loden, M. (1985) *Feminine Leadership–or–How to Succeed Without Being One of the Boys*, New York: Times Books.

Lukes, S. (1974) *Power: A Radical View*, Basingstoke: Macmillan.

McDowell, L. (1997) *Capital Culture: Gender at Work in the City*, Oxford: Blackwell.

McDowell, L. and Court, J. (1994) 'Missing Subjects: Gender, Power and Sexuality in Merchant Banking', in *Economic Geography*, **70**(3), 229–51.

MccGwire, S. (1999) 'Would You Give a Job to This Man?', *Guardian*, G2, Wednesday 9 June, pp. 6–7.

McKeen, C. and Burke, R. (1989) 'Mentor Relationships in Organizations: Issues, Strategies and Prospects for Women', *Journal of Management Development*, **8**(6), 33–42.

MacKinnon, C. (1979) *Sexual Harassment of Working Women*, New Haven, CT: Yale University Press.

McNay, L. (1994) *Foucault: A Critical Introduction*, Cambridge: Polity Press.

Maddock, S. (1993) 'Barriers to Women Are Barriers to Local Government', in *Local Government Studies*, **19**(3), 341–50.

Maddock, S. and Parkin, D. (1993) 'Gender Cultures: Women's Choices and Strategies at Work', *Women in Management Review*, **8**(2), 3–9.

Marsh, C. (1988) *Exploring Data: An Introduction to Data Analysis for Social Scientists*, Cambridge University Press.

Marshall, J. (1984) *Women Managers: Travellers in a Male World*, Chichester: John Wiley.

Marshall, J. (1985) 'Paths of Personal and Professional Development for Women Managers', *Management Education and Development*, **16**(2), 169–79.

Marshall, J. (1995) *Women Managers Moving On: Exploring Career and Life Choices*, London: Routledge.

Martin, J. (1992) *Cultures in Organizations: Three Perspectives*, New York: Oxford University Press.

Meehan, E. and Sevenhuijsen, S. (1991) 'Problems and Principles in Policies', in Meehan, E. and Sevenhuijsen, S. (eds), *Equality, Politics and Gender*, London: Sage.

Merit Systems Protection Board (MSPB) (1994) *Sexual Harassment in the Federal Workplace: Trends, Progress and Continuing Challenges*, Washington DC, US Government Printing Office.

Mill, H.T. (1970) 'Enfranchaisment of women' in Rossi, A. (ed.), *Essays on Sex Equality*, University of Chicago Press.

Mill, J.S. (1970) 'The Subjugation of Women', in Rossi, A. (ed.), *Essays on Sex Equality*, University of Chicago Press.

Mills, A. (1988) 'Organization, Gender and Culture', *Organization Studies*, 9(3), 351–69.

Mirza, H. (1998) *Black British Feminism*, London: Routledge.

Mohanty, C. T. (1991) 'Under Western Eyes: Feminist Scholarship and Colonial Discourses', in C. T. Mohanty, A. Russo and L. Torres (ed.), *Third World Women and the Politics of Feminism*, Bloomington, Indiana University Press.

Morely, L. (1994) 'Glass Ceiling or Iron Cage: Women in UK Academia', *Gender, Work and Organization*, 1(4), 194–204.

Morgan, G. (1986) *Images of Organisation*, London: Sage. .

Morgan, G. (1990) *Organisations in Society*, Basingstoke: Macmillan.

MORI (1985) *Working in Britain*, London.

Morrison, A. (1992) 'New Solutions to the Same Old Glass Ceiling', *Women in Management Review*, 7(4), 15–19.

Morrison, A. and Von Glinow, M. (1990) 'Women and Minorities in Management', *American Psychologist*, February, 200–8.

Morrison, A., White, R. and Van Velsor, E. (1992) *Breaking the Glass Ceiling: Can Women Reach the Top of America's Largest Corporations*, Reading, MA: Addison-Wesley.

Nelson, M. (1988) 'Women's Ways: Interactive Patterns in Predominantly Female Research Teams', in Bate, B. and Taylor, A. (eds), *Women Communicating: Studies of Women's Talk*, Norwood, NJ: Ablex.

Newman, J. (1995) 'Gender and Cultural Change', in Itzen, C. and Newman, J. (1995) (eds), *Gender, Culture and Organizational Change: Putting Theory into Practice*, London: Routledge.

Nicholson, N. and West, M. (1988) *Managerial Job Change: Men and Women in Transition*, Cambridge University Press.

Nieva, V. and Gutek, B. (1981) *Women and Work: A Psychological Perspective*, New York: Praeger.

Nippert-Eng, C. (1996) *Home and Work: Negotiating Boundaries through Everyday Life*, University of Chicago Press.

Nkomo, S. (1988) 'Race and Sex: the Forgotten Case of the Black Female Manager', in Rose, S. and Larwood, L. (eds), *Women's Careers: Pathways and Pitfalls*, New York: Praeger.

Noe, R. (1988) 'Women and Mentoring: A Review and Research Agenda', *Academy of Management Review*, 13, 65–78.

Northcraft, G.B. and Gutek, B.A. (1993) 'Point-Counterpoint: Discrimination Against Women in Management – Going, Going, Gone or Going But Never Gone?', in E.A. Fagenson (ed.), *Women in Management: Trends, Issues and Challenges in Managerial Diversity*, Newbury Park, Sage.

O'Leary, V. (1974) 'Some Attitudinal Barriers to Occupational Aspirations in Women', *Psychological Bulletin*, 29, 809–26.

O'Leary, V. (1988) 'Women's Relationships with Women in the Workplace', in Gutek, B. A. Larwood, L. and Stromberg, A. (eds), *Women and Work: An Annual Review 3*, Beverly Hills, CA: Sage.

O'Leary, V. and Johnson, J. (1991) 'Steep Ladder, Lonely Climb', *Women in Management Review and Abstracts*, **6**(5), 10–16.

O'Leary, V. and Ryan, M. (1994) 'Women Bosses: Counting the Changes or Changes that Count', in Tanton M. (ed.), *Women in Management: A Developing Presence*, London, Routledge.

OPCS (1991) *British Census of Population*, London, HMSO.

Opportunity 2000 (1994) *Annual Report*.

Orser, B. (1994) Sex Role Stereotypes and Requisite Management Characteristics: An International Perspective, *Women in Management Review*, **9**(4), 11–19.

Paludi, M. (ed.) (1987) *Ivory Tower: Sexual Harassment on Campus State University*, New York: Albany Press.

Parasuraman, S. and Greenhaus, J. (1993) 'Personal Portrait: The Lifestyle of the Woman Manager', in Fagenson E. A. (ed.), *Women in Management: Trends, Issues and Challenges in Managerial Diversity*, Newbury Park: Sage.

Parkin, W. (1993) 'The Public and the Private: Gender, Sexuality and Emotion', in Fineman, S. (ed.) *Emotion in Organizations*, London: Sage.

Pateman, C. (1988) *The Sexual Contract*, Cambridge: Polity Press.

Pemberton, C. (1995) 'Organisational Culture and Equalities Work', in Shaw, J. and Perrons, D. (eds), *Making Gender Work: Managing Equal Opportunities*, Buckingham: Open University Press.

Persaud, I., Sipley, B., Coutts, B. and Colwill, N.L. (1990) 'Gender Differences in Informal Social Supports: Implicating Women into Management', Paper presented at the 1990 ASAC Conference, Whistler, BC, June.

Peters, T. (1990) 'The Best New Managers Will Listen, Motivate, Support: Isn't That Just Like a Woman?', *Working Woman*, September, 142–3, 216–7.

Peters, T. and Waterman, R. (1982) *In Search of Excellence*, London: HarperCollins.

Pettigrew, A. (1979) 'On Studying Organizational Cultures', *Administrative Science Quarterly*, **24**(4), 570–81.

Phillips, A. (1991) *Engendering Democracy*, Cambridge: Polity Press.

Porter, H. (1997) 'Smashing the Glass Ceiling', *Guardian*, Monday 26 May, pp. 2–9.

Powell, G. (1986) 'Effects of Sex Role Identity and Sex on Definitions of Sexual Harassment', *Sex Roles*, **14**(1/2), 9–18.

Powell, G. (1988) *Women and Men in Management*, London: Sage.

Powell, G. (1990) One More Time: Do Female and Male Managers Differ?', *Academy of Management Executive*, **4**(3), 68–75.

Prince, J. (1993) Introduction to M. Hall, 'Private Experiences in the Public Domain: Lesbians in Organizations', in Jackson, S. Atkinson, K., Beddore, D., Brewer, T., Faulkner, S., Hucklesby, A., Pearson, R., Power, H., Prince, J., Ryan, M. and Young, P. (eds), 'Women's Studies: A Reader', Hemel Hempstead: Harvester Wheatsheaf.

Pringle, R. (1989) *Secretaries Talk: The Power and Paradox of Organisation Sexuality* London, Verso.

Quinn, R. (1977) 'Coping with Cupid: The Formation, Impact and Management of Romantic Relationships in Organizations', *Administrative Science Quarterly*, 22, 30–45.

Quinn, R. and Lees, P. (1984) 'Attraction and Harassment: Dynamics of Sexual Harassment in the Workplace', *Organizational Dynamics*, **13**(2), 35–46.

Radice, S. (1999) 'Careers Maketh the Man', *Guardian*, G2, Wednesday 16 June, p. 10.

Raitt, S. (1994) 'Sexual Harassment and Sexual Abuse: When Girls Become Women', in Brant, C. and Too, Y.L. (eds), *Rethinking Sexual Harassment*, London: Pluto.

Rees, T. (1992) *Women and the Labour Market*, London: Routledge.

Renshaw, J. (1988) 'Women in Management in the Pacific Islands: Exploring Pacific Stereotypes', in Adler, N. J. and Izraeli, D. N. (eds), *Women in Management Worldwide*, New York: Sharpe.

Ressner, U. (1987) *The Hidden Hierarchy: Democracy and Equal Opportunities*, Aldershot: Avebury,.

Rexford S. and Mainiero L. (1986) 'The "Right Stuff" of Management: Challenges Confronting Women', *SAM Advanced Management Journal*, Spring, 36–40.

Rich, A. (1976) *Of Woman Born: Motherhood as Experience and Institution*, London: Virago.

Rich, A. (1984) 'Compulsory Heterosexuality and Lesbian Existence', in Snitow, A., Stansell, C. and Thompson, S. (eds), *Powers of Desire: The Politics of Sexuality*, New York: New Feminist Library.

Richardson, D. (1993) 'Sexuality and Male Dominance', in Richardson, D. and Robinson, V. (eds), *Introducing Women's Studies*, Basingstoke: Macmillan.

Rigg, C. and Sparrow, J. (1994) 'Gender, Diversity and Working Styles', *Women in Management Review*, **9**(1), 9–16.

Roper, M. (1988) 'Fathers and Lovers: Images of the "Older Man" in British Managers' Career Narratives', *Life Stories/Recits de vie*, 4, 49–58.

Rosener, J. (1990) 'Ways Women Lead', *Harvard Business Review*, November–December, 119–125.

Rowbotham, S. (1989) *The Past Is Before Us: Feminism in Action Since the 1960s*, London: Pandora Press.

Rowbotham, S., Wainright, H. and Segal, L. (1979) *Beyond the Fragments: Feminism and the Making of Socialism*, London: Merlin.

Rowe, D. (1999) '5 Women Who Always Get Their Own Way', *She*, July, 102–06.

Rubenstein, M. (1999) *Discrimination: A Guide to the Relevant Case Law on Race and Sex Discrimination and Equal Pay*, London: Industrial Relations Society.

Sargent, A. G. (1981) *The Androgynous Manager*, New York, Amacom.

Sargent, A. and Stupak R. (1989) 'Managing in the '90s: The Androgynous Manager *Training and Development Journal*', December, 30–35.

Savage, M. (1992) 'Women's Expertise, Men's Authority: Gendered Organisation and the Contemporary Middle Classes', in Savage, M. and Witz, A. (eds), *Gender and Bureaucracy*, Oxford: Blackwell.

Scase, R. and Goffee, R. (1989) 'Women in Management – Towards a Research Agenda', paper presented at British Academy of Management Conference, September.

Schein, V. (1973) 'The Relationship Between Sex-Role Stereotypes and Requisite Management Characteristics', *Journal of Applied Psychology*, 57(2), 95–100.

Schein, V. (1975) 'Relationships Between Sex-Role Stereotypes and Requisite Management Characteristics Among Female Managers', *Journal of Applied Psychology*, 60(3), 340–4.

Schein, V. (1978) 'Sex-Role Stereotyping, Ability and Performance: Prior Research and New Directions', *Personnel Psychology*, 31, 259–68.

Schein, V. (1989) 'Sex-Role Stereotypes and Requisite Management Characteristics Past, Present and Future', paper presented at the Current Research on Women in Management Conference, Queen's University, Ontario, Canada, September 24–6.

Schein, V. and Mueller, R. (1990) 'Sex-Role Stereotyping and Requisite Management Characteristics: A Cross-cultural Look', paper presented at the 22nd International Congress of Applied Psychology, Kyoto, Japan, 22–27 July.

Scott, J. (1988) 'Deconstructing Equality-Versus-Difference: Or, the Uses of Poststructuralist Theory for Feminism', in *Feminist Studies*, 14(1), 33–50.

Schur, E. (1984) *Labelling Women Deviant*, New York: Random House.

Schwartz, F. (1989) 'Management Women and the New Facts of Life', *Harvard Business Review*, January–February, 65–76.

Scouller, E. (1992) *Equal Opportunities for Women in Banking: A Case Study of Lloyds and National Westminster Banks*, Occasional Paper no. 3, University of Bradford, Work and Gender Research Unit.

Sekaran, U. (1986) *Dual-Career Families: Contemporary Organizational and Counselling Issues* San Francisco, CA: Jossey Bass.

Serdjenian, E. (1994) 'Women Managers in France', in Adler, N. J. and Izraeli, D.N. (eds) *Competitive Frontiers: Women Managers in a Global Economy* Cambridge, MA: Paul Chapman.

Sheppard, D. (1989) 'Organizations, Power and Sexuality: The Image and Self-Image of Women Managers', in Hearn, J. *et al.* (eds), *The Sexuality of Organization*, London: Sage.

Shoenberger, E. (1994) 'Corporate Strategy and Corporate Strategists: Power, Identity and Knowledge Within the Firm', *Environment and Planning, A 26*, 435–51.

Skinner, J. (1988) 'Who's Changing Whom? Women Management and Organisation', in Coyle, A. and Skinner, J. (eds), *Women and Work: Positive Action for Change*, London: Macmillan.

Smart, B. (1988) *Michel Foucault*, London: Routledge.

Smircich, L. (1983) 'Concepts of Culture and Organisational Analysis', *Administrative Science Quarterly*, 28, 339–58.

Smith, D. (1988) *The Everyday World as Problematic: A Feminist Sociology*, Milton Keynes, Open University Press.

Snell, B., Glucklich, P. and Povall, M. (1981) *Equal Pay and Opportunities: A Study of the Implementation and Effects of the Equal Pay and Sex Discrimination Acts in 26 Organisations*, Department of Employment Research Paper no. 20. London.

Social Trends 28 (1998) London: The Stationery Office.

Somers, A. (1982) Sexual Harassment in Academe – Legal Issues and Definitions *Journal of Social Issues*, **38**, 23–32.

Spaights, E. and Whitaker, A. (1995) 'Black Women in the Workforce: A New Look At an Old Problem', *Journal of Black Studies*, **25**(3), 283–96.

Speakman, S. and Marchington, M. (1999) 'Ambivalent Patriarchs, Shiftworkers, Breadwinners and Housework', *Work, Employment and Society*, **13**(1), 83–105.

Spelman, E. (1988) *Inessential Woman: Problems of Exclusion in Feminist Thought*, Boston: Beacon.

Stamp, P. and Robarts, S. (1986) *Positive Action: Changing the Workplace for Women*, London: National Council for Civil Liberties.

Stanko, E. (1985) *Intimate Intrusion*, London: Routledge.

Stanko, E. (1988) 'Keeping Women In and Out of Line: Sexual Harassment and Occupational Segregation', in Walby, S (ed.), *Gender Segregation at Work*, Milton Keynes: Open University Press.

Stockdale, J. (1991) 'Sexual Harassment at Work', in Firth-Cozens, J. and West, M. A. (eds), *Women at Work: Psychological and Organizational Perspectives*, Buckingham: Open University Press.

Stone, I. (1988) *Equal Opportunities in Local Authorities*, London: HMSO.

Storey, J. (1993) *An Introductory Guide to Cultural Theory and Popular Culture*, Hemel Hempstead: Harvester Wheatsheaf.

Straw, J. (1989) *Equal Opportunities: The Way Ahead*, London, Institute of Personnel Management.

Sutton, S. and Moore, K. (1985) 'Probing Opinions: Executive Women – 20 years later', *Harvard Business Review*, *85*(5), 42–66.

Tangri, S., Burt, M. and Johnson, L. (1982) 'Social Harassment at Work: Three Explanatory Models', *Journal of Social Issues*, *38*(4), 55–74.

Tannen, D. (1992) 'Response to Senta Troemel-Ploetz's "Selling the Apolitical"', *Discourse and Society*, *3*(2), 249–54.

Tanton, M. (1992) 'Developing Authenticity in Management Development Programmes', *Women in Management Review*, *4*, 20–6.

Tanton, M. (1994) 'Developing Women's Presence', in Tanton, M. (ed.), *Women in Management: A Developing Presence*, London: Routledge.

Tashjian, V. (1990) *Don't Blame the Baby: Why Women Leave Corporations*, Wimington, DE: Wick.

Taylor, F.W. *Scientific Management*, New York: Harper & Row

Thomas, A. and Kitzinger, C. (1994) 'It's Just Something that Happens: The Invisibility of Sexual Harassment in the Workplace', *Gender, Work and Organization*, *1*(3), 151–61.

Thomas, A.M. and Kitzinger, C. (1997) 'Sexual harassment: reviewing the fields' in Thomas A.M. and Kitrzinger, C. (eds) *Sexual Harassment: Contemporary Feminist Perspectives*, Buckingham: Open University Press.

Thomas, R. (1997) 'Kate Barker', *Guardian*, G2, Monday 26 May, p. 6.

Thompson, D. and McHugh, D. (1990) *Work Organisations*, Basingstoke: Macmillan.

Thompson, P. and Ackroyd, S. (1994) 'Ain't Misbehavin': Power and Consent in Organisational Sexuality', paper presented at the British Sociological Association Annual Conference, University of Central Lancashire, Preston, March.

Townley, B. (1994) *Reframing Human Resource Management: Power, Ethics and the Subject at Work*, London: Sage.

US Department of Labor (1991) *A Report on the Glass Ceiling Initiative*, Washington, DC: US Government Printing Office.

US Merit Systems Protection Board (1981) *Sexual Harassment in the Federal Workplace: Is it a Problem?* Washington DC: US Government Printing Office.

Valdez, R. and Gutek, B. (1987) 'Family Roles: A Help or a Hindrance to Working Women?', in Gutek, B. A. and Larwood, L. (eds), *Women's Career Development*, Newbury Park, CA: Sage.

Valentine, G. (1993a) 'Heterosexing Space: Lesbian Perceptions and Experiences of Everyday Spaces', *Environment and Planning D: Society and Space*, 11(4), 359–413.

Valentine, G. (1993b) Negotiating and Managing Multiple Sexual Identities: Lesbian Time–Space Strategies', *Transactions of the Institute of British Geographers, NS18*, 237–48.

Vinnicombe, S. and Colwill, N. (1995) *The Essence of Women in Management*, London: Prentice-Hall.

Walby, S. (1986) *Patriarchy at Work*, Oxford: Polity Press.

Walby, S. (1990) *Theorizing Patriarchy*, Oxford: Blackwell.

Ware, V. (1992) *Beyond the Pale: White Women, Racism and History*, London: Verso.

Watts, P. (1989) 'Breaking into the Old Boy Network', *The Executive Female*, November–December, 32–72.

Webb, J. (1991) 'The Gender Relations of Assessment', in Firth-Cozens, J. and West, M. (eds), *Women at Work*, Basingstoke: Open University Press.

Weber, M. (1968) *Economy and Society*, Berkeley: University of California Press.

Weber, M. (1964) *Theory of social and Economic Organisation*, New York: Free Press.

Weber, M. (1986) 'Domination by Economic Power and by Authority', in Lukes, S. (ed), *Power*, Oxford: Blackwell.

Weedon, C. (1987) *Feminist Practice and Poststructuralist Theory*, Oxford: Blackwell.

West, C. (1990) 'Not Just 'Doctor's Ordered': Directive Response Sequences in Patients' Visits to Women and Men Physicians', *Discourse and Society*, 1(1), 85–112.

West, C. and Zimmerman, D. (1983) 'Small Insults: A Study of Interruptions in Cross-Sex Conversations Between Unacquainted Persons', in Thorne, B., Kramarae, C. and Henley, N. (eds), *Language, Gender and Society*, Rowley MA: Newbury House.

White, J. (1995) *Gender, Culture and Organizational Change*, London: Routledge.

Wilkinson, S. and Kitzinger, C. (eds) (1993) *Heterosexuality: A Feminism and Psychology Reader*, London: Sage.

Williams, C. (1988) *Blue, White and Pink Collar Workers: Technicians, Bank Employees and Flight Attendants*, London: Allen & Unwin.

Willis, F. (1966) Initial Speaking Distance as a Function of the Speaker's Relationship, *Psychometric Science, 5*, 221–2.

Wilton, T. (1992) 'Desire and the Politics of Representation: Issues for Lesbians and Heterosexual Women', in Hinds, H., Phoenix, A. and Stacey, J. (eds), *Working Out: New Directions for Women's Studies*, Brighton: Falmer Press.

Wise, S. and Stanley, L. (1987) *Georgie Porgie: Sexual Harassment in Everyday Life*, London: Pandora.

Witz, A. and Savage. M. (1992) 'The Gender of Organisations', in Savage, M. and Witz, A. (eds), *Gender and Bureaucracy*, Oxford, Blackwell.

Wollstonecraft, M. (1982) *A Vindication of the Rights of Women*, London: Dent.

Women in Management Review and Abstracts (1991) *Dedicated Issue: Breaking Through the Glass Ceiling*, **6**,(5).

Wood, N. (1985) 'Foucault on the History of Sexuality: An Introduction', in Donald, J. and Beechey, V. (eds), *Subjectivity and Social Relations: A Reader* Milton Keynes: Open University Press.

Woolf, N. (1990) *The Beauty Myth*, London: Verso.

Wrong, D. (1979) *Power: Its forms, Bases and Uses*, Oxford: Blackwell.

Young, K. and Spencer, L. (1990) *Breaking Down the Barrers: Women Managers in Local Government*, Local Government Training Board.

Zabalza, A. and Tzannatos, Z. (1985) *Women and Equal Pay*, Cambridge University Press.

Index of Authors

254

Index of Subjects